I'LL FLY A

I'LL FLY AWAY

A WORLD WAR II PILOT'S LIFETIME OF ADVENTURES FROM BIPLANES TO JUMBO JETS

John T. "Jack" Race

with

William F. Hallstead

SCRANTON: University of Scranton Press

Library of Congress Cataloging-in-Publication Data

Hallstead, William F.
I'll fly away : from grass strips to jumbo jets, a pilot's personal story /
William Hallstead, John T. Race.
    p. cm.
ISBN 1-58966-113-3
1. Air pilots–United States–Biography. 2. Race, John T., 1921-
I. Race, John T., 1921- II. Title.

TL540.R33H35 2006
629.13092–dc22   2006042110

Distribution:

The University of Scranton Press
Chicago Distribution Center
11030 S. Langley
Chicago, IL 60628

PRINTED IN THE UNITED STATES OF AMERICA

Dedication

For David
— Who has flown away and landed safely in
that land where joys shall never end.

The Airplane images at the beginning of each chapter were drawn by Richard "Ricky" De Nike, grandson of John T. "Jack" Race

CONTENTS

"I'LL FLY AWAY TO A LAND WHERE JOYS SHALL NEVER END"

–Southern gospel hymn

From a 37-horsepower Aeronca C-3 to the mammoth Boeing 747 jet-liner, John T. "Jack" Race has lived a fascinating 60-year odyssey in the air. He was the pilot who flew General Jodl to the surrender of the Third Reich, then went on to log 60 years aloft as flight instructor, crop duster, bush pilot, instructor for Afghanistan's Ariana Airline, consultant to Jordan's Alia Airline, around-the-world charter pilot, and Pan Am jet captain. He captained a cargo flight with Lindbergh on the jump seat then, at age 68, recreated Lindbergh's 1927 48-state tour in an open-cockpit biplane. Chief pilot for Orbis's flying eye hospital at age 70, he was one of the very few, if any, septuagenarian captains flying four-engine jet airline aircraft in the U.S. At the same time, he was also an American Baptist pastor serving as interim pastor in various American Baptist Churches.

This is his remarkable story of six decades aloft.

CHAPTER 1

THE GERMANS SALUTED CRISPLY

May 6, 1945. Twenty-six miles southeast of Hamburg, I banked the C-47 into the final approach to the airport at the just-surrendered town of Luneburg. The afternoon was overcast and murky, a bleak day in Germany. Fitting enough, I felt, for the collapse of Hitler's "Thousand Year" Third Reich.

We touched down, and at the end of the landing roll, taxied to the little knot of Nazi officers standing near the administration building. Four days ago, the German forces in Italy had surrendered. The day after that, the Hamburg garrison had capitulated to British Field Marshal Bernard Montgomery. Now he was headquartered in Luneberg. There a German delegation headed by General Admiral Hans Georg von Freideburg, an emissary of now-supreme commander Admiral Karl Doenitz, tried to work out a total surrender of all armed forces to Montgomery.

Because his authority was limited to his own sector, the famed British field marshal declined. Thus on May 4, Freideburg surrendered to Montgomery the German forces in Northwest Germany, Schleswig-Holstein, Holland and Denmark. General Admiral von Freideburg then hurried to General Dwight D. Eisenhower's headquarters at Rheims, France, to arrange the surrender of all remaining German armed forces.

That final surrender was to be signed by Colonel General Alfred Gustav Jodl. Only as we landed did my highest ranking passenger, British Major General Sir Francis Wilfred de Guingand—Montgomery's chief-of-staff—tell me who we were to take aboard. Through the cockpit side window, I stared at our priority passengers: glum Jodl himself and his pair of stone-faced officers, all standing stiffly in natty leather overcoats and high-peaked, silver eagle-crested garrison caps. Somewhere I've read the army with the most pretentious uniforms usually loses the war.

Our C-47, call sign "Bluenose B for Baker," was a U.S. Army Air Forces plane flown by an American crew on loan to the British Army. My co-pilot on this priority flight was 1st Lieutenant Pete Tumlinson. Staff Sergeant Emerson Autry, inevitably nicknamed "Gene," served as flight engineer. Our radio op was Corporal Joe Aaronson.

I cut the engines. General de Guingand and several of his high-ranking aides stepped down the narrow metal exit stairs. The Germans saluted crisply—but not with the infamous Nazi version of the Roman Legionnaires' outthrust stiff arm. Their salutes were the traditional old German Army style.

De Guingand's party returned the salutes in vibrating, palm-forward British style. Then an unexpected moment. Jodl, still rigid-faced, offered his hand. There was an embarrassing pause. In the dead silence, I found the whole scene surreal. Then de Guingand stepped forward and shook the defeated Nazi general's hand.

Next, something even more unexpected happened. An Australian fighter pilot strolled into this historic drama and tried to hitch a ride with us. Abruptly he turned on Jodl and began to chew him out unmercifully. At that point, one of de Guingand's aides yelled at him, "Shut up!" Which he did, then wandered back out of history and disappeared.

The Germans and Britishers climbed aboard Bluenose B. "It was a queer feeling," de Guingand wrote in his 1947 memoir, "to be in the same aircraft with the man who had for so long worked in the closest assocation with Hitler."

We took off into the muggy warm front. Destination Rheims, 430 miles southwest. When the ceiling lowered to less than a hundred feet, I had no choice but to climb through dense cloud hoping to break out on top before we reached 10,000 feet. Above that altitude, oxygen was routinely called for. At 10,000, though, visibility in the swirling cloud vapor was still zero. I took her on up. At 12,000, we finally broke through the overcast into bright sunlight.

Now oxygen was in order. We had the tanks and masks, but for our usual commuter-type short hops, oxygen had been deemed unnecessary.

The oxygen tanks hadn't been filled. But as long as everyone stayed put and didn't exert himself, we could manage.

Our flight path took us past Bremen, Osnabruck and the Cologne area—all heavily bombed by the U.S. Eighth Air Force and the RAF, and all invisible to us beneath the heavy undercast. We passed over Bastogne and the Ardennes where the Battle of the Bulge had raged not quite five months ago. Up to now, I'd depended on dead reckoning—heading and elapsed time. A precise directional bearing from ground radio would be far more reassuring. I had Aaronson transmit for a bearing. He reported atmospherics so poor he couldn't get through to any station.

Next, one of de Guingand's party tried contact with the "G Box," a British radio navigation device on board, the equivalent of American Loran. No response.

I fell back on the pilot's old stand-by. If you're not sure of your position, hold your heading. On what I hoped was our still-valid heading, I took us down through the cloud layer. Down, down . . . I had flown in as bad or worse weather during the past year and felt we would find ourselves pretty much on course when we broke out.

Down . . .

At a couple thousand feet, we broke into the clear. I spotted several familiar landmarks. And I felt a huge surge of relief. We were dead on course, 20 miles from Rheims.

In the lightning flares of flashbulbs, Colonel General Jodl stepped down from our drab C-47 to surrender what was left of the Third Reich's armed forces. For the former chief of staff of the German high command, that had to be an exceedingly bitter final duty. Jodl had been Hitler's personal emissary to inform *Wehrmacht* planners of the *Fuehrer's* determination to attack the Soviet Union in 1941. Four years later, Jodl had been wounded along with Hitler in the "Wolf's Lair" bombing attempt on Hitler's life. And a few days before appearing at Luneburg Airport, Jodl had been one of the last to confer with Hitler in his Berlin bunker. Just last week, on April 30 at 3:30 p.m., *Der Fuehrer* had committed suicide with a pistol shot in the mouth.

At 2:21 a.m., May 7, 1945, in a drab Rheims schoolhouse, Hitler's dream of a Nazi world officially ended as Colonel General Jodl, General Admiral von Friedeburg and Major General Wilhelm Oxenius signed the unconditional surrender document. General Eisenhower did not attend, sending in his place American British, French and Soviet emissaries. Though Soviet General Susloparov had co-signed the Rheims document, the following day the Russians insisted on a subsequent signing of a separate surrender document by Marshal Zhukov in Berlin. Thus, through Soviet finagling, May 8 became the official V-E Day.

On October 18, 1945, 21 German key military and civilian figures were indicted by Allied prosecutors for "crimes against humanity." Included was Alfred Jodl. Seven months later, the verdict: 10 of the 21 were condemned to death. To the surprise of many in the media, one of the 10 to be executed was Jodl.

"I have not merited this fate," he wrote his wife, but he remained defiant. "Death will find no broken, penitent victim, but a proud man who can look him coldly in the eye." On October 16, 1946, Jodl and the other nine were hung on black-painted gallows in the Nuremburg Courthouse gymnasium. Officiating as an experienced hangman was American Master Sergeant John C. Wood with a team of five. The bodies were cremated, the ashes taken to Munich and spread in a tributary of the Isar River. Recently, though, I've been told there is a Jodl gravesite marker in a cemetery on an island in Lake Chiem southeast of Munich.

The day my crew and I flew Jodl to the surrender signing and ultimately to his death, I was 23 years old. I had logged a total of 1672 flying hours, 360 of them in C-47s and their variations. What was to be a 60-year career in the air was just beginning.

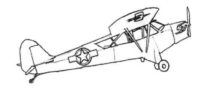

2
CHAPTER

"SPEEN!"

The slightly built, toothbrush-mustached pilot beside me in the snug enclosed cockpit eased the throttle forward. The pot-bellied Aeronca C-3 shuddered. Its 37-hp Aeronca E113C engine began to bang us along the lumpy sod strip. The squatty little plane, nicknamed the "flying bathtub," jounced on such stubby landing gear I could almost reach out the cockpit window and drag my fingers through the grass.

Then the turf strip fell away. A magic moment. We were airborne. Engine drumming in my ears, we climbed. Trees and scattered houses grew smaller. We chugged higher then crossed the ridge to the east. Sprawled along the valley beyond, the northeastern Pennsylvania city of Carbondale was transformed from my lofty perch into a picture postcard of autumn colors.

This was my very first escape from "the surly bonds of earth." I was thrilled, elated. To my further delight, the pilot let me take control briefly—well, at least touch the control "stick," actually a short rod topped by a leather-wrapped loop. There were no dual controls in the C-3, but the looped stick was in reach.

As we glided back into tiny Mid Valley Airport in the rolling Abington Hills, that first flight had already confirmed what I wanted to do with the rest of my life.

The year: 1939. I was 18. I had paid $2.00 for that Aeronca ride, money hard earned at 45¢ an hour working in my father's lumber yard. Dad—Niles Race—was one of five children. His father was a carpenter, and Dad and his two brothers had also taken up carpentry. After serving as a medic in WWI France, Dad with his brother Clayton in the 1920s and 30s had built most of the residences at Crystal Lake, a rural community in the wooded hills north of Carbondale. In addition to his building contract business, Dad now owned the Race Lumber Company in Carbondale.

My mother, Edith, like most wives of that era, made mothering her specialty. Her parents had emigrated from Wales. For a time, her father worked in the area's coal mines. A fine musician with an outstanding tenor voice, he was also an enterprising fellow. Eventually he became the owner of the Crystal Lake Hotel, and Mother now occasionally helped out at the hotel.

With my brother Don, two years younger than I, the four of us lived a quarter-mile from the lake. Some of the large Crystal Lake area estates had much more magnificent homes, though our modestly-styled house was one of the largest Dad and Uncle Clayton had built. Ours had three bedrooms and fine oak floors.

My fascination with aviation had been sparked at age six as Dad and I hung on every scratchy word coming over our radio May 20 and 21, 1927. Charles Lindbergh had the world's attention as he dared fly the entire Atlantic solo. Someday, I thought, maybe I, too, might . . .

But shortly, my more immediate interest was Sport, a three-legged stray dog I had taken in. With kids my age few and far between in our rural countryside, Sport became my best friend. Whatever the weather, I walked the mile to and from our one-room schoolhouse with Sport hobbling along beside me. There my devoted three-legged walking partner would patiently wait at the schoolhouse for recess, lunchtime and the end of classes. We would walk home together. We were inseparable—until one tragic day. The car came out of nowhere. Sport couldn't get out of the way. He was struck and fatally injured. That first tragedy in my life left me inconsolable for months.

Today the one-room schoolhouse seems like some sort of Norman Rockwell idyll, but I finished seven grades in that tiny frame building. My parents were told I could skip either the second or third grade. My thorough-going mother and dad would have none of that, so I took the full seven years there.

Due to Crystal Lake's isolation, my boyhood was a bit lonely at times. That prompted my early and avid interest in reading. From Aesop's Fables and the sometimes shivery tales of the Brothers Grimm, I read all the Oz books. In later years I was to reflect on the importance of their messages. The Scarecrow actually did have a brain, the Cowardly Lion needed only to realize he was not a coward at all, and the Tin Man found he indeed had a heart. These rites of passage parables are applicable to our own lives.

I eagerly moved on to popular boys' books of the time. Then I zeroed in on *Flying Aces, Wings* and other aviation magazines at a mere 10¢ per monthly issue. In warm weather, my favorite reading retreat was among the branches of a large maple tree near the house. One of the lake's summer resident families faithfully turned over their accumulated *National Geographic* magazines. One of those great stimulators of youthful imagination detailed the 48-state Guggenheim Tour Lindbergh flew following his historic Atlantic crossing. I still have my copy of that National Geographic issue, an especially meaningful one as will be seen.

Like many boys of that Golden Age of Aviation, I poured my heart into building model airplanes. With razor-nicked and cement-crusted (true model builders never would never say "glue") fingers I put together dozens of 10¢ "solid" model kits and more intricate 25¢ flying models. I spent hours hunched over a table in my room, piecing together balsa stringers and ribs then covering them with with "Japanese" tissue. These I launched at the mercy of the wind and a tightly wound rubber band. I wasn't an expert, but with the careful flying adjustments those models required, I had begun to learn aviation's basics.

For the eighth grade, this country boy found himself in Roosevelt School in the—to me—big city of Carbondale. Almost all of America's anthracite—hard coal—lies under five counties in Northeastern Pennsylvania. Carbondale sprawls across the northeastern tip of a major vein. From there, the rich lode of "black diamonds" runs southwestward beneath Scranton and on down to Wilkes-Barre. All three of these cities built by anthracite in the Lackawanna and Luzerne Valleys were to have profound influences on my future in aviation.

But not yet. My high school years at Carbondale's Benjamin Franklin High were, well, academically unremarkable. Unfortunatly I was unable to take part in any school sports. Transportation arrangements were such that I had to leave for home immediately after classes.

I spent many summer hours mowing lawns for Crystal Lake residents, handling my paper route there and helping unload freight deliveries at the lumber yard. By some of today's teen-age standards, that might sound oppressive. To me, it was entirely fair. You worked to earn your money.

At one point during those early years, our mother determined that Don and I must learn to play a musical instrument, capping that announcement with, "Choose your instrument."

Don opted for a cornet. I decided to try a saxaphone. Mother bought both. Mine was a Conn E-flat alto sax. This was to be no casual effort. My grandfather gave Don some early lessons, and Mother hired a tutor to come to the house once a week for my sax lessons. This went on for a year or so. During that time a little band was being formed in Elkdale, about three miles distant. Don and I signed up. The Elkdale Band, now including my brother and me, practiced in the Grange Hall. On Memorial Day and July 4th we marched along the road through tiny Lenoxville. Without uniforms and with ages ranging from 15 to 50, we must have appeared a shade on the humorous side. Don and I played taps at a Memorial Day cemetery ceremony, and I made a solo appearance at our one-room school.

After those few public appearances, I continued to play my sax at home, mainly to please Mother, though I did rather enjoy playing the thing. Ultimately flying would intrude in my musical life to the point where I would pick up the sax only occasionally, even years later. That venerable old sax is still in the family. My granddaughter has it.

My lawn and paper businesses eventually financed the purchase of a "previously owned" 1932 Excelsior motorcycle. Price: $12.00. After some mechanical work on the old bike, I had my own wheels. It turned out to be a real oil spitter. Unfortunately, about half the time the Excelsior gagged to full balk. Later I graduated to a big Harley, a $45.00 investment that reduced the unreliability factor to about 25%—twice as efficient as the Excelsior's 50% falter rate.

In 1939, I graduated from Benjamin Franklin High with two goals: (1) Learn to fly and, (2) Enter college to study aeronautics. Both were dream decisions.

That heady $2.00 flight in the flying bathtub out of Mid Valley confirmed my determination to become a pilot. A bit of research revealed the cost of flying lessons: a daunting $6.00 per half-hour. For a half-hour in the air, I was going to sweat 13 hours at the lumber yard. Not an encouraging prospect. But at 18, even with all my teen years spent in the Great Depression, discouragement was not in my vocabulary—and never has been. I often thank my family for that.

I signed up for the aeronatics course in Penn State's Extension Program down the valley in Scranton and began to grind out hours of part-time labor at the Race Lumber Company. On May 4, 1940, I received a diploma in aeronautics.

My part-time work had not only financed the motorcycle purchases; on May 19, 1940, I blapped the Harley 10 miles west to Mount View Airport near the farming town of Nicholson. That little town, by the way, is famed as the location of a railroad viaduct so massive it can be seen clearly from jetliners 30,000 feet overhead. The airport was not nearly as imposing, just a rudimentary sod field with a small frame hangar housing a Waco 10 biplane and an Aeronca Chief.

The Chief was no chugging, knee-high C-3 bathtub. This was a sleek two-place monoplane with side-by-side seating, powered by 50 horses of smooth Lycoming engine—a new plane with only a few hours logged.

My instructor? Hymie Wintersteen, the very same neatly mustached birdman who had first taken me aloft at Mid Valley a year ago. A bona fide veteran of the barnstorming 1920s, Hymie was already one of northeastern Pennsylvania's legendary aviators, dating back to the days of the Curtiss "Jenny" and the OX-5 engine. Literally a flying Dutchman, he featured picturesque treatments of certain aviation terms. After take-off, for example, he had you throttle back to "carousing speed" with an eye out for "owxilary" landing fields. His recollection of flying the old Jenny? "Eef you shifted your chewing gum, she would turn over."

Hymie's teaching technique was terse and no-nonsense. As we neared the end of my first 30 minutes of hard-earned dual instruction, he throttled back, pulled up in a nose-high stall then kicked in full rudder. As we whirled straight downward, he said simply, "Speen!" We were in a spin, all right, and it seemed all right to me. Today, "speens" aren't even part of private pilot training. When they were, they weren't introduced to a student in his first half hour.

I was able to scratch together enough cash for a weekly flying lesson with Hymie. We were making progress, but I realized only too well flying a mere half-hour a week, I was in for a long, long pull to get my hands on that private pilot certificate.

In June, I enrolled at the University of Scranton, a decision about to hugely accelerate my aerial progress. Alarmed by Hitler's increasingly obvious hunger for territory and Europe's unwillingness to do anything about it, President Roosevelt had won Congressional approval in January, 1939, for a $300 million appropriation to increase America's aviation personnel. The program included primary flight training for 20,000 men and women. Thus began the federally funded Civilian Pilot Training Program, soon known as simply CPT.

The nationwide project was conducted at hundreds of qualifying airports and administered through local colleges. Locally, Scranton Municipal Airport was approved for CPT flight operations, with the University of Scranton handling the ground school aspect. My enrollment at the university made me eligible for the CPT program. My slow plod into the sky was about to become a rush.

3

CHAPTER

NOTHING IS QUITE SO SILENT AS A DEAD ENGINE

Accepted for CPT private pilot training in mid-1940, I rushed along the 20-mile Carbondale-University of Scranton commute on my more or less faithful Harley motorcycle. On July 8, I reported to the airport for my first lesson under CPT auspices. My instructor: Mark Richards, chief pilot for Scranton Airways, the Airport's flight operations arm. Mark, I soon realized, was a superb pilot and top-notch teacher. A dashing figure in his early 30s, he closely resembled actor Errol Flynn. In those early days, flight instructors tended to be dramatically heavy-handed. Not Mark. He had the ability to calmly and patiently draw the very best from his students.

No sod field this time. Ten miles north of the city, Scranton Municipal Airport offered two paved runways and a spacious architect-designed cinderblock hangar with a broad concrete parking apron and a two-story office wing.

In the tiny town of Schultzville, tucked in the Abington foothills of the Endless Mountains, the airport had begun in the late 1920s as a private enterprise on purchased farm acreage. The venture was the inspiration of Scranton resident Harold Swank, who was to become one of Pennsylvania's best-known aviation pioneers. Assisting Swank in early flight operations was the ubiquitous Hymie Wintersteen.

In 1929, a group of area businessmen formed the Scranton Airport Corporation to foster development of the airport. Seven years later, for the sum of $1.00, the corporation deeded the airport to the city of Scranton to qualify the sod landing field for a federal Works Progress Administration (WPA) contract to grade the field and pave two 100-foot-wide, 2,500-foot-long runways.

For a few years, Scranton Airport was served by American Airlines flying Ford Tri-Motors and three-engined Stinson SM-6000 Airliners. American's switch to larger and more practical DC-3s ended tiny Schultzville's era as a scheduled airliner destination. The airport's runways were too short for DC-3 comfort, and several approaches had potentially hazardous obstructions. Airport revenues from private and some business flying declined to critical. Then came salvation. The CPT program approved Scranton Airport for pilot training.

The Scranton area's first CPT classes began flight training December 18, 1939, with three Piper J-3 Cubs. The Cub, acclaimed as one of the world's great airplanes, was a Pennsylvania product. The little two-seater monoplane first appeared as the Taylor Cub, built in several versions by the Taylor Brothers. In 1937, their Bradford, Pennsylvania plant burned down. Board Chairman William T. Piper moved the operation to Lock Haven and changed its name to Piper Aircraft Corporation. In 1938 the revised company began turning out an improved version of the Taylors' Cub, the Piper J-3 Cub. The little plane would have a long, long life. The last Cub, the PA-18—essentially the same plane with a bigger engine, flaps and other improvements—went out of production an astounding 55 years later in 1993.

On July 29, I soloed. A student's first flight alone is a nerve-twanging, never-forgotten experience. At 6:30 a.m., Mark climbed out of the Cub's front seat and leaned back in.

"Take her around." Then he cautioned, "She'll be a little light."

I wind in a nose-down trim and taxi back to take-off position. I find myself excited yet confident. I am sure Mark knows I am ready. I push the throttle forward. She's light, all right. We're off the ground almost immediately. Climb straight ahead, airspeed at its prescribed 60 mph to 400 feet. Then a climbing 90-degree left turn to 600. Another climbing left ninety-degree turn to 800 feet. Level off.

I actually begin to relax a little. Throttle back, turn left into the base leg. Hold the glide at 60. Turn final . . . a tad high. Left rudder and a bit of opposite stick to slip off a few feet. The bushes at the airport's edge flash beneath. Flare-out. Touch-down—hey! Nice three-point. I'm grinning. Mark smiles, too. And sends me on two more circuits.

After the third landing, I taxied back in, cut the switch and walked to the operations office still 10 feet in the air. Mark jotted something in my logbook. I snuck a look. "Good judgement—good T.O.s and landings." The world smiled.

Nine solo hours later, it frowned.

Mark had assigned me to a nearby practice area to work solo on precision spins while he watched from the airport. Just west of the field, I climbed to 3,000 feet then kicked the Cub into a turn-and-a-half spin, recovered and climbed back to 3,000 for another one.

On recovery from that second aerobatic whirl, the Cub's engine surged, faded. Surged again, faded.

With the engine popping and gasping, I sank in a wide spiral. The propeller slowly windmilled. Then it stood stark still. In a powered airplane nothing is quite so silent as a dead engine. The Cub had no self-starter. To kick in the engine, the propeller had to be yanked hard by hand. Not a chance of that up here. I had just become a stunned glider pilot. Eighteen hundred feet over Schultzville, I was sweatily committed to my first forced landing. And it *had* to be a good one. Neither Mark Richards nor Harold Swank was a believer in that old chestnut any landing you could walk away from was a good landing. At Scranton Airport, a good landing was one that inflicted not even a flexing of the plane's fabric covering.

With Mark, I had practiced simulated forced landings, always with the engine idling, ready to pull us out of the practice approach. This was the real thing. One shot at it. No way to go around and try again.

I headed toward the airport, swung into a much abbreviated landing pattern. Slipped off some altitude on final approach. Touched down with the engine dead and the propeller frozen. Rumbled to a stop midfield And let out my breath in a huge sigh of relief.

Mark had watched this whole chilling event. As I walked toward him, he said, "Not bad, Jack, not bad." Rare words of praise. I hoped he hadn't noticed my hands. They shook so badly I barely managed to sign the flight log sheet. Then he jotted into the log his commentary: "Solo spins, good entries and recoveries, one and a half turns. Motor gave trouble down from 720-degree spiral—quit entirely in 180-degree position—pattern, landing excellent."

Not quite two weeks after that unsettling experience, I passed the private pilot flight test. My first passenger was my mother, who had consistently supported my determination to become a pilot. Though she was afraid of heights, she gamely climbed into the Cub's rear seat for her first ever airplane ride. Airborne, she refused to look out at first. Then she peeked, was fascinated and sat back to enjoy the ride.

Next, my training hit a snag. The CPT secondary course wasn't yet offered at Scranton Airport. But word had it CPT secondary training was to start in the spring of 1941 at the Wyoming Valley Airport near Wilkes-Barre. I continued my studies at the University of Scranton via night courses. During the day, the need for cash called me back to the lumberyard—and I put in a brief stint harvesting ice at Crystal Lake for the John Booth Company.

In March, I was in the air again, this time in the Wyoming Valley Airport's Fairchild M62. Powered by a 180-hp Ranger in-line engine, this low-winged monoplane was the civilian version of the military PT-19 "Cornell." Its two cockpits were open to the raw spring wind. The fuselage was fabric-covered but plywood sheathed the wings. A bit under-powered for its weight, the sturdy little aircraft was somewhat reluctant to take off and not overly snappy during aerobatics in this essentially aerobatics phase of the program.

Wyoming Valley Airport lay in the town of Forty Fort along the north shore of the Susquehanna River. In severe summer rains it was prone to flooding, and the Scranton papers would publish photos of that airport with only the hangar roof above water. It didn't flood while I was training there.

Smith Flying Service was the operator of the flying portion of the CPT Secondary Course. The ground school aspect was taught at Wilkes-Barre's Bucknell Junior College. I was fortunate here, too, in being assigned an excellent flight instructor, Ed Barnes.

My most notable moment in the otherwise routine aerobatics curriculum took place during an hour of dual training on a pleasant spring day. We were flying inverted. My seat belt was holding me in place when suddenly I fell out. The seat retention mechanism had let go. I was sure I was on my way down with the seat but sans airplane. I fell 18 frightening inches. Then the seat retainer caught. Ed flipped us upright and I clunked back into place. Had the seat come entirely loose, the fall wouldn't have been fatal—provided I'd had the presence of mind to unbuckle the seat belt and free myself from its embrace. Fortunately regulations required aerobatics students and instructors to wear parachutes. But I rode the rest of that trip feeling profoundly grateful I was still aboard.

My other vivid memory of that flight course "down valley" was the required check ride with a different instructor at the end of each of the curriculum's four stages. At every one of those "stage checks," I was tight as a violin string. But I managed to pass all four. On June 3, 1941, I completed the CPT Secondary phase, flew a tense check ride with

CAA Flight Supervisor E.J. Fielder. The CAA—Civil Aeronautics Administration—was the forerunner of today's FAA. I passed the check ride and returned to Scranton Airport for the next challenge.

I was now eligible for CPT's cross-country training, including radio navigation and night flying. For that, I signed up July 2. Again I was privileged to have Mark Richards as my instructor. Dual cross-country flying and radio navigation instruction was flown in a 1937 245-hp Stinson SR-9B Reliant. Considered one of aviation's classics, the Reliant was a beautiful high-wing monoplane with a fully enclosed cockpit and a tapered gull wing design never since quite equalled for visual gracefulness.

Solo cross-countries, including nighttime trips, were flown in a Piper J-5 Cruiser, a souped-up Cub with a wider fuselage. With room for two in the rear seat and the pilot up front, the J-5 had position lights, a few additional niceties—and a two-way radio powered by a wind-driven generator. In pitch blackness over the Endless Mountains, the not-so-gutsy 75-hp Lycoming never faltered. The cross-country course was quite enjoyable. I completed it September 21 and now listed a total of 150 hours and 25 minutes flying time in my log book.

Next, the secondary instructor course; 20 hours of aerobatics in a Waco UPF-7 biplane and 20 hours in a J-3 Cub to learn the techniques of instruction. Yet again, my instructor was Mark Richards. On November 3, 1941, I passed the check ride. Now at age 20, I held a commercial license with a flight instructor rating. Total flight time, 194 hours.

This was an exciting time. Options were opening up in all directions, even in Canada where Mark had a friend at a flight school who was hiring instructors. If I was interested, Mark could arrange the job for me. I would be checked out on Avro Ansons then instruct Royal Canadian Air Force pilots. Though a yearning for adventure tugged at me, I wasn't all that keen on rushing off to Canada when there were instructor positions closer to home.

While I deliberated the Canadian possibility, I took on freelance instructing at Mount View Airport. This was the same turf field where I had taken my first flying lessons from Hymie Wintersteen. Now, eighteen months later, I soloed my first student there, Dr. Kenneth Wilson. Before that month as a temporary Mount View flight instructor ended, I was offered a full-time instructor position for a flying service near Portsmouth, Virginia. Unfortunately, a promising future there was to end the day I arrived.

I was assigned a student who was almost ready for his commercial pilot check ride. The idea was to give him a final flight check. In his mid-thirties, he was a good 15 years older than I. And he had logged more than 500 flying hours. I was a bit intimidated by his age and experience, a lapse that was about to prove disastrous. Off we flew in a Piper J-3. As instructor, I rode the front seat.

In the practice area, my far more experienced student flew my version of his check ride competently and we headed back toward the airport. At that point, I told him we should practice a few simulated forced landings. I closed the throttle. He selected an emergency landing area promptly and glided toward it. We went through this sequence several times. As we climbed up from the last of those exercises and reached 400 feet, I throttled back for one more forced landing simulation. This one was a tough test. In the J-3, a key caution was not to attempt a turn of more than 90 degrees if engine failure occurred below 400 feet during a climb.

I had noted an open field about 90 degrees to our course. If my student spotted it immediately, he could make a safe power-off approach. By the time he did notice the field, we had lost altitude gliding straight ahead. We were below the 400-foot danger point. To my horror, he racked the Cub into a steep turn. Our airspeed was crucially low and we sank like a brick.

"This isn't going to work!" I shouted. I leveled the Cub and rammed in full power. Too late. The ground rushed toward us. We smacked into a peanut field hard enough to total the airplane.

My student wasn't hurt, but I had three crushed vertebrae, was in a Portsmouth hospital for a week then wore a back brace for four months.

I had learned a bitter lesson. When I was in command of an aircraft, it was *my* responsibility—even if Lindbergh himself were in the cockpit with me—which, in fact, one day he would be.

When I was able to travel, I returned to Crystal Lake to continue recovery through the fateful month of December, 1941.

CHAPTER 4

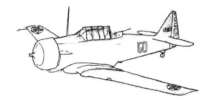

HIRED ON THE SPOT
BY THE AAF

This pilot's idea of supporting the war effort was not to hang around temporarily immobilized in the family home at Crystal Lake. But a brightness did shine through the gloom of my debacle: a young blonde, pretty and witty.

Through her brother Robert, a classmate of mine and a fellow model builder, I had met Katherine Adams during my senior year at Benjamin Franklin High.

A junior, she was a well-liked cheerleader at Benjamin Franklin—and an avid dancer. I didn't consider dancing to be of any use to humanity whatever.

Katherine tried to instruct me in that pagan activity. I wasn't at all cooperative, but she was so darned pleasant—and pretty. The best I could ever manage was a performance much like that of Rex Harrison's in the musical, "My Fair Lady." Rex, no singer, could talk his way through the lyrics. Under Katherine's tutelage, I, no dancer, finally managed to walk my way through the two-step.

My friendship with Robert continued beyond graduation, which frequently led to my seeing Katherine, then employed as a medical secretary. We dated casually until I was rendered hors de combat in the November, 1941, J-3 crash. During my recuperation, she was truly concerned and helpful, the bright light in that darkly painful chapter of my of my aborted flying career. Mutual thoughts of marriage surfaced, and we found ourselves engaged.

Robert was destined to join the Army Air Forces as an aviation cadet, then fly Douglas A-20 light bombers in the 9th Air Force in Europe. He would complete some 35 combat missions, including an emergency escape by parachute, and return home a captain.

During my recovery from the Portsmouth calamity, I received a phone call from the manager of Scranton Municipal Airport. Now that we were at war, the government had accelerated the CPT program and additional instructors were in demand.

Literally out of the blue, Harold Swank offered me a job as a CPT instructor to begin work as soon as I was fit to fly.

In February, 1942, just over two months after the accident, I reported to Scranton Municipal. Compactly built, balding and pleasant, Harold ran a tight ship. Compared to other airports in the Scranton-Carbondale area, Scranton could claim Cadillac status. Instructors were qualified and disciplined. The airport and aircraft were beautifully maintained by a small salaried staff. Despite its barnstorming beginnings, Scranton Airport had bloosomed into an adequately-financed and well-run operation.

Through the next 10 months, I was to teach a CPT primary course and five secondary instructor courses. The aerobatics were flown mostly in the Waco UPF-7, the sturdy, reliable biplane I would grow to love. Wacos—pronounced "Wahco," not "Wayco," as in Texas—were the products of the Ohio-based Weaver Aircraft Co. beginning in the early 1920s. In 1929 the corporate initials became the company's official name. The UPF-7, introduced in 1937, was powered by a 220-hp Continental radial engine. Six hundred UPF-7s were delivered to U.S. airports under CPT contracts. Scranton eventually would receive 12 of them. More than 60 years later, Waco UPF-7s are still in the air, including a pair of them flying passenger hops over Fort Myers, Florida, and a bright scarlet UPF-7 owned by—and still flown by—yours truly.

We also flew a Travel Air 4000 in the aerobatics course. This Wichita, Kansas-built, open-cockpit biplane was powered by a 220-hp Wright J-5 radial engine, the same engine that had powered Lindbergh's "Spirit of St. Louis." Because of engine torque plus the plane's control heaviness, I found performing a slow roll to the right in the Travel Air a real bear. The Wacos weren't so easy to slow roll to the right either, but not to the extent of the Travel Air.

The four primary students comprising my first CPT assigment included one of Lebanese descent, Khalil Bectar, who turned out to be the most promising of the group. The next month, April, I began teaching the CPT flight instructor course with three students. In June, I was assigned five students for the secondary instructor refresher course.

Despite all this military-related flight training, the war seemed quite remote to our bucolic countryside. Nevertheless, a temporary wooden aircraft watchtower was erected in a cemetery in Clarks Summit, five miles east of the airport. Shifts of binocular-equipped volunteers were assigned to report any suspicious aircraft passing overhead, Scranton Airport traffic excluded. The citizen volunteers relayed such observations via a dedicated line telephone in the tower. "Army Flash Six Nine Six" connected them immediately to a volunteer crew working a plotting board in the First National Bank basement down in Scranton. No Nazi bombers were ever reported, but plenty of scheduled airliners were.

After my departure from Scranton Airport, surviving legend has it that a contingent of military intelligence agents drove in one day to warn Harold of a disturbing rumor. A clandestine group of Nazi sympathizers might use Scranton Airport as a refueling point for "light bombing planes" intent on attacking New York and Philadelphia. If a suspicious fuel truck entered airport grounds, Swank was ordered to fire at it. "With this." They handed him a submachine gun and ammunition. Fortunately, Machine Gun Swank never had need to blast away an alien tank truck.

Despite my ineptitude on the dance floor, Katherine and I were married on July 4th, 1942, a sort of reverse observance of Independence Day. The Reverend Dr. S. Turner Foster officiated in the Presbyterian Manse in Carbondale. The wedding party included my brother Don, now a Navy ensign, and AAF aviation cadet Robert Adams. Parental approvals ranged from warm to lukewarm. I suspect both sets of parents may have felt neither of us had quite reached the age of reason.

For $25 a month, we rented a lovely little house on Grove Street in Clarks Summit with easy access to the airport, now via a secondhand 1939 Plymouth. Harold was a pleasure to work for. We instructors received moderate base salaries plus $2 per flying hour in Piper J-3s and $3 per hour flying Wacos and Travel Airs. I averaged $300 a month, a respectable amount in those early 1940s. And I was doing exactly what I loved to do—fly!

Near the end of the year, I learned the Army Air Forces were seeking experienced pilots to ferry military aircraft. I told Harold of my intention to apply. On December 13, as soon as I finished my last group of students, I drove to New Castle Army Air Base just south of

Wilmington, Delaware. Over two days, I was given flight tests in a Fairchild PT-19—no challenge after all my hours in the civilian version—and in a much gutsier 650-hp North American AT-6 advanced trainer. Passing both tests, I was hired on the spot by the AAF as a civilian pilot in the Ferry Division of the Air Transport Command. I now had logged a grand total of 940 flying hours.

A group of us newly-hired Pennsylvania pilots pooled our resources to rent what had once been an inn located in Odessa, Delaware, a dozen or so miles south of New Castle Army Air Base. George Colovos; Don Harding and his wife, Marie; Bill and Lois Hutchins and Katherine and I all took up residence there. Hutch was a native of Peckville near Carbondale, but I had just met him at New Castle. He had flown at Roosevelt Aviation School on Long Island, then instructed CPT courses at the University of Idaho. He was to log 600 hours flying the "Hump" during the war, and eventually put in 31 years with Pan American. Hutch was the co-pilot on the Pan Am plane that ditched off San Juan Harbor, Puerto Rico in 1952. Cited for saving the life of a panicked passenger who had burst into the cockpit, his version of the event was simply, "I shoved her through a cockpit window just so I could get out, then I pried her fingers off a radio antenna so the plane could sink properly." The captain of that flight, incidentally, was the husband of singing star, Jane Froman.

Colovos and Harding had been fellow CPT instructors with me at Scranton. From ferry operations at New Castle, George would join the USAAF and serve two years flying military cargo and passengers in the Southwest Pacific. After the war, he joined the family's restaurant business in Scranton then operated two area restaurants of his own.

Don Harding, a former Pennsylvania state trooper, had been nick-named "Herman" by his fellow Scranton Airport students because of his physical resemblance to the Luftwaffe's Hermann Goering. After Don had qualified for his flight instructor rating, Harold hired him as a CPT cross-country instructor. On one of his flights, he crashed the beautiful Stinson Reliant well short of a Scranton Airport runway. The engine had died during the approach, presumably due to ice in the carburetor. After flying in the Ferry Command, Harding would survive the war then leave the Scranton area to move with his family to Florida.

With housekeeping chores at our inn shared, we all got along well together. Lois Hutchins and Katherine were pregnant and both were to give birth five months hence in May, 1943.

I began ferrying L-4s, the military version of the familiar Cub. Taking delivery at the Piper factory in Lock Haven, Pennsylvania, we flew the little puddle jumpers to Orlando, Florida. In short-range Cubs destined for military liaison and observation use, these 1,000-mile cross-country ferrying trips were necessarily flown with several stops. After delivery, we would return to New Castle by plane or train. When we ferried these small aircraft, we flew in a loose group, usually five. We were supposed to stay together and make fuel stops at predetermined airports, but inevitably there was some wandering around. In such limited airplanes, there were no radios. Navigation was by checking landmarks on our maps and by dead reckoning, a computation of compass direction, airspeed and wind effect. A few of our group were bound to get lost. When I noticed someone straying, I would try to fly close and offer "follow me" hand signals. Despite the lengths of our trips in such small rudimentary planes, I don't recall any accidents during this phase of ferry flying.

Additional assignments included flying PT-19s from the Fairchild factory in Hagerstown, Maryland to AAF training bases in Texas. I also ferried PT-26s, a 200-hp version of the PT-19. These were destined for the Royal Canadian Air Force, and we delivered them from Hagerstown to Toronto.

In January, 1943, I was selected to attend New Castle's officer training program, a blitz of how to salute, march, observe proper military courtesy and the code of conduct, plus firing the Colt .45 sidearm. On February 7, I was commissioned a USAAF 2nd lieutenant. My silver pilot wings were embossed with a large S on the shield designating me as a service pilot, an identification sometimes referred to not so charitably as "snake pilot."

Off I went to St. Joseph, Missouri for multi-engine and instrument training with the 1st Operational Training Unit of the Air Transport Command. The multi-engine practice was flown in twin-engined, low-wing Cessna AT-17 Bobcats and similar Curtiss AT-9 Jeeps. The Jeep was a two-place trainer; the Bobcat seated five.

One day out there, I noticed a commotion on the flight line. One of the Cessnas had crunched down on the runway with its wheels still retracted, a precise reenactment of the classic excuse, "I couldn't hear the control tower tell me the landing gear wasn't down because the landing gear warning horn was making too much noise."

At the OTU, I was also checked out in the North American B-25 Mitchell. Jimmy Doolittle and his group had flown the same type of medium bomber from the aircraft carrier *Hornet* to attack the Japanese mainland April 18 the previous year.

While I was in Missouri, Katherine returned to Carbondale to stay with her parents during her final months of pregnancy. On May 11, I completed the operational training requirements and hurried back to

Delaware. At New Castle Air Base May 14, word came of our daughter Jacqueline's birth in Carbondale.

I rushed to the base parking area for my car. To my dismay, the Plymouth was nowhere in sight. In the midst of my frantic investigation of where in heck the car might be, in it rolled—driven by Don Harding.

"I'm sorry, Jack. Really sorry. But I was so desperate for transportation, I jumped the ignition and I've been using your car myself. I was sure you wouldn't mind."

My friend, a former cop, had in effect stolen my Plymouth! I was stunned.

"But look, it's still all in one piece," he assured me.

I checked it over. No dents. "But look at the tires, Don. You've worn them almost through to the fabric!"

"Don't worry, don't worry. I'll get you a whole new set."

He never did.

I had called Katherine and sent her flowers, but I was so anxious to see her and our daughter, I cut short the infuriating confrontation with Don and headed north in my reclaimed machine. In those pre-interstate highway days and at the federally-imposed 35-mph national speed limit, that was not a fast trip. Rolling across the open countryside to Allentown then winding through the Pocono Mountains, the abused tires managed to hold out.

Mother and daughter were doing nicely. Two days later, an elated new father returned, as ordered, to New Castle to sign in with the 2nd Ferrying Group.

The new assignment? Ferrying Baltimore-built Martin B-26s, that bullet-nosed, twin-engined medium bomber initially termed the "widow maker." Several modifications and some intensified transitional training ultimately made it one of the USAAF's most respected and effective weapons.

Katherine arrived in Wilmington by train to be with me on my 22nd birthday on the 30th. We shared the cake she had brought, a wonderful celebration in a Wilmington hotel. Shortly, we—now including our infant daughter—rented a little house in Middletown, a few miles west of Odessa where we had co-habited in that old retired inn with Hutch and the car-appropriating Don Harding. These were good days. When I wasn't flying a ferry trip, I would from time to time check out a B-25 for a training flight, always easily finding another pilot to go along on these fun rides.

Then, in September, new orders. I was to be transferred to the 9th Air Force in England.

5
CHAPTER

FIERCE ACCELERATION GLUED ME TO THE SEATBACK

October, 1943. The staging area at Taunton, Massachusetts, 15 miles east of Providence, Rhode Island featured one primary activity: waiting. For a couple weeks. That was time enough for Katherine to join me briefly, and we spent several pleasant days together in Providence. While she was with me, new orders were cut, including train fare to Halifax, Nova Scotia. This dedicated aviator was about to cross the Atlantic by boat. Katherine returned to Pennsylvania, and I climbed aboard a train for the long pull to Halifax. There I boarded the good ship *Mauritania* for a five-day crossing to Liverpool, England.

Officers were given quarters near the deck, a far better arrangement than the alternative bunks down in the bowels of the ship. We whiled away the first four days playing cards or reading. The crossing was smooth and uneventful—until the final day.

We awoke to rapidly deteriorating weather. Through the day, heavy seas racked up a roster of retching passengers. I came close but fortunately managed to "weather" it out without embarassing myself.

From Liverpool, the gritty home port of the ill-fated *Titanic* and *Lusitania,* we pilots destined for ferry assignments boarded a train for Matching Green, not far from London. Here a bustling USAAF replacement depot offered a sprawl of hump-roofed Quonset huts seemingly adrift in a sea of mud. As we awaited assignments in this bustling mire, we had more than enough free time and several of us became lasting friends. Californian Dan Sjoberg, a gifted cartoonist and one of the wittiest people I've ever known, was a joy to be with. Jim Fisher, Morgan Sleppy and Wilson Tayloe also became good and true friends of mine.

When November rolled around with still no assignments, we were free to visit London, usually staying at the officers' Red Cross Club at Princess Gardens. Britain was under frequent attacks by the Luftwaffe, and we all developed a great admiration for the beleagured Brits.

A wonderful British lady, Emilie d'Alexander—Alex, we called her fondly—worked the desk at the club. She knew London well and directed us to theaters, cinemas and museums. And, of course, pubs. Though I didn't drink, I did enjoy pub crawling with the "lads." Alex called me "father," and informally appointed me chaperon to see that all in our party returned safely after nights on the town. Since our group had no really dedicated drinkers, that wasn't a tough job—except one particular evening.

One of our friends had hoisted a glass or two too many. When he became wobbly-kneed and a trifle boisterous, I thought it time to escort him back to the club. As I hailed a cab, a group of high-ranking American officers, including a general and several others of elevated rank, strolled into the scene. Our friend, a lowly flight officer—the USAAF equivalent of a warrant officer—lurched in front of them. He then addressed the general as "Buddy" and offered a not exactly reverent remark concerning high brass.

All of them bristled. "Time to call the military police," one growled.

At that point, chaperon 2nd Lieutenant Race stepped forward. "It's possible, sir," I said to the offended general in as placating a voice as I could muster, "that Flying Officer Adam may be reacting to the stress of combat."

I don't believe they took my explanation seriously, but the general hesitated. I hoped he wouldn't study our silver wings closely. Service pilots weren't assigned combat flying, and Adam hadn't had a moment of it. "I'll see that he gets home immediately, sir," I promised urgently.

Adam attempted a pitiful salute. Possibly the general was thinking of the red tape involved in an arrest, insubordination charges, etc., etc. Fortunately the cab I'd signaled still stood by. While the high rankers appeared to be digesting all the complexities of running Adam in, I hustled him aboard the cab and we hurried out of there.

Another—and far more genteel—London incident concerned an invitation delivered to Alex at the club by a British couple. They would like to host dinner for two American officers. Alex decided Sjoberg and I were good candidates, and we accepted gladly. We arrived at the Britishers' impressive "flat" and immediately felt we were a tad beyond our depths at this level of British society.

The conversation began with our hosts asking us about our homes and, of course, our schools. I muttered something about the University of Scranton, hoping it might be assumed an equivalent of Yale or Harvard, but it didn't come within binocular range of our host's venerable public (British private) school followed by his prestigious university. Dan and I did our gentle best to steer the conversation back to our hosts. During the marvelous dinner, we observed carefully to be certain not to grasp a spoon when a fork was called for, and I felt we came through with colors still flying. Then we were offered a glass of port. I declined, a churlish reaction, I decided too late, in comparison with Dan's graceful acceptance. Throughout the visit, the warmth and hospitality of these two members of the gentry were irresistible. We enjoyed a truly grand evening.

None of us had flown for two months. To qualify for flight pay, Army Air Forces regulations required four hours of flight time per month. Thanks to an AAF detachment at Heston, an airport nearby, several of us were finally able to fly one of Heston's Piper L-4s and log the required air time.

On one of those flights, I landed at an RAF field at Watford and spotted a sporty little de Havilland Tiger Moth. I asked if I might take the 1930s vintage open-cockpit biplane "around the patch." Permission granted, I flew my first British airplane.

An American P-47 squadron was in operation near Matching Green. Still awaiting an assignment, I hoped that base might have a need for an unassigned and temporarily idle ferry pilot. I checked out a Jeep from Matching Green's motor pool, drove to the P-47 base and asked to see the commanding officer, a Colonel Peterson. The executive officer heard me out, and together we went to the colonel, a surprisingly young chap in his late twenties.

Peterson hoped I'd had some P-47 experience. I admitted I hadn't, but he was interested in my 100 hours in B-26s and over 1,000 flying hours total. For a heady moment, I saw the possibility of finessing the system and becoming a P-47 fighter pilot. Then he asked how much gunnery training I'd had. Zero. My hope evaporated.

At last in December I was assigned to the 326th Ferrying and Transport Squadron of the 9th Air Force at Grove. The airfield was in the vicinity of Reading, a town in the lovely countryside along the Thames about 35 miles west of London.

Shortly after I arrived, I was given an instrument flying check in a Link Trainer. This nefarious machine consisted of a miniature airplane on a boxlike base. The stubby-winged plane's fuselage seated one victim. When the hood was in place covering the cockpit, the pilot within had a set of realistic controls but was entirely dependent upon the instrument panel. If mishandled, the little plane could stall, drop into a spiral, whirl around in a simulated spin and sink to zero altitude. The Link instructor, most often an enlisted man, sat in full charge behind a desk on which a three-wheeled "crab" crawled around a radio range chart. The crab's marking wheel indelibly recorded in red ink the pilot's navigational success or failure.

I passed the Link check. Next came a successful and brief check ride in a C-47, the military cargo version of the airlines' DC-3.

Grove was to be my home for about six months. Life there was not at all bad. I lived in a fair-sized Quonset hut with the same hutmates I'd had at Matching Green: cartoonist Sjoberg, Wilson Tayloe, Jim Fisher and Morgan Sleppy.

Grove's airfield lay close by the village of Wantage. Since strict blackout regulations were observed, not a single light gleamed at night. Occasionally we walked into town to catch a movie, a challenge each way in the pitch blackness.

An important part of each day was mail call. Katherine never missed a single day's writing. Often I would be delighted to receive two "V-Mail" letters from her in one day. Hers weren't the only letters I read. One of my duties as an officer was to censor letters written by enlisted men before they could be mailed home. The purpose, of course, was to eliminate anything of a revealing military nature. I found this duty so distasteful I'm afraid I gave those personal writings mere cursory scans.

My first flying assigment at Grove—ironic after the turn-down at the P-47 fighter base—was to ferry a P-47 from Filton to Chilbolton. Filton, near Bristol in western England's Cottswold Hills, was the staging area for Republic P-47s and North American P-51s. The fighters were shipped from the U.S. to England semi-disassembled. At Filton, the wings and tail surfaces were reattached, each fighter was flight tested, then we service pilots would ferry them to operational bases.

The fat-bodied, seven-ton P-47 was powered by a huge Pratt & Whitney 18-cylinder radial engine that generated 2,000 howling horses at take-off. The plane was officially and aptly named the Thunderbolt. Its chunky appearance earned it the pilots' nickname, the Jug. Since I'd never flown a P-47, I had never had access to an operating manual.

My sole introduction to this massive fighter was a quick cockpit check, and assurance that when I landed this powerhouse 80 miles distant in Chilbolton, a British Airspeed Oxford three-place trainer would be waiting to fly me back to Filton for the next ferry trip.

The winter weather was murky with visibility a scant two miles. This was absolutely not the best day to strap on the first fighter I had ever sat in—especially this imposing Thunderbolt.

Take-off was . . . exhilerating. The fierce acceleration glued me to the seatback. Promptly airborne, I made a cautious turn toward Chilbolton and howled through the muggy afternoon at 235 mph. I felt as if I were trying to keep up with aerial events racing ahead of me and had only a slight hope of spotting Chilbolton before I roared on across the English Channel. If I were only a mile or so off-course, I could easily tear right on past, and Chilbolton would become a name to haunt me.

Then, sheer luck! Twenty minutes into the flight, there it lay. Dead ahead. Now to slow this monster so I could keep the airfield in sight. I throttled back, cut the airspeed to 150, circled, lowered the flaps a little and turned downwind. When I swung into the base leg, the airport had disappeared. I turned to the runway heading for final approach through a wall of mist.

The airfield popped back into view. I was coming in way too high and much too fast. I rammed the throttle forward, retracted the flaps, swung around again.

The second approach was just as bad. On my third try to put this thundering machine on the ground, I tightened the pattern for a shorter final approach leg to the intermittently visible airport.

Gear down, flaps full down. I rushed across the end of the runway at 120 mph to manage quite a smooth landing. Taxied in. Parked the beast and walked to Flight Control trying to look as if I customarily made three approaches. Nothing to it.

"Surprised to see you come in, Lieutenant," said the ops officer. "In this sort of muck, we here at Chilbolton do not fly at all."

This presumably crazed ferry pilot sat down to wait for the promised twin-engined Oxford to return me to Filton for the next P-47 trip, now that I as such an experienced Thunderbolt pilot. Dusk deepened the airfield's gloom. Mine too. I waited all night. The Oxford pilot wasn't flying at Chilbolton either. He had become lost, landed elsewhere and didn't show up until the next day.

Dicey flying in England's wintertime murk was the norm. That flight wasn't to be my only close call.

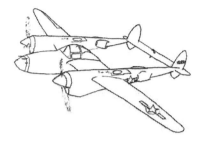

6
CHAPTER

A REAL HANDFUL OF
NO-NONSENSE AIRPLANE

Through the ensuing few months I ferried a lot of P-47s and P-51s to bases all over England. My next memorable flight from Filton in what the RAF termed "filthy" weather was a wintertime delivery of a P-51, North American's superb shark of the air. The P-51 Mustang has been said by many aviation experts to have been the best fighter plane of World War II. Its trim profile was deepened by a prominent ventral airscoop, the Mustang's trademark. The otherwise sleek fighter was powered by a Packard-built Rolls-Royce Merlin in-line engine that booted out 1,400 hp at take-off. The P-51 cruised at a then-impressive 362 mph.

My edge-of-the-seat P-51 flight began with my ship as the second of three Mustangs to take off from Filton. We intended to make a short hop to Charmy Down, only 15 minutes distant. The base of thick clouds hung a scant 100 feet over the airfield at Filton. Off into the murk roared the first P-51. Just moments later out there in the gloom, he crashed. The pilot did not survive.

With that morale flattener starkly in mind, I gunned off next. I kept her down on the deck, skimming chimney pots in the nearby town. I knew I was approaching the tethered defensive barrage balloons around Bristol well below their level. The balloons were hidden in the clouds overhead. Their steel cables, intended to ensnare low-flying enemy aircraft, also were invisible. But the tethers were equipped with "squealers" on a secret radio frequency to warn Allied aircraft of their locations. Thanks to the squealer signals, I wound my way through the cables unscathed.

Charmy Down lay on a slight plateau, just high enough to put the airfield up in the cloud layer. I made two abortive attempts to put the P-51 in there, then discretion became the better part of needless determination. I swung away, headed east deciding to land at the first minimally open airfield I could find. That turned out to be Grove, my home base. I glued the Mustang down there and was told the third pilot in our little group—he had taken off just after I had—also had managed to land in one piece. Elsewhere, not at Charmy Down.

My first flight in a P-38 Lightning, Lockheed's twin-engined fighter the Germans called the "fork-tailed devil," turned out to be another self-taught happening. In February, 1944 a P-38 landed at Grove. Our squadron was on call to ferry P-38s, but only Dan Sjoberg had ever flown one—and then just briefly. He was directed to give me a cockpit check, then I would fly the single-place fighter and qualify others.

I won't forget that day. A thick overcast hung 500 feet above the field. Snug in the pod between the big fighter's twin booms, I sat surrounded by a bewildering array of switches and gauges. Perched on the wing root, Dan tried to explain the essentials. Starting procedure, power settings, take-off and approach speeds, flap settings—all were fairly understandable. There was no check list in the airplane, and when I asked Dan about several gauges and switches that seemed part of the cooling system, he admitted he wasn't quite sure which did what.

"So it's probably a good idea not to concern yourself too much with them." Not exactly reassuring advice.

The Lightning had an impressive 52-foot wingspan and two Allison 12-cylinder in-line engines that supplied almost 3,000 hp at take-off. This was a real handful of no-nonsense airplane.

Dan gave me a thumbs-up and stepped to the ground. I started the engines, taxied to the runway and took off without trouble. But my usual procedure to check out an aircraft new to me was impossible because of the hovering clouds. No stalls, no tests of flap setting effects, no way to check single-engine performance. I just circled around and landed.

The next morning Colonel Feldman, our group commander, asked me to give him a cockpit check on this plane I had first—and too briefly—flown only yesterday. With a show of confidence I certainly didn't feel, I did my best. The checkout moved along nicely until the colonel pointed at a particular switch among the myriad of knobs and toggles.

"What's that one for, Lieutenant?"

A lowly lieutenant instructor did not fake it with his colonel student.

"Colonel," I said, "I honestly have no idea what that switch is for."

Silence.

Then I added in what I hoped was an authoritative military tone, "However, I do not think it will come into play at this time."

Fortunately he decided not to fly that day because of the persistent low ceiling. A few days later, we found a P-38 operating manual and the remaining cockpit mysteries were solved.

Through the winter of 1943-44, I ferried a raft of P-47s, 51s and 38s to bases all over England. During that period, I passed a flight test to qualify as a fully accredited AAF pilot and was promoted to 1st lieutenant. I retired my service pilot wings in favor of the S-less plain shield wings of a fully qualified AAF pilot.

A flight where I came close to losing it was a ferry hop from Green Castle, Ireland across the Irish Sea to Matching Green. The aircraft, a Martin B-26, had a torpedo-like fuselage slung between two big Pratt & Whitney Double Wasp engines, 1,850-hp each. Soon after take-off, the oil temperature soared and oil pressure sank. Disaster impended. Fortunately the flight was a short one. A few more minutes and the B-26, disparaged by some as the "widow maker," could have made another widow. The problem: The thin "pickling" oil used in aircraft for shipment had not been replaced with heavy duty oil for flight operations.

From January to May, 1944 the murky English weather was a constant problem. One gloomy day, I flew the lead P-38 in a flight of two from Burtonwood to Memsbury. Worsening weather forced us down to treetop level and we diverted to an RAF base near Tilstock. We spent the night there, including an invitation to the officers' club. I declined an offer of scotch, but my fellow pilot accepted a bit too readily. In the morning the weather had cleared but my traveling companion was seriously hung over.

"Just follow me," I suggested as he struggled up into his cockpit. I fired up my P-38's engines then glanced over at my friend's fighter. Its two propellers were stark still. Something was wrong. I cut my engines, stepped back down, walked over to his plane, climbed up on the wing root and leaned over the cockpit. He looked up at me, a goofy grin on his face.

"I forgot how to start the engines, Jack."

I tried to talk him out of flying at all this particular morning, but he insisted. So I reviewed the starting procedure for him, and off we went. A normal flight, to my relief—except during touchdown and taxiing he came close to running me down.

During those first five months of 1944, I experienced other trying moments. While ferrying a twin-engine A-20 attack bomber, I shut down one of its engines in flight to check the bomber's single-engine performance. When I tried to restart the engine, I couldn't get the propeller to "unfeather." Its blades stayed edge-on into the slipstream. With that engine now useless, I had to make an emergency single-engine landing at the nearest available airfield.

Another day, this time ferrying a P-47, I was struck by an overwhelming impulse to slow-roll the big fighter. We ferried Jugs at an economical 235 mph. I knew from previous slow-rolls in the P-47 that 250 was the minimum speed for such a maneuver. But somehow I ignored that bit of personally acquired knowledge. As I rolled through the inverted position at my relatively leisurely 235 mph a mere 500 feet above the ground, I felt the controls begin to go slack. I rolled the plane upright and found I'd lost 200 feet during the rollout. Not exactly what I had planned.

More often than not, the weather was bleak; poor visibility and low ceilings. Several pilots in our squadron crashed and died, almost always because of the marginal weather. My own poignant moments included landing a P-47 in a hair-raising squealer on a landing strip 500 feet shorter than the lightplane runways back at Scranton Airport. And I had the eerie experiences of flying a C-47 and a B-26 absolutely solo. No co-pilot was available for either flight in those big multi-engined planes.

Other flying assignments included Cessna UC-78s, Airspeed Oxfords and an occasional Canadian-built Noorduyn Norseman. The trips in these light transports were mostly passenger hops carrying military personnel.

In May, we began flying C-47s. Except for that brief check made months ago, my first trip in that military version of the airlines' DC-3 was a ferry flight. No one checked me out this time, but I did have a C-47 operating manual. Not only did I fly that C-47 mostly on "book learning," the co-pilot on the trip turned out to be the base intelligence officer, a non-pilot. Fortunately, the flight went off without a glitch.

The C-47 and its multi-seat version, the C-53, were military adaptations of the Douglas DC-3, the "plane that saved the airlines" back in the late 1930s. The DC-3 had first flown in December, 1935. With its relatively high speed, passenger comfort and economical operation, the all-metal, 24-passenger airliner had introduced a whole new concept of air travel. The DC-3 was to be a Methuselah of airplanes. Officially named the Dakota in battle dress, but affectionately called the "Gooney Bird," the C-47 and variants would also serve in Korea and Vietnam where some flew in combat refitted as gunships. Even past the turn of the century, DC-3s would still serve as low budget Caribbean airliners, cargo planes, even as low-flying insecticide sprayers. The 70-year-old design just may be the most successful airplane ever built.

When Gooney Birds were added to my assignments, I had no inkling of the unusual direction in which a DC-3 in warpaint was to take me. In late May and early June, we experienced an increase in C-47 cargo and personnel flights. D-Day loomed and an out-of-the-ordinary assignment came my way. In a P-51 I made several quick dashes from Grove across the channel to the French coast. All the fighters we ferried were armed and the guns were charged. So for these over-the-channel missions the guns were loaded and ready to fire. I flew the recon trips at fairly high altitude for an overview of coastal weather conditions and was debriefed in detail on my return. No enemy aircraft sighted.

On June 5, the day before the invasion, I flew an A-20 to Little Walden where Katherine's brother Robert, my old model-making buddy, was based. What a delight to see him!

The next morning, the invasion of France began. Shortly I was appointed a quasi-airline pilot, flying American generals between various destinations in the United Kingdom. Barely off the bottom of the commissioned ranks ladder, this 1st lieutenant found my new assignment quite unnerving. During flights in sticky weather, I would sometimes become aware of a star-wearing command pilot hanging over my shoulder. Such attention was not highly relaxing. I much preferred flying cargo or ferry flights.

In early July we began flying across the channel into France. I flew my first such trip July 4 in a C-47 cargo carrier, landing on a temporary strip surfaced with perforated steel matting: Emergency Landing Strip (ELS) #1. This quickly scratched-together landing site only a couple miles inland from the Normandy beachhead lay close to German-held territory. While the battle raged not so comfortably distant, we began frequent cargo and personnel flights into ELS#1 and returned to England with essential personnel and sometimes wounded troops. I also continued to fly various and sundry generals in and out of that crude strip.

As the Allies pushed further inland, I ferried P-51s and P-47s to ELS#1 and two additional landing strips—A-2 and A-3—now open for business. I found all of this demanding and undeniably exciting, but fate's fidgety finger was about to point me in a wildly different direction.

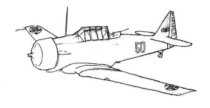

7
CHAPTER

BLUENOSE B

A few weeks after D-Day, General Eisenhower visited British Major General Sir Francis de Guingand, Field Marshal Bernard Montgomery's Chief of Staff.

"Might there be anything you need?" Eisenhower asked.

"Yes!" de Guingand answered with no hesitation, "An aeroplane."

Although the RAF would provide him with a flight on request, he told Ike, "That's not the same as having one's own."

Within 30 minutes, AAF General Carl Spaatz phoned de Guingand to ask where he would like his plane and crew delivered. The Britisher was pleasantly jolted. "There is no doubt the Americans had less rigid and narrow-minded ideas about air transport," de Guingand was to recall in his memoirs.

That same afternoon, Lieutenant Colonel Allen, our squadron commander, told me, "Fly one of our C-53s to Thorney Island. That's where Field Marshal Montgomery and his chief of staff of the British 21st Army Group are. Fly them wherever they want to go, Lieutenant."

Colonel Allen could see by my stunned expression I wasn't at all delighted with this surprise. I had no enthusiasm for flying our own high brass around. Now I was about to fly the high brass of another country's army.

In fact I said, "Colonel, would it be possible to find someone else to do this? I've been flying high-ranking people for quite awhile and it's no fun."

"Relax, Lieutenant. It's only a two-week asssignment while a C-47 is being customized for Monty's chief of staff. I've chosen you over all the others in the squadron. The orders are already cut. You can pick your own copilot."

In other words, just do it.

I decided on dependable 2nd Lieutenant "Deacon" Galbraith. The son of a Texas pastor, Deacon was a mild-mannered fellow with corn-silk hair, a drooping mustache and a pure Texas accent. Slight in stature, he was in his early 20s.

On July 28, off Deacon and I grumbled to Thorny Island on Britain's south coast. At that point, I had flown a mere 25 hours on C-47s and their C-53 versions.

We were met by de Guingand's aide-de-camp, Captain Bill Culver. An American, Bill was a member of a distinguished St. Louis, Missouri, family. Culver Military Academy was part of his "family tree." In his mid-20s, well-spoken and personable, he was the perfect general's aide. We were to become good friends.

Bill arranged lodging, and to my surprise, we were assigned a "batman," as were British officers. He would attend to uniform pressing and shoe shining, and would make sure we were awakened each morning with tea. Deacon and I realized for all practical purposes we had just become part of the British Army.

All the British protocol attention to this low-ranking Yank pilot was strangely discomfiting, but it was the system, so far be it for me to protest. In fact, such high living would last only a week or so until Main Headquarters moved to France. With that, our recently enjoyed posh existence abruptly gave way to tents.

After settling in that first day, I was escorted by Culver to the General Officers Club and there briefly met General de Guingand, at age 45 a youngish-appearing man but with tired eyes. The next day, I was briefed on the assignments we would be flying, primarily from Thorny Island to Heston near London and to "A-9," an airfield close to Caen, France, in the British sector.

Following our cushy introduction, my crew and I were airborne every day, usually with seven or eight generals aboard, including de Guingand. In less than a week, Culver told me the general would like to know if I were willing to continue this assignment when his new, far more plush American aircraft was ready. Surprising myself at how comfortable I already felt working with the British, I said I would be glad to carry on indefinitely.

I did have to fly back to Grove several times to tidy up an administrative impurity. Though I continued to draw U.S. Army pay, I was now a pilot for the British having minimal contact with the USAAF. The only negative concerning this unusual arrangement was it took me out of any slot for promotion. General de Guingand tried to circumvent that red tapery, but the U.S. units I was attached to for pay purposes understandably filled promotional openings with their own people. Also, I detected a trace of rivalry between the camps of Ike and Monty at the higher levels of command—and I was identified closely with the British.

Colonel Allen's promised "two weeks" lengthened into six. By then, I had become quite fond of the 21st Army Group and our British general passengers. I especially liked General de Guingand.

A temporary assignment? At the end of the six weeks, I was officially transferred on detached service to the British 21st Army Group—a Pennsylvania Yankee now in King George's service. I had begun wearing British insignia and found myself coming close to rendering that palm-out, vibrating British salute.

Copilot Deacon Galbraith, not altogether happily, was soon returned to the 326th Squadron. He was replaced by a highly ambitious 326th pilot—a 28-year-old 1st lieutenant with about 3,000 flying hours. We got along well enough, but he obviously wanted my job. He spoke to Culver about his vast experience and C-47 time—a wrong move. Neither Culver nor de Guingand was thrilled. After a few weeks, the new copilot went back to the 326th. His replacement, Smokey Callahan, was a pleasantly gregarious 25-year-old, a good pilot who looked like the public's vision of an heroic fighter pilot type. Smokey stayed with us two or three months, and we got along well.

Bill Culver told me General de Guingand insisted I make all take-offs and landings when he was aboard, which was most the time. That inevitably became quite boring to Smokey, and he returned to the squadron. My next copilot, 25-year-old Pete Tumlinson, was a pleasant chap, well-liked by all of us, and he fitted in well.

Most of our flights by now were from the A9 strip to London and Thorny Island with some welcome overnights in England. We also landed at other UK destinations, with our VIP passenger list energizing many an arrival or departure into quite a military scurry.

In late August I flew to Burtonwood near Liverpool to check progress on our promised C-47. On September 7, we flew back there and took delivery. Now more an airliner/office than a military plane, our new C-47 was informally christened *Mary Lou* in honor of General de Guingand's daughter. Officially, though, our call sign was "Bluenose B for Baker." The aircraft had been beautifully reworked, and Bluenose B and I were to become very close.

By now, I had a permanently assigned all-American enlisted crew. Sergeant Emerson "Gene" Autry served as flight engineer and Corporal Joe Aaronson handled our liaison radio.

As the Allies continued their advance through France and into Belgium, our flights ranged further inland. We flew nearly every day to destinations in both countries. Airport runways had suffered a lot of bomb damage. We often landed on and took off from improvised strips, usually with perforated steel matting surfaces laid by combat engineers.

In September the 21st Army Group's headquarters moved into Belgium. To our delight, my crew and I were given an entire spacious apartment in residential Brussels, quite a step upward from A-9's gritty tents.

The Allies had marched into Paris in late August. In mid-September, we flew there, making a celebratory circle around the Eiffel Tower before we landed just outside the city on an airstrip designated A-42. The crew and I spent the night in the city welcomed by the citizens and enjoying the euphoria that still swept the newly liberated populace. Paris had survived a very close call. In a maniacal fit, Hitler had ordered the entire city destroyed, constantly asking, "Is Paris burning?" At his personal peril, the local commander had defied the order, and the city was delivered intact into Allied hands.

In the autumn of 1944, we were confronted with deteriorating weather. With navigational aids virtually nonexistent, almost all of our flying had to be low level with careful map reading, or between cloud layers with reliance on dead reckoning. Often we navigated entirely on instruments. For landing approaches we would ease down low enough to see the ground. Low enough was under 500 feet. At Brussels we sometimes arrived after sunset. Low approaches in miserable weather and increasing darkness with no airport lighting in evidence were often rather dicey.

All our flights were essential to the Allied advance, and the general staff did not appreciate turn-arounds because of weather conditions. The go or no-go decision for every flight was mine. I cancelled only when the weather was absolutely unflyable. Though sometimes in flight the situation deteriorated to marginal, I never had to turn back. But had safety been in question, I would have aborted no matter how our high-ranking passengers may have reacted.

In addition to his military brilliance, General de Guingand was an extremely kind and thoughtful man. In December, he arranged a delivery of turkeys for Christmas dinner for a group of fortunate British troops. Regular RAF military transport was unavailable for this morale mission, so de Guingand designated his personal aircraft to bring in the birds. My crew and I flew impeccably maintained Bluenose B to Watts Corner, Ireland where we crammed every available inch of the plush transport with as many specially bagged turkeys as the plane could possibly hold. Then we flew them back to an RAF field on England's south coast for distribution to the troops.

After we tidied up the airplane, we flew back to London where the general was attending a War Office conference. While the conference was in session, stunning news flashed in from the combat zone. A sudden attack by the Germans through Belgium's Ardennes Forest the morning of December 16 was developing into a major breakthrough.

De Guingand and several of his officers insisted on returning to Brussels immediately. But a stretch of fog and low cloud all the way from London to Brussels kept us agonizing on the ground. I spent all the next morning at Northolt checking and rechecking the weather. Finally I spotted what I felt was a small "window of opportunity" to fly at virtually tree-top and wave-top levels from Northolt to Amiens, 70 miles north of Paris and about 40 miles inland from the French coast. If we didn't take off promptly, that window would close.

I called Bill Culver. "If you can rush our generals here in the next few hours, we should be able to make Amiens."

That afternoon, December 21, 1944 we took off with just enough visibility to see the end of the runway. We skimmed across the English Channel never above 200 feet and made landfall at the mouth of the Somme. I followed the river to Amiens and landed just as night closed in. The next day I flew *Mary Lou* back to England to collect the rest of the 21st Army Group's officer staff and returned to Brussels on the 23rd. After a Christmas Eve flight to Eindhorn in Holland then back to Brussels for Christmas dinner at Main Headquarters, we stood down for several days.

Not far to the south, seasoned German veterans were pushing back some of America's greenest troops in the most confused confrontation of the war in Europe—the Battle of the Bulge. In the opening days of the historic battle, the Germans made alarming progress. In spite of frantic American and British efforts, the Germans rolled west through Allied lines. When the weather cleared at the turn of the year, the battered Luftwaffe managed a final offensive burst, including an unexpected attack that was to was doom *Mary Lou.*

On New Year's Eve, I flew back to Brussels from a tiring round-trip to Paris. I went to bed early And I was jolted awake early—to the howls of alien aircraft engines roaring low overhead. Then I heard machine gun fire.

I leaped to the window. German Focke-Wulf fighters were strafing the airport. After long noisy minutes, they were gone. I called for transport, and my crew and I rushed into a scene of confusion and stunning damage. Our C-47 had been heavily strafed. Bullet holes were everywhere, especially along the fuselage. Though the cockpit was intact, the plush interior was in shambles. *Mary Lou* was mortally wounded. I was told a replacement would not be available for six weeks.

The clear weather had only briefly benefitted the tattered Luftwaffe. Now it helped doom Hitler's desperate offensive. Allied air support swarmed into the fight. Reinforced American and British ground forces shoved the Germans back—50 miles back—to where they had been at the start of their offensive. In this last and failed *blitzkreig*, Hitler lost 120,000 men killed, wounded and captured.

While we waited for a new C-47, I found an available Stinson L-5 two-place liaison plane and flew it in the British sector, one general at a time, until we took delivery of the replacement *Mary Lou* in mid-February.

A few weeks later, Main Headquarters moved to Venlo, Holland. We gave up that great Brussels apartment and returned to tent living. As the Allies pushed deeper into Germany, we flew nearly every day. Flying over the Ruhr Valley, Hamburg and Cologne, I was struck by the utterly devastated landscape. We knew the war could not last much longer.

When we landed at German airfields, we sometimes encountered American and British prisoners of war from nearby liberated *stalags*. Hoping for a quick ride out, many of these former POWs gathered at the airfields. With turmoil everywhere, my crew and I had great compassion for these often bewildered men. General de Guingand shared that feeling and he would allow us to pack in as many of the ex-POWs as we could. Our C-47 had 12 plush seats, but we would jam in three dozens of these bedraggled guys, many of them sitting on the floor. Then off our repatriation flight would rumble to Holland, Belgium or England with a load of reclaimed soldiers elated to be leaving Germany.

With the pace of the war accelerating, we flew daily through April and into May, sometimes close to territory still held by the Germans.

On only one of those flights we had fighter escort but we were fairly comfortable to be on our own. A lone C-47 closely shepherded by fighters could have attracted some unwanted enemy attention.

On May 6, we were directed to fly from our "camp" in Venlo to Luneburg, Germany. On our arrival there General de Guingand told me our passengers were to be General Jodl and his small party. Our mission: fly them to the surrender ceremony at Rheims, France—the historic flight I have already detailed.

Before I left the British Army in early June, 1945, I and copilot Pete Tumlinson were invited to tea with General Montgomery at 21st Army Group Main Headquarters in Brussels. And it was tea. Our little tête-à-tête was not in Monty's office, but in his private quarters. Pete and I wore our class A uniforms. The general wore his battle jacket but not his familiar beret. The only other person present was his aide-de-camp who bustled about to accomodate us.

Monty neither drank nor smoked, nor did I—which appeared to please him mightily. As tea and crumpets were served by a batman, General Montgomery asked what I planned to do now that the war was over.

"I hope to continue flying," I told him, "possibly with an airline."

"Can I do anything to help?" he asked.

I thanked him but explained the airlines system of starting new applicants as copilots at the bottom of the seniority lists.

His piercing, deep-set eyes blazed. "Nonsense! With your experience, your flying as a copilot simply will not do! You must let me know to whom I should speak."

That was a magnificent offer from one of history's best-known British generals to a lowly USAAF 1st lieutenant, and his naivety in the face of American unions and corporate tables of organizations was . . . well, refreshing. But I knew the flight rosters of Eastern or American or Pan Am would not be entered by way of a call from the hero of E1 Alamein.

The British aspect of my military career climaxed in Washington, DC at the British Embassy where Lord Halifax presented me with the Air Force Cross. In December, I was honorably discharged as a first lieutenant—with a promotion to captain arriving well after that date. The USAAF mailed me the Bronze Star, perhaps a properly low-key presentation mode for one of their people who had spent most of his military flying with the British high command.

With airline employment offices surely jammed by legions of hopeful ex-military pilots, what now?

8
CHAPTER

IMPRESSED BY THE TRIP BUT NOT BY THE CAPTAIN

December, 1945. I left the USAAF to return to Katherine and Jackie, our 2½-year-old daughter, in Carbondale. The war in the Pacific having ended three months earlier, Northeastern Pennsylvania shared the optimism that swept the country. No less optimistic myself, I applied to several airlines' employment offices, though I knew hundreds of ex-military pilots had the same idea.

No immediate openings were available. New applicants were placed at the bottoms of the airlines' seniority lists then were told to go home and wait for possible calls.

Katherine, Jackie and I couldn't live on "waiting," especially with Katherine pregnant with our second child. I drove to my old former center of the flying universe, Scranton Airport. Fortunately my old boss and still good friend, Scranton Airways manager Harold Swank, had just invested in a surplus Vultee-built BT-13. He planned to use the wartime basic trainer for instrument flying courses. The federal government had come to airport operators' financial aid once again. Flight training had been approved under the G.I. Bill, and Harold was making ready for a business boom. Early in 1946, he hired me as instructor for the instrument course. The low-wing, two-place BT-13 was officially named the Valiant. Overpowered by its 450-hp radial engine, the plane had earned the derisive AAF nickname "Vultee Vibrator." Several students signed up for instrument training, and I also instructed private pilot students in the airport's J-3 Cubs.

In these optimistic post-war days with federally-funded students again pouring in, this time with no looming military service to worry about, the airport seemed in a recreational mode. Harold's staff included peppery Gasper Barone, a former pilot himself but now our chief mechanic. Gruff-acting but good hearted Bill Rusinko served as groundsman, lineman and general handyman. Motherly Helen Rawlings kept the airport's paperwork in order. Harold, possibly because of his high energy level and the vivid color of his Buick, had acquired the nickname "The Green Hornet." These were pleasant days at Scranton Airport.

One of Scranton's first G.I. Bill students was 22-year-old AAF vet Bill Hallstead. He had served as a Morse Code instructor, then as a Link Trainer instructor finally as a radio operator/gunner on 15th Air Force B-24 bombers in Italy. Before he was assigned to me, he had logged a few dual hours with instructor Tommy Davis. "He's the first student I've had," Tommy told me, "who could fly on his first lesson—until he looked out the window. Then he was all over the sky."

That, Bill told me, was what happened when you learned to "fly" in a closed-up Link Trainer. Davis left Scranton ultimately to fly for famed aviatrix Jacqueline Cochran, and I felt Bill was ready for solo. On a muggy afternoon I climbed out and told him to take the Cub around by himself. I started to walk away, then sensing he shared my streak of wry humor, I stuck my head back in.

"Don't crash," I told him.

He didn't, but he came in too high and landed in the last half of the field.

"Why didn't you go around?" I asked.

"Starting to rain," he said. "I didn't want you to get wet."

Some excuse.

Bill completed the private pilot course, then the commercial and instructor courses. A year after that first rainy-day solo, he was a Scranton Airport flight instructor soloing his first student. In the meantime, we had become good friends and he is my co-author of this saga.

It had taken me a while to realize applying to an airline employment office was not at all productive. Now I went straight to flight operations and spoke to the chief pilot. Most new hires had taken that route. When I learned that was the way to do it, I applied to Capital Airlines and American Overseas Airlines. Both notified me within days of each other to "come on down."

My first choice was AOA. I reported to Long Island on the designated date, August 6, 1946. "You're hired," chief pilot Captain Thompson, told me, "but first you need to go to the personnel office to fill out some forms."

I trotted over to personnel. "I'm here to fill out the forms for my being hired as a pilot."

"Sorry," said the impersonal personnel person. "We're not hiring pilots right now."

"But I've just been hired—by the chief pilot."

"Oh? Let me check on that." His next comment: "You're right." And he handed me the forms.

AOA conducted its ground training classes in Flushing. I was enrolled, and the airline offered help find lodging in the nearby community. I appeared at an address in Jackson Heights and found a room in a marvelous home owned by an elderly, aristocratic lady and her daughter. My third floor room was small but quite comfortable. I was given a key so I could come and go as I pleased, and my trusty '39 Plymouth was handily parked in the street out front.

The six-week ground school was quite intense with fine instructors, and included time in Link Trainers. All 12 of us were ex-military pilots, and friendships were formed, particularly with Andy Strba and Ray Russell. Both had been naval aviators. Russell had been a lieutenant commander and would sometimes appear in class in full Navy uniform, though he had been discharged. He may have joined the reserves.

While I was enrolled in AOA's ground school, I managed to log some freelance instructing time at Flushing Airport. Then those of us with a minimum total flight time of 1,200 hours were sent to the American Airlines Flight Training Center at Ardmore, Oklahoma. We lived in a barrackslike building at the airport, close to the action. To serve as first officer on long range oceanic flights, you were required to have a DC-4 type rating. Those who did not were relegated to second officer status. I finished the program in late December, air transport rated with DC-4 type rating and returned to New York ready for my first AOA flight as first officer.

I found all of this a heady experience. My longtime ambition was about to be realized. On January 9, 1947 I was launched on my maiden flight as a DC-4 first officer, the new term for copilot. Our route was New York to London with intermediate stops at Boston, Gander, Newfoundland and Shannon, Ireland. The Douglas DC-4 was a four-engined, long-range airliner carrying 44 to 86 passengers, depending on seating configurations. Designed in 1939, it saw military service as the

C-54 Skymaster. Now it was one of the last piston-engine airliners in major airline service at the brink of the jet age.

On this first flight as an airline crewmember, I was impressed with the trip but not with the captain. He moaned and groaned at being stuck with a first officer making his maiden transatlantic flight. I felt the captain wasn't particularly adept as a pilot but he had no problem being abrasive toward me. During our layover in London I noted his fondness for the grape, a trait that would lead to his ultimate dismissal by AOA. Our return trip wasn't any more fun than the flight out.

Yet I believed I was on my way. A month of much more pleasant transatlantic flying followed. But only a month. Then I was dismayed to be furloughed. The airline's program to increase the number of flights had faltered. Some 25 of us at the foot of the seniority list were declared redundant. We were released with a vague parting promise: the furloughs might last only six months.

Six months. What to do now? Our son John Jr. had been born five months ago, September 6, 1946. Now we were four. Fortunately I hadn't yet moved Katherine and the children to the New York area, but my $225 monthly salary had evaporated. With a degree of desperation, I returned to Pennsylvania where Katherine and the kids had been and still were living in a $25-a-month apartment in her father's house.

When I had left Scranton Airport the year before, Harold had offered a little counseling. "Airline flying means being away from home and family a lot of the time, Jack. Why don't you give some thought to Scranton Airways as a long term possibility?"

Obviously, I hadn't listened. With his words still vividly in mind, I gave Harold a courtesy call and told him I'd been furloughed. Though I didn't ask him for a job, he told me he didn't need anyone. I suspected he was letting me know I should have listened to his airline pilot advice.

I next stopped at Wyoming Valley Airport down the Susquehanna River near Wilkes-Barre where I had flown my CPT secondary training in what seemed a lifetime ago.

"How are you doing, Bill?" I asked flying service owner Bill Klish.

"Okay," he said, "but I need another flight instructor."

Talk about luck! "Just so happens I have some spare time on my hands, Bill. I'll be glad to help you out."

"When can you start?"

"Tomorrow."

"Fifty a week or three bucks an hour, whichever is higher. Okay with you?"

"Anything to help a friend, Bill."

Financially paroled but with no real enthusiasm, I'm afraid, I began instructing Klish's flight students in Aeroncas. "Air Knockers," Piper Cub pilots called them. "Paper Cubes," the Aeronca pilots fired back. I did manage to fly some twin-engine instruction hours for Klish in Wyoming Valley's surplus Cessna Bobcat.

After four months of this hand-to-mouth employment, AOA actually called. "Come on back. We need you."

Returned to DC-4s, I renewed my first officering across the Atlantic. Now the outlook was cheerfully bright. Katherine and I began seriously to consider buying a house on Long Island. Then on October 1, furloughed again!

This time, there were two differences. One was good—more new pilots had been added to the bottom of the seniority list and I was closer to the line separating furloughees from non-furloughees. The other difference was not so good. No encouraging words were offered concerning possible recall.

Still intent on an airline pilot career but again at loose ends, I instructed part-time at Clifford Airport, a little turf strip about 10 miles northwest of Carbondale. And Harold decided he could use me after all, again in Scranton Airport's rackety BT-13. There, just a few days later, I became part of a fascinating fiasco.

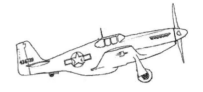

"RELEASE! RELEASE!"

Three of us launched our grand adventure in the "Bloody Thumb" restaurant. Near the entrance drive to Scranton Airport, the rustic ma-and-pa eatery had been informally awarded that name when one of the airport's instructors was served a plate bloodied around its rim by a cut on the server's thumb.

My former student, Bill Hallstead, now a flight instructor, had just returned from the Schweizer Aircraft factory's glider school in Elmira. Scranton Airport commercial pilot graduate Gordon Wills, the second member of our trio, was a Navy veteran. Energetic, fun-loving and impulsive, Gordon had been a gunner on Grumman Avengers. On my second AOA furlough, I was the third party at this fateful hamburger lunch in October, 1947.

"We can buy a Schweizer utility glider and trailer for only $1,200," Bill told Gordon and me. "Somewhere there must be a second-hand plane we can get cheap to use for the tow plane."

"Harold would never let us operate a glider business here," Gordon pointed out. "Scranton Airport's too busy, too much traffic."

"How about Mid Valley?" I suggested. "And I can check on a tow-plane."

The idea of hopping passengers and teaching students in a glider struck me—struck all of us—as absolutely fascinating. The novelty of it surely would generate a bunch of publicity. People would be trampling each other to try powerless flight.

How would we finance this heady dream? We decided we each could pony up $800. With $2,400 venture capital pending, we next kicked around suitable names and settled on reliable-sounding "Northeastern Soaring Association." We exited the Bloody Thumb elated.

In just a few days, the elements fell into place. The Davis Brothers, who now operated Mid Valley Airport, readily agreed to let us base our proposed glider operation at that relatively isolated turf field. No charge. The publicity potential for his little operation was enough of a sell for manager Homer Davis.

The tow plane? None other than Hymie Wintersteen would be willing to sell us his 1931 Bird Model B biplane for a mere $800. The Brooklyn-built relic's 5-cylinder Kinner engine should be more than adequate to tow a glider aloft. The Schweizer Brothers confirmed the $1,200 price Bill had quoted, and we could pick up our 2-22 two-place utility glider whenever we were ready. NSA was about to take off.

We drove to a little airport at Berwick, 20 miles down the Susquehanna River from Wilkes-Barre. Hymie had already rolled the Bird from the hangar. The cream-colored biplane sported its low registration number, NC 94V, in bright red. The front cockpit seated two. The pilot perched aft.

We handed Hymie the check. I climbed aboard and he gave me a cockpit run-through. I felt my flying was about to come full circle. Eight years ago, this same Flying Dutchman with his little toothbrush mustache had taken me on my first airplane ride—at Mid Valley, the Bird's destination.

"Switch on," I called.

Hymie hauled down on the big metal propeller. The Kinner belched, caught then chucka-chucked that rare sound only archaic radials produce. I gave my two partners a wave, fed in the gas. The Bird took off in a surprisingly short run. Towing the glider should be no challenge to this graceful old lady. We headed up the Susquehanna toward Mid Valley.

That little airport a few miles beyond a high ridge southwest of Carbondale, had an aging hangar flanked by a small lean-to office. The hump-roofed, wooden hangar housed a few lightplanes and had room for the Bird and the glider-to-be. On October 22, Bill, Gordon and I rolled the Bird out early and fueled it for the flight northwest to the

Schweizer factory at Chemung County Airport, a few miles north of Elmira.

Bill climbed into the front cockpit. Gordon stood by the propeller. "Switch on," I called.

He swung the prop. Swung it again—then yelled, "Switch *off!*"

A stream of gasoline splashed to the ground. I cut off the fuel valve. We unsnapped the cowling behind the engine. The problem: the carburetor's cut-off float had sunk. That opened up the fuel feed and kept it open, flooding the carburetor until it overflowed.

We detached the float and found it had developed a pinhole leak and was full of gasoline.

"I can fix that," Gordon announced. "I'll borrow some soldering gear from the garage down in Justus."

Justus, the nearest town, was not "Justice" misspelled. The name meant Just Us—a lonely little burg in a fold of the surrounding hills. But a helpful one; in a few minutes Gordon and his Jeep bounced back with blowtorch and solder.

The idea was first to heat the float and vaporize the gasoline inside it. That seemed to Bill and me a lot like melting dynamite. We insisted he perform this hazardous operation seated, reaching around a chest-high board between his knees. That way, when the float exploded, he would lose only his hands, face and kneecaps. Bill and I retreated to a more than safe distance.

Gordon went about his gasoline blowtorching as if he handled such explosive potentials every day of the week. A few minutes later, the float was repaired and the carburetor reassembled.

Promptly all three of us climbed in the Bird, were airborne and bound for Chemung County Airport.

By mid-morning, the glider and trailer were ours. Things were sailing right along—then, a snag. The tow line mechanism newly installed on the Bird had to be certified by a CAA inspector. The nearest one was in Syracuse, 75 miles northeast. Bill and Gordon stayed in Elmira overnight while I flew on to Syracuse planning to return the next day CAA-approved to tow them in the glider back to Mid Valley. A couple days after that, Bill would drive back to the Schweizer factory, have a trailer hitch installed on his '41 Chevy and haul down the trailer.

The next day dawned cold and blustery with a strong wind out of the northwest. The CAA man approved the tow line hitch promptly, and through bumpy air I flew the Bird back to Chemung.

Laying out the 100-foot sisal towline, we hooked the glider to the Bird. With Bill flying the glider from its front seat and Gordon in the seat behind him, we took off smoothly enough. When we turned southeastward over the Endless Mountains, we flew into heavy turbulence. In powerful updrafts the Bird would balloon upward with the glider wallowing far below. If the glider stalled, Bill would have to release the line to avoid pulling the Bird out of the sky; if he didn't, I would be forced to cut loose the tow rope at my end. While we both hung on the verge of stalling out, the glider would hit the same updraft and rush upward behind me. Bill later told me each time this happened, Gordon would yell, "Release! Release!"

"But," Bill said, "I didn't see any landing places big enough to be towed out of by the Bird, and the trailer was back at Chemung."

After an hour and a half of breath-stopping towplane leaps and glider catch-ups, Mid Valley finally came in sight. A small crowd had gathered to watch the arrival of the first glider tow the area had ever seen. Bill cut loose over the airport then rode the rising current along the east ridge for a few minutes before landing across the turf strip at barely walking speed into the stiff wind. The crowd was agog.

A few days later I had the unique experience of being soloed in the glider by the same fellow I had soloed in a power plane 20 months ago.

"Take it around yourself," Bill said, climbing out of the narrow cockpit. Then he leaned back in. "Don't crash."

I closed the canopy. Bill lifted the single-wheeled glider's wings level, the signal to Gordon in the Bird to begin take-off. The towline surged the glider forward and I was airborne. At 1,000 feet, I pulled the release knob. The towline snapped free. Gordon dived clear, and I drifted in silence, the most surprising aspect of glider flying. I could hear sounds from the ground—a car winding along the country road past the airport; a tractor at a nearby farm. Another surprise was the rate of sink. A Piper Cub with its engine throttled back can glide six feet forward for every foot of altitude it loses. Our 43-foot-wingspan model 2-22 utility glider could do almost three times better than that: 17 feet forward for every foot down. Sailplanes can manage an astounding 30+ feet forward for every foot of sink.

From my mere 1,000-foot release altitude with no really strong rising air currents to assist, I managed 12 minutes of absolute joy in unpowered flight.

Gordon's glider lessons did not go smoothly. On a low approach, he pulled up sharply to avoid a row of small bushes at the end of the field. The glider stalled and he and Bill smacked down hard enough to split the single tire. They flew the Bird to Elmira for a replacement.

Every time we towed the glider aloft, we had a small crowd. But it was essentially the same crowd. In retrospect, if every soul in the Greater Justus Metropolitan Area—too tiny to rate even a dot on the map—had bought a ride, that would have paid for about a week's worth of gas for the Bird. We did manage some early publicity in area newspapers but should have kept up a sustained PR effort.

Having failed to master the glider, Gordon became our most frequent towplane pilot. One dramatic day, he settled in critically low on his tow rope release pass and mistook our frantic "go higher" signals for "go lower." Go lower he did and dragged the tow rope into a high tension line near the field's north end. A bolt of blue lightning flashed to the ground. Dry grass began to burn. He landed staring over his shoulder at by-standers rushing off the premises to stamp out the fire that had erupted in his wake.

Off to Chemung he and Bill flew again, this time to buy a new tow line.

While NSA struggled at Mid Valley to become a viable force in soaring circles, I handled an occasional spot of instructing and charter work out of Clifford Airport, a few miles to the northwest. On one charter, I flew to Flushing Airport on Long Island to pick up a Clifford-bound passenger. The aircraft was a tired surplus AT-6, a two-place low-wing trainer with retractible landing gear and a big, remarkably noisy radial engine. By the time my passenger climbed aboard, night had fallen and I was well aware Clifford had no runway lighting. After take-off, I discovered one of the landing wheels lingered halfway up. It stayed there all the way to Clifford, with hydraulic pressure decreasing.

The AT-6 was heavy iron for that airport's short dirt strip. As we neared the area, I released the retracted wheel and by wildly skidding the plane left and right, managed to lock both in place. Gear down, I spotted the lights of Airport Manager Duane Johnson's farm near his blacked-out airfield. A couple of low, window-rattling circles around his house brought him in his car to the strip. In 1920s barnstorming mode, he aimed his headlights down the field, and I brought the AT-6 to ground. Enough hydraulic pressure remained to stop the landing roll just in time to avoid our lunging off into the dark scrub. Mightily relieved, I taxied back to Duane's car, shut down the engine and turned toward my passenger, certain he was scared voiceless.

"Great flight," he said cheerfully. "Enjoyed it. I hope I might do it again some day."

After a 10-minute glider tow November 2—my last flight in the Bird—Homer told us part of the space we were taking up in the hangar was needed for paying customers. The Bird could remain but the glider had to go. The early winter weather wasn't conducive to much flying anyway, so we dismantled the glider and Bill stored it on its trailer in his family's barn in Dalton.

We had flown 23 glider flights from Mid Valley, most of them with paying passengers. We hadn't made a profit yet, but who knew what the future would bring?

Within days it brought disaster. On a crisp Sunday afternoon in mid-November, Gordon fired up the Bird for a solo ride from Mid Valley and headed toward Carbondale. A couple thousand feet over the hilly countryside, the engine suddenly rattled. Then stopped.

Gordon frantically searched for an emergency landing site. He spotted tiny Clifford Airport and managed to plunk the dead Bird in there.

One of the old Kinner's cylinders had swallowed a valve. We quickly placed ads in the weekly *Trade-A-Plane* classified advertising sheet for a replacement antique Kinner K5 cylinder. But the Bird would sit outside all winter, not recommended for a fabric-covered airplane.

Now that we were rendered flightless, a stern order arrived from the CAA. Stripped of federalese flourish, it directed us to notify every airport in the vicinity each time we lofted the glider. That seemed like a red-taped death warrant of its own, but now I realize our compliance— say six to eight phone calls per day to Scranton and Clifford and maybe—heh, heh—even to Wyoming Valley Airport would have driven them all to begging the CAA to suspend that directive. Since we currently had no towplane and the glider had been barned for the winter, the whole CAA thing was academic.

Shortly after Gordon had inadvertently removed the Bird from Mid Valley, its hangar burned to the ground, including all the planes therein. Cause undetermined. Mid Valley Airport was no more. The glider had lucked out by being kicked out. The Bird had been saved by strangling itself.

With NSA in winter abeyance, I finished 1947 as an instrument instructor in Scranton's BT-13 then instructed at Clifford Airport through April, 1948. Scranton rehired Bill. Lacking an instructor certificate, Gordon invested in a snow plow attachment to his jeep and waited for the usual Northeastern Pennsylvania blizzard season. That winter, it never arrived.

I also attended journalism night classes at the University of Scranton. Bill, too, had signed up there for a couple night courses in writing. We were coincidentally together in a Journalism II headline writing course and felt we mastered such complexities in the first session. We found that course of no value in itself, but we shortly did collaborate on several aviation articles that appeared in *Flying* and *Open Road for Boys*.

In the spring of 1948, we finally tracked down that rare replacement Kinner cylinder. Gordon and several volunteers took it to Clifford

Airport and installed it in the wounded Bird. NSA's tottering treasury paid one of Scranton's licensed mechanics to inspect and okay a ferry flight to Scranton for a more complete inspection. Gordon flew the Bird down there, and while he washed off the winter grime with a long handled brush, the brush end fell through rotted fabric on the top wing. He'd been lucky to have made it from Clifford without plummeting to earth trailing fabric tatters.

While we pondered, the Bird sat forlornly on Scranton's tie-down line between an airport-owned Cub and a Cub owned by the local squadron of the Civil Air Patrol. With only a couple hundred dollars in NSA's shaky account, we faced the staggering expense of completely replacing all the Bird's fabric. That problem was about to be resolved by a mean-spirited spasm of Mother Nature.

On a benign-appearing late winter day, Gordon and Bill volunteered to install a new anemometer for the airport. With the wind velocity measuring device in place, they yearned for at least a gust or two to see if it worked.

In the early afternoon, the sky to the west darkened. Unseasonal thunder rumbled out there, and my two NSA partners were hopeful their work on the anemometer might be proved successful this very day.

The sky suddenly changed from gray to black. The still air boiled into a howling gale. Chief Mechanic Barone burst into the lobby. "Stay outta the hangar, everybody! The west wall is bending in!"

Sheets of rain pelted across the hangar apron. The needle on the anemometer's dial leaped to 50 . . . 60 . . . 70, then quivered at 96—class 2 hurricane velocity.

Someone shouted, "There goes the Bird!"

The grand old lady of the air tore loose from our double tie-down ropes, stood on her left wingtips then crashed down on the CAP's Cub.

The wind faded as fast as it had risen. Behind Gordon and Bill, Harold Swank—never a fan of our NSA venture—said quietly, "Well, boys, that just may have saved your lives."

Fortunately the CAP's commanding officer decided the crunching of his Piper J-3 was not our fault, but God's. There was no financial liability. For about what we paid for it, we sold the glider on its trailer to the Kodak Soaring Club in Rochester, New York. The Bird's mangled cadaver was purchased for $200 by an Ohio collector of such relic remains. A compelling, long-shot adventure, NSA had collapsed.

. . . And the airlines still did not need my services. Freelance instructing was no reliable way to support my family of four. My brother Don told me one of his fellow ex-Navy fliers, Leroy Berkebile, was hiring pilots for his company in Illinois. Don, also flight instructor rated, planned to work for Berkebile through the coming summer. Why not give Leroy a call?

"What kind of flying service is he operating, Don?"

"Crop dusting."

CHAPTER 10

WEAR YOUR GOGGLES!
DON'T LOOK BACK!

In May, 1948, Scranton Airport instructors Bill Hutchins, Stanley "Stosh" Zaramskas and I—plus recent Scranton commercial pilot grad Vince Jacoby—headed west. Vince, a World War II vet, had earned his private and commercial ratings via the G.I. Bill. Our transportation was my 1939 Plymouth and a Triumph motorcycle owned by Hutchins. Our destination: Leroy Berkebile's and Roy Nealy's crop dusting operation in northern Illinois.

We took turns riding the Triumph. As we headed toward South Bend, Indiana, Vince was in the saddle. With no warning, a car darted out of a side road into his path. He smacked it broadside, flew straight up then sprawled back down on its hood. The impact knocked the wind out of him, but neither Vince nor the car's driver was injured. The Triumph, though, was grievously wounded. Hutch arranged for its repair in Fort Wayne and returned several weeks later to retrieve it.

After a day's delay to clear up the unfortunate car-cycle encounter, we drove on with all four of us in my car the rest of the way.

At a gas station in the Rockford area, we convulsed the attendant by asking directions to "Pecato*neec*a."

"Pecato*nic*a's up a county road ten miles west of here," he told us. Shortly thereafter, we pulled into Canners Aerial Dusting Service at

Pecatonica's rustic airport; a small office building, a hangar and a collection of hard-used Piper J-3 Cubs. The planes had been modified into dusters with big hoppers in place of their second seats, and their standard wooden propellers replaced with metal ones. "In case you fly through wires," we would be told. The aircraft industry did not design and produce planes specifically for agricultural work until the 1950s. Up to that breakthrough, any plane that could make money carrying an overload would do, including the little Cubs.

Mild-looking, quiet-spoken Berkebile checked our credentials and the others were given flight checks. Perhaps because Berkebile had been a Navy pilot with my brother Don, I was given only a demonstration of dusting techniques. The check and demo pilot was Berkebile's sun-scalded, tight-jawed partner, Roy Neely. "All you pilots from the East fly high and careful," he pronounced, then proceeded to show each of us how to fly low and risky.

Hutch and Stosh passed their flight tests. No doubt due to lingering trauma from his flight from cycle seat to automobile hood, Vince did not pass. He returned to Pennsylvania.

After a detailed briefing by Leroy, I was assigned a 65-hp Cub. Designed to carry no heavier than a 176-pound passenger in the rear seat, the little duster now had a looming sheet metal hopper back there. Recommended load: 300 pounds, though sometimes I was to cram in 350 pounds. The pay would be a penny per pound of insecticide distributed, an arrangement conducive to frequent overloads.

I was dispatched to Rochelle, about 25 miles directly south of Rockford. My career as an agricultural pilot officially began June 8, 1948, dusting new peas on acreage leased by the California Packing Company. Through those initial dusting days, I took a room in Rochelle, living solo for the first few months.

What had sounded like a sure cruise to riches was obstacle strewn. Weather could be a serious limitation. Even on the sunniest of days, dusting was halted if the breeze exceeded a mere five miles per hour. Any higher and the dust drifted away from its intended target. In dead calm air, dusting passes could be flown as high as eight or even 10 feet. A little breeze put you lower, recommended minimum three feet, but most pilots said the minimum altitude really was "don't damage the crops."

From the company's flight insurer we each received a cautionary list of dire warnings:

WEAR YOUR GOGGLES
DON'T LOOK BACK.
DON'T DUST INTO THE SUN

DON'T TAKE OFF OVER OBSTACLES (Easy for the insurance folks to say . . .)

CHECK FUEL SUPPLY

REPETITION BREEDS CARELESSNESS

The goggles were to protect against insecticide dust that could burn the eyes like tear gas. And when you are three feet off the ground and racing toward a tree line at 70+, looking back for whatever reason could be your last look ever.

I usually assisted my loading crew with filling the hopper. I relied on the flagman out in the target field with a small flag to make sure I lined up precisely for each pass. And, of course, there was the need to put each 25- to 30-foot wide swath where it was supposed to go, resist the impulse to pull up too soon—or worse, to stay down too long. Then zoom clear of shrubs, trees, pole lines and make turn-arounds tight enough to save time but not so tight as to stall and drop out of the sky. Agricultural flying has been considered the second most hazardous civil flying occupation. Surprisingly, the most hazardous is said to be instructing.

On days with calm air throughout, substantial money could be made. On one such, I flew nearly eight hours straight with several $30.00 trips per hour, a most profitable day's outing.

On several of my early dusting assignments in the Rochelle area, though I didn't notice him, a balding fellow in his sixties intently watched my performances. Roy told me about my audience of one. I found that odd but thought no more about it. Then a few weeks into the season I was surprised by an invitation to the impressive home of the Atwood family up in Rockford. Seth Atwood, owner and CEO of the Atwood Vacuum Machine Company, told me he had been the mysterious observer of my dusting work. Leroy Berkebile had told him of my flying for the British high command and for American Overseas Airlines. What was going on here?

"Would you be interested in flying a Grumman Goose I've just purchased?" Atwood asked me. My salary would be $500 a month, twice my AOA copilot pay."

The twin-engined, seven-passenger amphibian—a seaplane adaptable to land use via retractible wheels—was a replacement for the company's smaller Grumman Widgeon. The ill-fated Widgeon had dug in one of its wing-mounted pontoons during a crosswind take-off in Canada and crashed. Its replacement was being luxuriously refurbished at Palwaukee Airport near Chicago and soon would be ready for use.

I found Atwood's proposal intriguing, "But," I told him, "I've had no seaplane experience."

"I'll arrange training for you, Jack. And when you have your seaplane rating, it will be perfectly all right with us for you to continue dusting when you're not flying the Goose."

After clearing that with Berkebile, I was delighted to accept Atwood's offer.

Whenever I had time during the weeks that followed, I flew one of the Rochelle area dusters the 50 miles east to Palwaukee Airport to check the refurbishing of the Grumman G-21A Goose. The 51-foot wingspan amphibian, powered by two impressively large 450-hp Pratt & Whitney engines, was ready for delivery July 22.

I checked myself out in the big Grumman and flew it as a land plane from Palwaukee to Rockford's Machesney Airport. Atwood had signed me up for a 10-hour course in seaplane training. Three times I flew the Goose from Rochelle to Milwaukee Airport and picked up my seaplane instructor, a seasoned older pilot. We would then fly out to Lake Michigan for practice on the water. After our session, I would fly back to Milwaukee, drop off the instructor and return to Rockford. Seth Atwood the younger, a pleasant man in his 30s, went along on these flights. After the third one-hour training stint, he said, "I don't see why you need seven more hours of training. We have a lot of flights planned. I'm going to make an appointment for you with a CAA examiner."

True to his word, he contacted an examiner who operated a seaplane business on Lake Calument near Hammond, Indiana.

August 2, I landed the Goose on Lake Calumet where the operator/examiner gave me a run-through for the multi-engine sea rating. With him aboard, I flew the sequence, except for crosswind landings. The wind was too light. He recommended I put in a few hours of crosswind landing practice then return on a breezy day for that element of the flight test.

The next day flying solo at Lake Geneva a few miles above the Wisconsin-Illinois border, I put the Goose through the test sequence which included docking and crosswind take-offs and landings. The most demanding aspect was the crosswind landing, the very same maneuver that had doomed Atwood's Widgeon amphibian. Banking into the wind to counteract drift, an unwary pilot could all too easily dig in the upwind pontoon and come to quick grief.

So here at Lake Geneva I saved the crosswind landing for last. With a spanking breeze ruffling the water, I flared out and dipped the upwind wing—just a little. I was increasingly aware of how close its pontoon was to the surface. When the hull touched the water, I was still drifting sideways a little. At that instant, some small voice within me warned,

"You are crazy to try to complete this landing." I gunned the engines and departed in one piece.

A few days later, I returned to Lake Calumet for the flight test. Everything went swimmingly with the examiner well pleased—and to my relief, no crosswind landing. Then he said, "I guess we'd better do a crosswind landing."

I circled the lake, throttled back, and made the best crosswind landing I was ever to make in the Goose.

"Well, sir, said the examiner, "that shows you what practice can do."

I combined flying the Grumman with dusting for a really busy summer. From early June to the end of August, I logged 175 dusting hours, all flown from whatever fields or roadways were available; almost never from an airport. The sacks of insecticide and the aviation fuel were trucked to the loading sites. The dust of choice was DDT, not yet banned, and several other dusts, including eye-searing rotenone. I'm sure we breathed in more of all that stuff than was healthy. A story went around claiming the local DDT rep would sprinkle some on a bowl of cereal that he would then eat with gusto to show how harmless it was to humans. None of us was inspired to try that.

My dusting work that summer was fairly uneventful, but not entirely. On one take-off, I found I had almost no elevator control. With its 300-pound load, the Cub was sluggish anyway, but this was not good and there was not enough room to abort my take-off.

An empty dust sack had jammed the control. I gingerly tapped the rudder pedals to try to free the offending paper sack lodged back there in the tail assembly, and at last it flew off in the slipstream. Luckily no high obstacles reared across the end of the field and I managed to climb out of there unscathed.

My fellow duster pilots and I felt a special compassion for the flagmen. They had to stand in our target fields waving flag-topped poles to line us up for each pass. As we dived in, they would dash aside to try to avoid the thick plumes we laid right beside them.

A late-in-the-season incident involved anti-aircraft fire of a sort as I raced overhead. I had been reluctant to dust a field where migrant workers continued to gather tomatoes but tight scheduling forced me to go ahead anyway. After a couple of passes, the migrants' tempers flared. On the next pass, a barrage of tomato flak sailed toward me. A lucky shot splattered the fuselage, and I didn't blame those irate Mexicans one bit.

On one delayed pull-up, I zipped under a utility line, not an advised procedure but better than my pull-up August 30. With only a few days left in the season, I flew *through* wires, about 10 of them I deduced from the succession of ping-ping-pings I heard over the engine's yowl. The only damage was the nicked metal propeller. Fortunately the light copper wires still strung between the poles at the field's edge were no longer in service and weren't connected to adjacent poles.

I ended the 1948 dusting season with virtually no damage to the airplane. Many of the other pilots had not been so lucky. Trees had been flown through, propellers broken—and there had been one fatality.

My Goose flying that summer had been mostly to lakes in Wisconsin, Lake Geneva in particular. The Atwoods had a summer home there. With the dusting season over, I began flying the amphibian almost daily. The Atwood Vacuum Machine Company manufactured and supplied automobile hardware to General Motors and Ford in Detroit. I flew plenty of business trips there, plus PR fishing trips to Canada with Atwood customers. Most of those flights were to lakes north of International Falls. We cleared customs at Fort William (now Thunder Bay) then flew on to lakes where campsites and guides were waiting. With no navigational aids or satellite positioning in those days, the fishing flights demanded careful map reading and dead reckoning experience. Up in the wilds, lakes were about the only landmarks.

When Katherine and the children joined me, we rented a comfortable second floor apartment in Rochelle, and between Atwood flights, I squeezed in some freelance instructing at the Rochelle Airport. The Canadian trips tapered off in the fall, but frequent Detroit flights continued. On September 1, when I least needed it, I was notified by American Overseas Airlines to report October 1. I talked the situation over with Seth Atwood senior and proposed my going to New York to ask AOA for an official leave of absence.

Armed with an excellent personal letter from Seth, I sped off in my Chevy to Long Island. There I discussed the whole matter with AOA's chief pilot, C.T. Robertson, a remarkably understanding fellow. He granted me the maximum permissible leave of six months. When that expired, he would make possible another six months by putting me on AOA's payroll for one day between the two leave periods.

With the Atwoods planning a two-week mid-January Florida holiday, I flew the Goose in mid-December to Palwaukee for interior refurbishing. The work was completed January 12, and I returned there to flight test the plane. Except for a minor oil leak in the right engine, all seemed in order. I had the leak repaired and took the Goose back to Rockford January 13 for departure to Florida the next day.

When I landed at Rockford's Machesney Airport in mid-afternoon and parked the aircraft, I was stunned to find the right side of the fuselage drenched with oil. What had been a small leak supposedly fixed was now a big leak desperately needing immediate major attention. With departure scheduled early tomorrow morning, the problem threatened to scuttle all plans—not a comfortable situation for a corporate pilot. Worse, no hangar space was available and the winter afternoon air had taken on an arctic edge.

I phoned Palwaukee maintenance and they promised to send over one of their top mechanics immediately—a two-hour drive. He rushed in well after sundown in a pickup truck loaded with equipment. On the airport's icy parking apron, we rigged lights, stripped off the spattered cowling and washed down the engine. Then I fired it up. Oil sprayed from a leaking gasket. With the temperature now in the teens, we replaced the gasket—a job that took us into the wee morning hours. I finally made it home with just enough time for an all-too-brief nap then rushed back to the airport. With Seth G. Atwood and his wife, both in their 60s, and his son, Seth B. Atwood, and his wife, both in their 30s, comfortably aboard, we actually departed on schedule.

First stop would be Louisville, a three-hour 20-minute leg. With the engines operating nicely and the weather clear, all of us were elated to be on our way—until Seth senior leaned into the cockpit.

"Jack, old man," he said in my ear, "a window on the right side has a streak of oil on it."

My heart thudded. But the engine was running smoothly. Oil temp and pressure in the green. I reassured him that all was well and I would check the engine in Louisville. Which I did. It was still leaking oil. Not a large amount but . . . a leak. I located a qualified mechanic. This time the fix turned out to be retorquing the base of one of the push rods. With all shipshape by sunset, we decided to push on to Atlanta. That pleasant night flight was followed the next day by a four-hour 15-minute cruise to Fort Lauderdale. The Atwoods went off to their luxury hotel; I to a more modest arrangement.

The following day, I returned to the airport, hired a pair of competent line boys and we gave the Goose a thorough cleaning, inside and out.

On the 19th, we flew to Nassau for the day, stood down in Fort Lauderdale four days, then decided to take a look at America's second-largest fresh water lake, Okeechobee, only a few minutes' flight from Fort Lauderdale. To avoid possible floating logs or other debris in that vast, largely deserted expanse, I landed in the middle of its 730-square-miles of glittering water. When I shut down the engines and released the anchor, I was jolted to discover the water way out there was only six feet deep.

On the 25th, we took off from Fort Lauderdale for home. The weather forecast was iffy. Flying on instruments from Atlanta, I diverted to Bowling Green short of Louisville. In the morning, icing levels were such that an instrument flight at standard altitude in the Goose with no deicing equipment was unthinkable. I told the Atwoods a low-level visual flight should be possible. They understood the situation and agreed to a low-level attempt. Off we went, flying a mere 1,000 feet over the ground. When we were still a half-hour from Rockford, the ceiling lowered to about 500 feet and visibility deteriorated to one or two miles. Shades of flying in Merrie Olde England. Fortunately I knew the terrain well, there were not yet any surprise cell phone relay towers to loom out of the mist, and we landed safely at Machesney Airport, all of us glad to be on the ground.

The rest of that winter, I flew a few business trips to Chicago; Tecumseh, Michigan and Toledo. By April, Berkebile's operation began to gear up for the 1949 dusting season. With several other duster pilots, I traveled to Sikeston, Missouri to fly back with a selection of war surplus Stearman PT-17s. The 225-hp biplanes were selling at Sikeston for a mere $1,000 to $2,000 each.

In May, the Canadian fishing trips resumed. Ontario's Gulliver Lake was a favorite destination with its primitive but comfortable facilities and skilled native guides. On a notable expedition to Gulliver Lake May 16, we unloaded the Goose then decided to fly on to nearby Lake Irene to check the lake's fishing potential. After an easy 15-minute flight, we put down at Lake Irene, and I spotted a sandy beach—unusual in that part of Canada—just the place to taxi my passengers ashore.

I lowered the landing gear and when I felt the wheels touch ground, increased power. We moved a few yards shoreward, then in about three feet of water, the left wheel dropped into a soft spot. We listed heavily to port. Stuck. Deep in the wilderness. No tow truck or Sea Rescue tug for hundreds of miles. Now what?

I helped my middle-aged passengers into our little inflatable dingy and saw them safely ashore. Then I tried to dig out a slope ahead of the sunken wheel. The water felt just a few degrees short of ice. My frantic digging made the plane list even further—so much so that the fuel feed line access from the left wing tank was no longer submerged in gas and I couldn't start the left engine.

Next, I tried bleeding air from the right wheel strut to help level the plane. That didn't work either. Shadows lengthened. We faced a cold night with no shelter except the chilly plane. And we had brought no food on this short recon flight.

Then—with my passengers on shore wondering how in the world I was going to get out of this mess—an inspiration. I dug sand from beneath the *right* wheel. The boatlike hull settled deeper in the water. I retracted both wheels and the Goose floated free. With everyone back on board, we returned to Gulliver just as the sun disappeared behind the hills.

We stayed at Gulliver about 10 days, shuttling from there to Irene—but I kept well clear of that seductive beach. The fishing was superb. The evenings at Gulliver were quiet, sometimes with bridge games by lamplight. When the Goose needed refueling, I flew it to Ignace where aviation gas was available to bush pilots, hand-pumped from 55-gallon drums.

Late one night at Gulliver, the silence was shattered by violent thunderstorms. I began to worry about the safety of the Goose anchored 100 yards offshore. I dressed, plodded into the downpour and launched a canoe into the chop. Capsizing became a real threat, but I managed to paddle to the Goose and tie up to the hull. Several lightning strikes out in the lake had me wondering what would happen if a bolt hit the plane. The anchor seemed to be holding fast, but I decided to stay aboard through the night to keep a watchful eye on the situation. Not until first light did the storms die out. Hugely relieved, I paddled ashore for a moosemeat breakfast.

Back in Rockford, I found a few days to devote to dusting. At Pecatonica, I picked up the Stearman I had ferried in from Missouri, now equipped with a 1,000-pound capacity hopper in place of a front seat. I flew the sturdy biplane to Rockville with a stop at Polo Airport, a few miles north of Dixon. There I greeted Bill Hallstead, currently the airport manager.

After the demise of our glider venture, Bill had instructed at Scranton Airport until he and Gordon Wills found the lure of crop dusting too strong to resist. They passed their flight tests at Pecatonica and were sent 25 miles southwest to the small turf airport the dusting company had leased near the minuscule town of Polo. Here they were given a blitz course in crop dusting by former P-51 pilot and veteran duster Kirby Smith.

By the time I visited Polo, Gordon and Kirby had been assigned to Beaver Dam, Wisconsin to begin dusting for the Jolly Green Giant. Gordon, engaged to an Ohio girl, was especially eager to begin making some money. Bill had been asked to remain in Polo to manage the airport.

"I'm not sure I've made the right choice," he told me." But impending calamities were about to convince him he had.

11
CHAPTER

THE STEARMAN SLOWED, THEN IN A SHOWER OF SPARKS, IT LUNGED FORWARD

Almost invisible in the middle of pasture and crop acreage Polo Airport had two turf runways in the shape of a T. Miniscule though it was, the airport boasted two large hangars and an office shack with a shaded veranda. I was impressed by an incredible sight. Neatly parked between the hangars loomed a B-17 Flying Fortress.

"The town barber flew it in," Bill told me. How he had managed that on either of the short sod runways, I hadn't the remotest idea. Was this a put-on? No indeed. Lester Weaver, Polo's barber and a veteran B-17 pilot, had a fascination for relics of the air. He was to be prominently mentioned in Martin Caidin's 1979 book, *The Saga of Iron Annie,* a Junkers Ju-52 Weaver would buy in Ecuador in 1970.

In October, 1948, Bill had married a striking auburn-haired Clarks Summit girl, and they were presently living at Ma and Pa Shenafelt's rooming house in "downtown" Polo. To keep from going bonkers in Polo's limited environment, Jean served as volunteer custodian at the airport.

By now, a quarter of Pecatonica's 24 pilots were Scranton Airport alumni—Hutchins, Zaramskas, Bill, Gordon and the brothers Race. Katherine, the two children and I were comfortably situated our apartment in Rochelle, about 25 miles east of Polo.

With the dusting season underway, I enjoyed the power and load-carrying ability of my Stearman, though I would discover it, too, could fly into trouble.

Trouble began early. Up in Wisconsin in mid-June, Gordon pulled up a moment too late at the end of a dusting pass. He flew through utility wires, kept climbing—and stalled. The Cub pancaked into an adjoining field. The nose crumpled, the wings collapsed and the fuselage broke just forward of the front seat. So did both of Gordon's legs.

Then his luck turned. The gas tank stayed in one piece. The wreckage pinning him did not burn.

Gordon's betrothed rushed in from Ohio. He was transferred from Beaver Dam to a hospital in Youngstown. Weeks later, with the aid of canes, he struggled back to his feet but not back into the air. The wedding did take place, and his love affair, her bedside vigil and the marriage had such appeal it was featured in the *American Weekly*, a Hearst Sunday magazine of that era. We lost track of our old glider partner until the 1970s when Bill heard Gordon was working in corporate security in Ohio. But a letter failed to bring a response.

Still flying a Cub duster, Bill Hutchins took off from a small loading field bounded by a fence and felt an odd jolt. On his first dusting pass, the cockpit filled with a cloud of eye-searing insecticide. He landed in a hurry and discovered he had grazed a fence post on take-off. The top of the post had stripped away much of the fabric covering the bottom of the fuselage behind the hopper's venturi outlet. The instant he had opened the hopper, the dust swirled into the fuselage.

Not long after that mishap, Hutch pulled out of a tight corner under full power. The engine quit cold. He rammed the stick forward. The Cub nosed down to pick up speed, but he was too low to recover. The J-3 plowed in and flipped over. Miraculously unhurt, Hutch crawled out then supervised the loading of his inert aircraft onto a truck. The problem: water in the gas.

A few days later, he resumed dusting operations in the same airplane. Pulling up from a dusting pass, he shoved the throttle forward and heard a loud *pop*. A spark plug had blown out of a cylinder. Down he went again, this time landing right side up.

Hutch wasn't the only duster with a rebelling engine. Another Pecatonica pilot recalled only that his engine quit on take-off. "Next thing I knew, I was standing in the corn a hundred feet away. There was my Cub, upside down, and I don't remember one single thing about how it got that way."

After several days' dusting in the Rochelle area, I received a request from Atwood to conduct another of the company's fishing escapades.

This one took us back into the Ontario bush: Worthington Lake, Quirke Lake, Algona and Caribou. The flight was a delightful break—days of leisure with cooking fires ashore for freshly caught walleyes, and quiet evenings in camp. I especially enjoyed the occasional visit from a bush pilot in a de Havilland Beaver, a Canadian-built single-engine light transport designed specifically for bush flying.

When we returned, aphids were infesting fields of peas. Now both my jobs were demanding. The days dusting in the Stearman were interspersed with long trips in the Goose.

A flight in the amphibian from Wellington, Ontario to Detroit still gives me a twinge. As we neared Detroit, I detected a distinct heaviness of the left wing. I had no idea what could be causing such an unusual condition. Though the wind was from the west, it was fairly light. I decided to make a straight-in approach to Detroit City Airport's longest runway. Because of the strange wing heaviness, I came in crosswind and hot but touched down with no trouble.

As we taxied in, the tower called. "Grumman 38N, you have a large section of fabric missing from your wing."

Sure enough, when we deplaned we could see a gaping hole about three feet square in the wing's upper surface. On the plane's most recent annual inspection, the fabric had tested in the green—but just barely. All the covering was to be replaced at the next annual check but it had already reached critical. Luck had been with us. Had I not landed straight in rather than circling to land on the east-west runway, more fabric could have been torn away with a possibly fatal result. A temporary patch was promptly applied and we flew—carefully—on to Rockford. A couple days later, I ferried the ruptured Goose to Palwaukee for replacement of all its fabric.

In August I dusted almost non-stop—almost, because of several intervening business trips in the now resplendently re-covered crimson Goose.

Flying so many dusting hours together, Stearman N53181 and I became very close. When I occasionally flew an alternate Stearman, I could immediately sense the difference. The aileron travel would not be quite the same. Control pressures would differ just a tad. Normally I might not have noticed such subtleties, but the critical nature of crop dusting made them obvious.

Most of my dusting take-offs and landings were from cut-over pea fields or dirt roads. I usually carried 600 pounds, but occasionally I would have the crew load her up to the maximum 1,000-pound capacity. The half ton of dust would boost the Stearman at least 500 pounds over certified maximum gross weight. The take-off run would be much longer and on the first few passes, I would be extremely gentle. For such overload trips, we had to keep the fuel's weight at minimum— a policy that led to my second forced landing.

On a late afternoon, fieldman Arvo Kallio asked me to dust a location several miles from our loading site. I had never dusted in that area, and when I finally spotted the field, it turned out to be surrounded by trees. For full coverage, I had to make extra passes along all the tree lines. Those finishing touches took up another 10 minutes.

The fuel gauge in a Stearman was a "sight gauge" projecting from the 50-gallon center section tank. By the time I headed back toward the loading field, the gauge was covered with dust and unreadable. I knew I had already used more than intended of the quarter-tankfull I normally carried. But I figured there still should be enough in there to get me back to the loading field.

The sun had set and darkness was closing in. About two miles from the landing site, the engine sputtered—then quit. Out of gas. Dead silent. All of 100 feet above the ground.

Just ahead I spotted a small field behind a row of trees. No time to deliberate. I threw the plane into a maximum slip, cleared the tops of the trees and plunked down to see another line of trees at the end of the field rush toward me. I hit the brakes and we stopped just a few feet short of the oncoming trees.

Now what? I didn't see a sign of habitation in any direction. In the near dark, I climbed out of the cockpit and began to walk east. I knew a north-south road lay out there somewhere. With luck, Arvo should be driving along that road wondering what in the world had happened to his pilot.

Eventually I reached the road and walked it for 15 or 20 minutes. Then I saw lights approaching. Arvo in his pick-up. Having driven around for a half-hour hoping I would turn up, he was a lot more distraught than I was. He drove me home to Rochelle.

Early next morning we located the Stearman and poured in 10 gallons of gas. I had landed the short way across the rectangular field. I fired up the Stearman and took off the long way. Back at the loading field, I began another day of dusting.

Not long after that incident, I had finished dusting on another late afternoon. As I was about to fly back to Rochelle Airport for the night, a field man bounced his truck into the loading site.

"Would you lay a quick 300 pounds on an experimental plot of mine? It's only a couple miles from here. Very important project."

The sun had just set, but the field lay close to my route back to Rochelle, so. . . . Okay.

Bordering a road to the town of Flag, the field to be dusted had trees along only one side, the field man promised me. Though a row of poles paralleled the road, he didn't think they supported any wires—not an unusual situation in that sparsely populated area. A flagman would be in the field to line me up for the dusting passes.

We loaded the Stearman. I took off and soon spotted the flagman in the fading light. I dived down across the road bordering the field for my first pass, pulled up at the far end, made the turn-around, roared back over the field and zoomed back across the road. As the field man had said, no wires were visible. I swung around, let down over the road again—and this time I felt as if I had flown into a huge rubber band. The Stearman slowed, then in a shower of sparks it lunged forward.

Six feet over the field, I continued that pass wondering what in the world had happened. The plane handled normally, so I completed the job then flew back to the loading field. There I discovered gashes in the metal farings of the landing gear, not a reassuring sight but easily repairable.

The field man thanked me for hanging in to dust his plot, "but," he added, "I understand the town of Flag is in total darkness."

Both of us had failed to see on those "abandoned" poles the power line that supplied the town. I had caught the wires on the landing gear struts just above the wheels, luckily below the propeller arc. The wires had stretched then snapped. I was thankful of that but mortified not to have inspected the field closely before dusting it. A lesson learned.

That same month, the impossible happened. Kirby Smith, Polo's veteran dusting instructor, the former fighter pilot who had taught Gordon and Bill the finer points of the crop dusting art, stalled out of a low altitude turn. His Cub slammed into a hillside and he was killed.

Beneath the counter at Polo Airport, he had stored a carton of his belongings. Bill and Jean sealed it and Bill flew it to Pecatonica for shipment to Smith's family. He said he found that as depressing as every such episode in any aerial combat movie ever made.

A tragi-comedy crash involved one of Pec's pilots who hit the ground at the edge of a housing development where a woman was watering her backyard. He scrambled from the Cub's burning wreckage with his clothes aflame. As the panicked pilot dashed past her, she raced after him and successfully hosed him down.

When the 1949 dusting season ended, I was given one last assignment. As bean harvesting began, a night of potentially damaging frost was forecast. To protect a large acreage of beans from a fatal frosting, I was asked to fly the Stearman over the threatened area through the night. Optimum altitude: six feet. The venturi under the fuselage was expected to produce enough turbulence to prevent frost from forming on the threatened bean pods.

The field was not far from Rochelle Airport. I would fly for two hours, return to the airport to refuel, then rush back to the bean field for another two-hour grind. The night was moonless and black. The field contours undulated and during several passes I rolled my wheels through the beans. I flew seven hours that early September night but I never became tired. The cold and intense concentration took care of even the thought of fatigue, and the beans survived.

I was paid the handsome sum of $10 per hour, $70 for the job, a princely amount in 1949.

As the season ended, Bill and Jean Hallstead returned to Pennsylvania. Bill instructed flying and ground school courses at Scranton and Clifford Airports through 1951 then left flying for more dependable pursuits—and a less dependable one, freelance writing. His first book, published that year, was number 31 in the famous Hardy Boys series.

American Overseas Airlines informed me my appearance was required at LaGuardia no later than October 1. I had already agreed to one final fishing expedition September 26 to 30. So informed, AOA granted me a few extra days to fulfill the commitment. My last flight in the Goose was that five-day jaunt—Irene Lake-Fort William-Duluth then back to Rockford—the final leg a pleasant night flight. The Atwoods, kind and generous people, made me an offer of permannt employment should I so decide in the future. Leaving them was not easy.

I reported to LaGuardia as directed. After a 30-minute requalifying flight, the check pilot recertified me as a DC-4 co-pilot. I returned to the familiar New York-London-Frankfurt run. A few months later, to my surprise, I would no longer fly for AOA.

12
CHAPTER

FROM AOA'S DARK BLUE TO
PAN AM'S BLACK

While flying the now-familiar New York-London-Frankfurt run for AOA in early 1950, I managed to squeeze in a fair amount of part-time instructing and charter flying at Clifford Airport. On a particularly interesting charter flight, a group of us representing the Carbondale Chamber of Commerce flew a Navion and a Stinson Voyager to Leesburg, Virginia. There we invited famed radio personality Arthur Godfrey to fly his DC-3 to Clifford for an appearance at an airshow scheduled in September at Clifford Airport.

On the day of the show a goodly crowd was thrilled not only by the appearance of an international celebrity. They were also treated to the remarkable sight of Godfrey's big DC-3 making its approach over high ground and wires then squeezing down into Clifford's 2,400-foot runway. The relatively huge DC-3 was the largest airplane ever to land at that grass field lightplane airport.

In August, 1950 I was no longer flying for American Overseas Airlines. AOA had merged with Pan American Airways. I changed from the dark blue uniform of an AOA pilot to Pan Am's black.

In the late 1920s, Marylander Juan Trippe had formed Pan American Airways as a marginal passenger and mail service between Key West and Havana, Cuba. His technical advisor: Charles Lindbergh. In 1936, Pan

American began the first transpacific airline service. As his great "Clipper" fleet opened the Orient to airline passengers, Trippe became an aviation celebrity, "the man who shrank the earth." In the 1950s, Pan Am was serving much of the world and, as I would discover, was involved in some highly unusual projects.

My first Pan Am mission was to report to Miami to requalify yet again as a DC-4 first officer. After that brief sojourn south, I was posted to Frankfurt on a six-month assignment flying intercity routes in Germany.

After World War II, Germany had been divided into sectors: East Germany, occupied by the Soviets, and West Germany occupied by the Allies. With Berlin entirely in the East zone, that city was partitioned into Soviet, American, British and French sectors, an arrangement the Soviets determined to make intolerable for the Allies. On April 1, 1948, hoping to oust the Allied powers from Berlin, the USSR closed all roads and rail lines into the city from the west—the infamous Berlin Blockade. After scores of American and British planes had airlifted more than 2,000,000 tons of food and coal into the beleagured city, the Soviets relented, opened the roads and railways—but insisted on strict adherence by aircraft to designated air corridors.

The Berlin Blockade had ended a year before I began my Pan Am assignment, but the air corridors were still strictly observed. The Soviets made sure of that. Each of the three 10-mile-wide corridors also had a 10,000-foot maximum height restriction. Straying outside or above those corridor boundaries was absolutely forbidden. We were tracked continuously by Soviet radar, and several times I spotted MiG fighters monitoring our flights.

Our Berlin-bound flights from Hamburg, Hanover and Frankfurt all ended at Tempelhof Airport in downtown Berlin. Though much of the city had been devastated by Allied bombers, we found Berliners most hospitable. For all the Communists' bluster concerning occupation protocol, access to the Soviet section of the city was unrestricted. Our crew often attended the opera and concerts there. Good seats were had for the equivalent of about 50¢, and the performances were first rate.

Despite constant Soviet heckling, we enjoyed flying the corridors. We made plenty of take-offs and landings on our relatively short hops—and in the winter months, logged a lot of instrument flying experience. Even with that day's relatively primitive instrumentation, most of us could take an ILS (Instrument Landing System)/GCA (Ground Controlled Approach) right down to the runway.

We were a small group of eight Pan Am crews seemingly independent of the Pan Am egis, almost as if we were operating our own little airline With experience levels about equal, captains and first officers differed only by their seniority numbers. The captains often shared "left seat time" with their first officer copilots.

Flying into and out of Tempelhof was a unique experience. The airport had a main east-west runway 5,000 feet long, and a slightly shorter parallel runway we used only occasionally. Approaching from the east, we made the final approach between apartment buildings. The terminal offered a huge overhanging roof that we would taxi beneath to deplane our passengers.

In May, 1951 I completed my overseas assignment and returned to New York with lasting impressions of Germany. The cities still showed the ravages of all-out war. Though civilian casualties had surpassed those of the military, almost all the German people I encountered had been kind and generous—the Berliners still most grateful for the 1948-49 Berlin Airlift.

The next month, I qualified on the Lockheed Constellation, that graceful four-engined airliner with three vertical stabilizers. The "Connie" had been designed to meet specific Pan Am and TWA requirements, the ultimate in piston-powered aircraft. But the jet age loomed and the Connie's days were numbered.

One of my first Constellation postings was on an African flight to terminate in Johannesburg, South Africa. Because of some scheduling glitch before departure, I was taken off that crew and rescheduled for a later flight. Near Monrovia's Roberts Airport in Liberia the Connie crashed. No one survived. I was stunned. A routine scheduling change had spared me.

After several flights to Africa and elsewhere during the summer, I was enrolled in Pan Am's navigation school at the airline's Training Center in Flushing, Long Island. I found the long and complex curriculum fascinating, including celestial navigation and the use of Loran, then a rather cumbersome system. At the time, all oceanic flight crews required a CAA-licensed celestial navigator. I qualified in December as a flight navigator on the Constellation then on Boeing's 112-passenger Stratocruiser. The Stratocruiser had been developed from Boeing's C-97 military transport, which in turn had been derived from the B-29 Superfortress. Of the 55 Stratocruisers built, Pan Am operated 27.

Most of us involved in celestial navigation would use first magnitude stars—Betelgeuse, Castor, Pollox—relatively easy to identify. But fellow navigator and old friend from AOA ground school, Andy Strba, challenged himself by using only second and third magnitude stars such as Caph, Schedar and Ruchbah, much more difficult to identify. Navy vet Andy was a good navigator—very good—and literally colorful. When he was on duty, he would shed his uniform jacket and pull on a brightly checkered vest stuffed with pencils of various hues plus a big chronometer.

His parents were Czech immigrants, his father a wine steward at one of New York's luxury hotels. Andy had graduated from Syracuse University as a math major. He was adept at figuring odds on almost any gambling game. He was well known in many European casinos, and I joined him on a visit to the casino in Bad Homburg, Germany.

Sporting a gambler's thin mustache, smoking a long, thin cigar and with his overcoat draped over his shoulders European style, he was greeted at the door with great respect. Room was immediately made for him at a roulette table. He would place his bets then wander off to check other tables. If in his absence he won, the croupier would hold his chips for him. In the dining salon, he was surrounded by eager waiters. There would follow a connoisseur-level discussion of available wines. All of this was marvelous to behold, especially since I knew his financial backing was solely his Pan Am copilot salary.

During much of our downtime, Andy and I played marathon games of Scrabble. He was sharp but since he always played with a libation at his elbow, sometimes I would win. He was also adept at bridge—even when he drank heavily.

Alas, Andy never did check out as captain. Alcohol got the better of him, and he died before he reached 50. I remember him as one of my greatest friends and miss him to this day.

Through 1952 and much of 1953, I flew as navigator or first officer on Constellations and Stratocruisers. During this routine and uneventful period, I did have an unusual experience—one I would describe as spiritual. I suspect every pilot has such moments in the air, but this one took place on the ground. After landing at Idlewild, I sat in my car unusually depressed. I think the difficult circumstance of long absences from family and the tensions of frequent international flying all weighed in at once as I faced another long drive back to Carbondale.

I had been brought up in the church and had actually read the Bible cover to cover—with a bit of trouble accepting some of the Old Testament's teachings. I found the words of Jesus in the New testament true and real guidance, particularly "Be anxious for nothing" and "Cast all your troubles on me."

There in the deserted parking area, I offered a fervent prayer of faith. In moments, I found myself free of every concern and worry—and I knew the power of the Holy Spirit. The impact of that incident has stayed with me and in large measure would lead to an important part of my life.

In September, 1953 I bid on a vacancy in Germany. In accordance with Pan Am's seniority system, I was awarded the position, a three-year assignment as a DC-4 first officer in Frankfurt, this time with my family. Katherine, 10-year-old Jackie, seven-year-old John and I took up residence in Frankfurt's Niederaad Section. A fine German family, the Saans, occupied the floor above ours. They became good friends of ours, along with many Pan Am crew members and their families stationed in the area. We attended church at the U.S. Rhein-Main Air Base and Katherine taught a Sunday school class there. We played golf at the Frankfurt course, attended the local opera, enjoyed Frankfurt thoroughly, then traveled throughout Germany, France, Switzerland and Italy. Katherine, the children and I tried to master the German language. For a time, Jackie attended a German private school, and we did learn enough to get by. But mastery? No. Since English was a German school subject, most of the local populace spoke a lot better English than we spoke German.

In August, 1954 our third child was born. By now we were so at home in our German surroundings some of our friends thought we should name him Wolfgang, a solidly Teutonic suggestion. But Jackie, Johnny and . . . Wolfgang? We named the newcomer David.

Though the war had ended almost a decade ago, some of the people were still in dire straits. Only a few Americans continued to regard Germans as enemies. Fellow Pan Am pilot Bob Rickard was already trying to assist destitute families. I joined in and began to learn the true meaning of helping your neighbors.

Again I flew primarily in the Berlin corridors, this time with Stuttgart, Munich and Vienna as added destinations. The airport at Stuttgart offered a novel feature—sheep grazing on the grass along the runways. Shepherds controlled their flocks beautifully, and I never spotted a single sheep astray.

For overnights in Berlin, we crew members stayed at Tempelhof Airport in the same quarters occupied not so long before by Nazi officers. The Soviet sector was still easy to visit and I saw my first performance of "Madame Butterfly" in East Berlin. American films were becoming popular in the city, and several Hollywood notables appeared in person. Among those on my flights were John Wayne and Douglas Fairbanks. Layovers in Vienna were high points of our German experience, primarily as culinary triumphs.

In 1955, a truly memorable moment: After a landing at Frankfurt, I walked down the corridor to Pan Am's scheduling office with my ears still tuned to DC-4 engines. Chief Pilot Tom Flanagan called to me, "Come on into my office, Jack. I want you to meet General . . . ."

I didn't catch the name. A general?

"General Lindbergh," Tom said as I walked in, "I'd like you to meet Jack Race." He added some complimentary words but I wasn't listening. The pilot I had idealized in my youth, aviation legend Charles A. Lindbergh, now in his 50s, and I shook hands. And we had a brief conversation concerning flying in then-divided Germany. I walked out of there three feet in the air.

One of my good Pan Am friends during this period was Dartmouth grad and former Navy pilot Everett Wood. Woodie was exceptionally well-read and spoke fluent German. His heroes were not Rickenbacker, Lindbergh or Doolittle but Thoreau, Conrad, Hemingway and Albert Schweitzer. Convinced that no one should own much more than he could carry under one arm, Woodie lived in a cold-water flat surrounded by books and little else. Yet he knew the vineyards of Germany so well he became a recognized authority in that esoteric subject. By the time I first met him, Woodie had placed a number of articles in classy magazines including *Field & Stream* and *Gourmet.* Then a first officer, he was to become an excellent captain, though he seemed to have little understanding of things mechanical. In the 1960s, he would involve me in one of the most unusual flying episodes of my life, and we remain great friends to this day.

Other Pan Am pilots from that era whose friendship meant much were Bill Malcolm, Len Goodman, Rad Clausen, Lodi Lodeesen and still others.

Katherine, the three children and I returned to the U.S. in December, 1956. This time we settled in Ridgefield, Connecticut where several of our Pan Am friends from the Frankfurt days now lived, a 90-minute drive from Idlewild Airport.

Until March, 1957 I flew as first officer on DC-4 cargo flights from Long Island to various cities in Europe. In April I was assigned to DC-6 training. That Douglas-built aircraft was essentially a DC-4 with a longer fuselage and more powerful engines, still piston-driven. The most notable DC-6 had served as President Truman's aircraft, the "Independence." I co-piloted "Dizzy Sixes" on European and South African runs through September.

I certainly was not moving up the seniority ladder at anything near a blistering pace. Monty's words came back to me: "Flying as copilot simply will not do!" In October, I was once more assigned as first officer on DC-4s flying the corridors to Berlin. This was déjà vu all over again.

But life in Ridgefield was novel. Katherine and I were active in the town's Methodist church, and on flights to Germany I would take along boxes of clothing from church members for the many needy familes there. A German colleague saw to the clothing's equitable distribution. In the course of this charitable effort, I learned of a small bombed-out Lutheran church north of Wiesbaden. Its displaced parishioners were temporarily meeting in a barn. They hoped to rebuild their original church, a project I found compelling. Borrowing a car from my German friend, I drove the 20 miles from Frankfurt to Wiesbaden. The pastor, a warm, gentle man, seemed quite pleased to introduce me to a number of his parishioners.

During layovers at Frankfurt I visited that Weisbaden group as often as I could manage. Each time I brought greetings from our church in Ridgefield, gifts of clothing—and cash to help in their rebuilding efforts. In turn, I was given letters of appreciation to be read to our congregation.

Our church also sponsored a refugee couple from Greece. Several of us picked them up at Idlewild and had difficulty pronouncing their names on the entry visas. The best we came up with was "Flash" for him and "Fotty" for her. We had arranged a place for them to stay in Ridgefield and we found a job for Flash. They were fast learners and picked up English in a hurry. Soon Flash needed a car to travel to and from work. One small problem with that; he didn't know how to drive. I volunteered to teach him, something of a struggle. His greatest drawback was his lack of "speed sense."

Despite that problem, Flash eventually passed his driver's test in my 1954 Ford Falcon. While he saved up for his own machine, I sometimes loaned him mine. One quiet evening as he drove the Falcon along a broad street in Ridgefield's outskirts, Flash lost control. He bounced across a grassy stretch, rolled over a lawn and banged into the front porch of a residence.

Fortunately for a change, Flash had not been traveling very fast. Injury to both porch and car was slight. Mightily embarrassed, he insisted on paying for the damage. The lady of the house and I told him to forget it. After a time, Flash and Fotty moved elsewhere, kept in touch, and they did well in America.

Up a notch in the seniority numbers game by May, 1959, I began flying as first officer on Boeing Stratocruisers. During check-out, I was one of two trainees on a flight at Long Island's MacArthur Airport. The training captain, a grizzled old-timer named Meredith "Merry" Warren, demanded top-notch performance. The other trainee took over the controls first and had trouble mastering the ILS. Merry's unhappiness became evident.

When my turn came, I flew several three-engine and four-engine approaches. Merry was pleased. He called the other pilot trainee forward.

"Observe Race on this next ILS approach. This is the way it should be done."

And, of course, my next approach turned out to be noticeably shabby. An inflight demonstration that flattery will get you nowhere—and pride goeth before a flub.

For the next few months, I flew as a Stratocruiser first officer from New York and Boston to—not London and Berlin—but Bermuda, a refreshing change.

Ever a devotee of lightplane flying, during that summer I bought a 1939 Aeronca Chief for $900. I kept the single-engine two-place Chief at Danbury Airport about 10 miles north of Ridgefield. From time to time, Charles Lindbergh would rent a little Aeronca Champ at Danbury, sometimes flying alone, sometimes with one of his children. His daughter, Reeve, tells about one of her Danbury flights with her father in her book, *Under A Wing*.

Quite often I flew the Chief to Crystal Lake with son John, then 13, sometimes taking the controls. I quickly realized he was a natural.

After some 75 round trips to Bermuda, I resumed navigating on DC-6s than came many more months of DC-4 flying out of Frankfurt

In May, 1960 I entered the jet age.

13
CHAPTER

BRASS BANDS AND
RED CARPETS

The DC-8, Douglas Aircraft Company's response to Boeing's early 700 series jetliners, looked much like the Boeing 707. Its four jet engines were suspended on pylons beneath the swept-back wing, and the tail assembly was also rakishly swept back. The 189-passenger DC-8 won FAA approval in August, 1959.

I began DC-8 training in the spring of 1960. After completing the required DC-8 ground school on Long Island, I was sent to Miami for flight training. My first training hop took place May 24, 1960 with the second one the next day. Total flying time, 3 hours. The two main differences I noted between a propeller-driven transport and a jet were the jet's noticeable lag on sudden power applications, and the jet's reluctance to slow down once it got up to speed. When power was reduced, the jet was so aerodynamically clean, it didn't decelerate as promptly as would a prop-driven plane. On, say, a DC-6 if airspeed dropped a bit, just a nudge on the throttles would bring you back to speed. On a jet, the thrust levers would go well forward and you would wait for the airspeed increase. Another difference, of course, was the ability to fly much higher in the jet. Cruising along at 30,000 feet in a pressurized jet put you in a much different environment. A few propeller-age pilots could not master the transition to jets, and in those days Pan Am's cut-off age for upgrading was 56. Fortunately I was not yet 40.

My instructor, Lew Oates, was a pleasure to fly with. I qualified at the end of the second flight. This was not type rating training; my qualification cleared me to fly as second officer copilot. My seniority number still was not high enough to advance me to a DC-8 first officer slot.

Aside from the impressive acceleration at take-off, I found jet flying quite routine—except on a refresher training flight later that year. Each of us two "refreshees" aboard was required to make three take-offs and landings. The first up, I had completed my three. Next, my colleague took the controls while I rode the jump seat. As he brought the jetliner into Peconic Airport, Riverhead, Long Island, too low, I cringed. Then instead of shoving in full power as required in a jet, he just nudged the thrust levers forward. That slow advance of the thrust levers was too little and too late—even when the instructor took over.

About 100 feet short of the runway, we hit down hard, rolled onto the runway, then turned off on a taxiway. The flight engineer took a look out the bottom door and reported everything still appeared to be in one piece. The instructor pilot decided we could safely return to Pan Am at Kennedy Airport on the other end of Long Island. I felt certain we had to have broken something in that jolting touchdown, but the flight to Kennedy seemed routine. There, however, a more thorough inspection revealed two twisted engine pylons. The plane was pulled out of service for repairs.

All DC-8 oceanic flights required two copilots. Since I held a flight navigator license, I also navigated on our transatlantic flights. I soon became comfortable in the DC-8 and enjoyed flying it. Type rating training would wait for awhile. I was destined to fly transatlantic as second officer/navigator for a year or so. Then in early April, 1961 Pan Am's Chief Pilot "Jooge" Warren called me into his office and proceeded to amaze me with a remarkable assignment. The airline had contracted for two high-priority, essentially PR junkets arranged by the State Department. The purpose: to help win the allegiance of Indonesia's President Sukarno.

"Bung (Brother) Karno," as he was known to his fellow Indonesians, had helped found an independence movement in 1927. After World War II, he declared the 17,000-island state of Indonesia independent of 350 years of Dutch rule and was elected president. With Communism an increasing threat worldwide, the Kennedy Administration was courting Sukarno and his Guided Democracy effort. Pan Am was about to become part of that project.

Captain John Rowe headed our crew. Don Rice served as first officer and I as second officer—the two required DC-8 copilots. We took off April 14 from Idlewild for Rome's Ciampino Airport. From there we continued to Karachi along Pakistan's Arabian Sea coast. Next stop, Calcutta on India's eastern tip. Then down the Bay of Bengal to Singapore at the eastern end of Malaya. On April 15 we landed at Djakarta's Halim International Airport, a not so busy facility at the time. A few French-built twin-jet Caravelles of Garuda Indonesian Airways were all that were in evidence at the single-runway airfield. The small terminal was not in a state of elegance.

There we boarded 60-year-old President Sukarno. A short man at five-feet-six with a swarthy complexion, he was dressed in Indonesian garb and stayed in his native dress throughout our travels. I didn't see him smile often, possibly—as I recall—due to some health problems. There was, though, a certain attractiveness about him which did charm some people.

Our DC-8 had been refitted to provide the president his own personal compartment curtained off amidships. His entourage consisted of perhaps a dozen Indonesians—and an American. Some were his personal staff to attend to his comfort wherever we went. The others were higher ranked government personnel. The American? She was an attractive young Pan Am flight attendant, one of four in our cabin crew. She served as Sukarno's personal flight attendant. I felt the other three were a bit resentful since she didn't share any of their duties. She and Sukarno were openly affectionate and she spent most of her time with him in the first class section.

A Pan Am representative also traveled with us. No State Department people were aboard, but they met us at almost every stop.

Our first official call on this U.S. taxpayer-supported head-of-state tour was Bangkok International Airport, Thailand. The last 50 miles of that flight were especially memorable as we were escorted by a squadron of U.S.-built Thai Air Force fighter jets. We were welcomed by a brassy band and a red carpet reception with King Bhumipol Adulyadej himself on hand to greet Sukarno.

During our four days' stay in Bangkok while royal-level festivities and meetings abounded, the crew was housed in the modest hotel customarily used by Pan Am for crew layovers.

Following an elaborate send-off ceremony, we next flew President Sukarno to California with brief intermediate stopovers on Guam and in Honolulu. We arrived in Los Angeles April 20 for several days' layover with no strain for the president or his Pan Am charter crew in the City of Angels.

Finally we flew Sukarno to his ultimate destination, Andrews Air Force Base outside Washington, D.C., for talks at the White House with President Kennedy. We in the crew flew on to New York. Following the Washington meeting, another Pan Am crew took over from there.

A month later, May 25, with Captain Bob Crane replacing Captain Rowe but the rest of the crew intact, we flew our specially configured DC-8 to Vienna to pick up his excellency once again, still under State Department egis. Whether he had returned to Indonesia before visiting Vienna, I'm not certain. There was talk of his having flown straight to Vienna from Washington for some medical treatment. In view of frequent coups in his part of the world, I suspect he did "show the presence" briefly in Indonesia.

On the first leg of this second odyssey we lofted Sukarno to cool and rainy Dublin. Though the Dubliners greeted him graciously, Ireland apparently offered little to hold his interest. That same day, we flew on to Prague, Czechoslovakia behind the Iron Curtain where all seemed quite drab. Perhaps the State Department hoped the west-to-east contrast would be evident to our primary passenger. Our three-day layover in Prague did give us crewmembers a marvelous opportunity to explore what turned out to be a fascinating city with its dominating Castle of Prague, many ancient churches—and the tomb of Good King Wenceslas of enduring Christmas song fame.

Next, a short hop to Budapest, Hungary, for two days. There, as in Prague—as it was to be in destinations to come—the crew was invited to certain of the state dinners. One of these occasions in Budapest fell on May 30, my birthday. A fellow crewmember asked the musicians to play *Happy Birthday* for me, which they did with considerable gusto. Sukarno, whose birthday was a week away, acknowledged my musical salute with great enthusiasm. We of Pan Am diplomatically let that perception stand.

Then we were off to Bucharest, Romania, another Balkan nation enduring Communism's heavy hand. Again Sukarno's hosts toured him through the better parts of the city, though grinding poverty was evident to any of us who looked past the pomp.

Our next port of call was Moscow, heart of the Soviet Empire. We landed at Sheremetievo Airport at noon, June 5 for a 10-day stay. Following the official greeting ceremonies at the airport, the crew was invited to lunch by the chief pilot of the Soviet airline, Aeroflot. A comparable number of Aeroflot pilots, engineers and flight attendants joined us at a long table, with the chief pilot and his translator at its head. A small glass of vodka was placed in front of each guest. Our host began the festivities with a toast. We noted sipping was bad form; the vodka was to be knocked back in its entirety.

We had eaten nothing since early morning and the vodka hit all of us hard, especially those of us not used to drinking—or who didn't drink at all. And that first shot was just the beginning. We realized we were expected to reciprocate. Glasses refilled, we toasted Aeroflot. Then came toasts to the brotherhood of pilots, of engineers, the sisterhood of flight attendants. . . .

Becoming progressively stoked, we Amerikanskis were doing our not-quite-level best to maintain some illusion of decorum. Then one of the Soviet flight attendants sitting beside one of our crew dredged a cigarette from her purse. She was about to strike a match when our man, playing the perfect gentleman, flourished his lighter.

"May I?"

A sequence of wobble-handed flame-wielding and futile cigarette-drawing triggered all of us into giggle fits. When he finally succeeded in lighting the cigarette—in its middle—the whole table broke into gales of knee-slapping hilarity. Mercifully that performance ended the toasts. Lunch was served, and we all became aeronautical brothers and sisters forever.

While we were treated well in Moscow, we couldn't shake our feeling that all of us were closely watched. We also believed our rooms were bugged. Aside from that oppressive undertone, we did enjoy much of what Moscow had to offer. Our crew was treated to a hydrofoil ride along the Moscow River, visited Lenin's tomb on Red Square, then enjoyed a 700-mile train trip to the Black Sea where we spent the night. Back in Moscow, I attended a Baptist Church, impressed to find standing room only for the three-hour service. The parishioners courteously shared sitting time.

The greatest treat of all was an invitation to us pilots to fly an Aeroflot Tupolev Tu-104. Entering Aeroflot service in 1956, the twin-engined jetliner could accomodate up to 100 passengers and would serve the airline for the next 20 years. Its 590-mph maximum cruising speed was comparable to our DC-8's 600 mph.

We Pan Am pilots climbed aboard eagerly. The Tupolev's crew consisted of pilot, copilot and flight engineer. During take-off, we noticed both the pilot and the copilot hauling hard on their dual control yokes. We soon found out why. At several thousand feet, Captain Crane and I were offered turns in the left-hand seat, each of us flying about 15 minutes in a designated area.

When my turn came, I found the Tu-104 extremely heavy on the controls, obviously lacking the boosters common on American jetliners.

I made a few turns, climbs and descents. After about 45 minutes, we returned to the airport with Aeroflot's pilot and copilot both on the heavy-handed controls, again with biceps bulging.

Hoping to reciprocate their courtesy with a flight in our DC-8, we cleared that proposal with Pan Am and the State Department. But the Soviets declined. The Aeroflot pilots would never have been the same, once they experienced the ease of American-style boosted controls.

On our last night in Moscow, we were invited to an informal reception in a government building remotely located in a Moscow suburb, and apparently designated for entertaining foreign visitors. As we worked our way along the receiving line, I was stunned to be shaking hands with a chubby, elfin fellow. There stood Premier Nikita Khrushchev with his wife, both with twinkling eyes and firm handgrips. When dancing began, Nikita and the missus tread the boards with surprisingly impressive style. No hint of the coming Cuban missile crisis nor Khrushchev's deposal by Leonid Breshnev two years hence.

The next day, we took off for Belgrade and more of what had become routine high-level events, including a big reception where maverick Communist Tito himself spoke—at considerable length— clearly still *the* man in Yugoslavia.

Then off to Rome for two days and on to Copenhagen, Denmark. There ended Sukarno's all-expense-paid global-hopping state visits. Now he needed return passage Indonesia. The best route to get him there was Copenhagen-Fairbanks, Alaska-Djakarta. That great circle route would take us a couple hundred miles south of the true north pole and much closer to the magnetic north pole. Sukarno informed us of his desire to fly over the true north pole. Furthermore, he wanted us to circle it. Navigationwise that would be challenging, all the more so because the flight was to be in daylight with the sun as the only available celestial body.

Pan Am arranged for Pat Reynolds, the airline's chief navigator, to join us in Copenhagen. Pat, a top-notch pro, had made navigation his life, dating back to Pan Am's flying-boat days. Plotting a position over the true north pole with the technology of the early 1960s was no stroll in the park. A major problem would concern the compass pointing to magnetic north on Prince of Wales Island, Canada at 73° north latitude with variation changing rapidly.

When we arrived over the top of the world with the President of Indonesia staring expectantly from our DC-8's windows, Pat worked a miracle. We performed Sukarno's desired 360° turn around the true north pole—at 30,000 feet above a dense cloud layer. Then a second miracle. A small break appeared in the heavy undercast right over the pole—though Pat later confided there was a two-to-three-mile margin of error. No need to tell our delighted VIP passenger of that small technicality.

Eight hours after leaving Copenhagen, we landed in Fairbanks. And there we left the President of Indonesia, and the dozen people in his entourage and his special flight attendant. Another crew and plane flew them the rest of the way to Djakarta.

In 1963, an overly-optimistic Sukarno named himself President for Life. Two years later, an attempted Communist coup gone awry led to the military take-over and dictatorship of General Suharto. Stripped of title and power, Sukarno was placed under house arrest until his death in 1970.

I finished out 1961 and the early months of 1962 flying DC-8s on the transatlantic run. Then came a fascinating offer that would completely change my and my family's life for the next three years.

CHAPTER

14

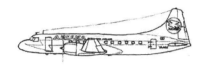

"WHAT ARE YOU DOING IN THAT THING, JACK?"

After finishing out 1961 flying DC-8 jets, I was offered an unusual and compelling opportunity. My old friend, Everett "Woodie" Wood, had been posted to Afghanistan as chief pilot for that country's Ariana Afghan Airline. That unique assignment was part of a project financed by the United States Agency for International Development (USAID). Woodie asked Pan Am, which had a 49% interest in Ariana, to send me over there as the airline's assistant chief pilot and chief flight instructor. The airline was operating with foreign nationals doing most of the flying and maintenance. The objective was to build Ariana into a truly Afghan airline.

In August, 1962 I reported to Pan Am's training center in Miami where I requalified on the piston-engined DC-6 and received my FAA type rating. Back in New York, I was given a series of State Department briefings. In September, Pan Am flew me to Teheran, Iran. And there ended civilization as I knew it.

The day after my arrival in Iran, I boarded a long-outmoded DC-4 for Kabul, Afghanistan's capital city. The flight took four and a half hours and I was mightily impressed by the terrain. Every foot of the way, I felt as if we were flying over the surface of the moon. Both pilots were foreign nationals; I had yet to meet an Afghan.

Kabul's airport lay a full 6,000 feet above sea level. The city was a bustling primitive sprawl in the shadow of the Hindu Kush mountain range a few miles north, its jagged, snow-capped peaks rearing in some areas past 24,000 feet.

Woodie, a five-month veteran on the project, met me at the airport. After our old-buddy greetings, he told me I would be staying with him and his wife, Barbro, until I arranged digs for my abbreviated family. Daughter Jackie had married and was happily settled in Connecticut. Son John was currently in a Massachusetts prep school and would be with us during vacations, so at the moment only Katherine and our eight-year-old son David would be joining me in Kabul.

Woodie and I piled into his car, a small tired Chevy complete with an Afghan driver. Car and driver were provided us by USAID.

"Jack, old man," said Woodie, "this evening I have a very special treat for you." Off we bounded to a house much like a Southwestern U.S. adobe dwelling. Barbro, a lovely Swedish woman who spoke three languages fluently, welcomed me like a long-lost friend. She had come to Pan Am in the 1950s as a flight attendant, married Captain Woodie and voilà, here they were in Afghanistan.

In Moslem Kabul alcoholic beverages were available at the American Embassy commissary, and Woodie believed in a preprandial glass or two. One glass was more than sufficient for me.

"And now," Woodie announced as he brought out the drinks, "the surprise!"

Proudly, and with a flourish, he set out three plates of the finest Beluga caviar.

"Ah," I said, and waxed properly—but insincerely—appreciative. I would much rather savor a bowl of cornflakes than dip into caviar. But I dipped, and the party went well.

The next day I met Ariana's management and discovered the airline's entire fleet consisted of four DC-3s, one DC-4—the plane that had brought me from Teheran—and one DC-6.

Since I hadn't flown a DC-3 in 17 years, Woodie and I toured one around for a couple hours until I felt right at home. In a few more hours, I began training Afghan pilots.

At that point, Ariana had only two Afghan captains, and one of them was in prison on a highly questionable gun-running rap. Prisons in Afghanistan were miserable; dirt floor, no sanitary facilities and prisoners ate only when family or friends brought food.

All the Afghan pilots were initially trained in the U.S. at Parks Air College in St. Louis or American Flyers in Ardmore, Oklahoma. Those who were successful—and most were—returned to Afghanistan with commercial licenses, instrument ratings and about 250 flying hours. We would put them through additional instruction, usually 50 hours of base training and route flying. In 1960s Afghanistan, visual flight was the rule. Kabul and Kandahar did have NDBs—non-directional beacons—but their output was limited and they were notably unreliable. The beacons were powered by diesel-fueled generators. More than just occasionally, certain citizens would drain an NDB generator's fuel tank for their own uses—often just when we most needed the beacon to guide us through a blinding sandstorm.

The Afghan pilots were devoted to their training and I found them a pleasure to work with. As Woodie and I agreed, they made the transition from camels to airplanes quite competently. I learned to admire the Afghans in general. They struck me as a noble people, most of them exceedingly hospitable and generous. I was to make friendships there that have lasted to this day.

In a few weeks, Katherine and David arrived and we moved into a little one-story building behind compound walls that became our home for the next three years. The house was rent-free but I was required by terms of our USAID project to employ a houseboy and a gardener. At the going rate of $20 a month each, Rajab and Alishofa became part of our family. Life was not easy for many Afghans, and we helped our two employees as best we could.

We enrolled David in the Ahlman Academy, a small school for children of our foreign community. Katherine soon devoted herself to volunteer work at a Kabul hospital where many of its needs were being met by the UN's CARE/MEDICO program. As we had done in Germany, all three of us tried to learn the local language, Farsi, a Persian dialect spoken in that part of Afghanistan.

To us, Kabul was the capital of a never-never land. Then ruled by King Zahir Shah, the nation was at peace, and several countries were providing aid. Germany and Belgium had sent advisory groups. The Soviets assisted the small Afghan army and air force. American help included education in cooperation with Columbia University and agriculture with the participation of the University of Wyoming. U.S. engineering projects—roads, dams and airport construction—were contracted through an American company. And, of course, Pan Am had the USAID contract for the development of a truly Afghan international airline.

Afghanistan at that point had two major airports. The one at Kabul had been built by the Soviets. The other, almost 300 miles southwest at Kandahar, had been constructed with American input. The contrast was striking. A state-of-art facility, American-built Kandahar Airport boasted a 10,000-foot runway, a beautiful terminal building, and a hospital, dental clinic and motel on the airport grounds. Because of its location as a logical fueling stop for flights from the Near East to the Far East, the airport had been designed as a major international facility. Its planners also believed the airport could be a busy terminal for tourism in the near future. A moving force behind the airport's development was a fine USAID representative, first name Michael. The sprawling project became identified by some awed observers as "Mickey's Madness."

Neither of the hoped-for supporting events came about, at least in the 20th century. Jet travel with its long-range airliners eliminated the need for an intermediate airport in Afghanistan. Oncoming political turmoil erased the possibility of tourism as a viable industry.

Pan Am had established a maintenance base at Kandahar. Ariana used the airport for some of its training and for certain domestic flights, especially during the annual Haj pilgrimages to Mecca. But the magnificent U.S.-built Kandahar Airport has yet to come even close to its potential.

Within a week of my arrival in the "Beloved Kingdom," I was to give one of the Afghan pilots, Habibullah Balki, his check ride for upgrade to captain. For several years Habib had been flying the airline's DC-3s as copilot. For him to earn the stamp of approval from the Director General of Civil Aviation, a DGCA inspector was required to accompany two flights to judge Habib's performance. I was stunned when I was told the nation's only DGCA inspector, a young Afghan named Bajawri, had fewer than 100 total flying hours and held only a private pilot license.

Since I had never been in the cockpit with Habib, he and I flew one of the DC-3s on September 20 from Kabul 150 miles north to Kunduz, 100 miles west to Mazar-i-Sharif then returned to Kabul. Habib knew the route well and handled the aircraft like the pro he already was. Forty years later, those cities would be in U.S. wartime headlines But that peaceful day we had a great flight—my first over the towering Hindu Kush range at the 14,500-foot minimum altitude above 11,000-foot high Salang Pass.

The following day Habib, Inspector Bajawri and I gathered at Kabul Airport. Local custom demanded more than a simple American "Good morning."

"*Salaam alakum.*" Peace be with you.

"*Walakum a salaam.*" And to you, peace.

Then followed polite inquiries concerning the health of yourself, your wife, your children—and all others in your household, including everyone working for you.

That acomplished, we planned our flight from Kabul 300 miles southwest to Kandahar, from there 300 miles northwest to Herat, back to Kandahar and finally home to Kabul, a 1,200-mile haul with each leg about two hours' flying time.

Off we droned in fine weather, Habib in the captain's left seat, I in the right seat and private pilot Inspector Bajawri hanging over candidate Habib's shoulder. My man did a fine job throughout, including his answers to the inspector's occasional and quite rudimentary questions.

On our return to Kabul, Habib made a good landing, considering the 10- to 15-knot crosswind—which I was to discover was a Kabul Airport norm. He did drift a bit, and Bajawri was critical of that. Our hugely unqualified DGCA rep surely was covering a sense of inadequacy, but we needed his approval and accorded him all the respect we could muster. As diplomatically as I could manage, I assured the inspector that Habib had the aircraft under complete control.

The DGCA upgrade regulations still required Inspector Bajawri to observe Habib's expertise on a flight over the Hindu Kush to Kunduz and Masar-i-Sharif. We scheduled that for the day after next.

In between, I had a training flight scheduled with Kahlil Youssuf, another Ariana co-pilot close to qualifying for captaincy. I arranged for Habib to come along and shoot two or three landings in the day's light crosswind. He did well and I planned to so inform Bajawri tomorrow.

In the morning, enroute Kunduz with Bajawri again aboard, Habib and I were informed our inspector had a new requirement. Though Afghanistan airline flying was strictly VFR—visual flight regulations— the inspector decided to check out his candidate's instrument flying skill. This would be no problem for Habib. He already had an instrument rating.

We had no instrument training hood aboard, so Bajawri scratched around and dredged up a piece of brown paper. We taped it inside the windscreen, only partly obscuring vision outside. Habib flew a few minutes straight and level. The whole procedure struck Habib and me as ludicrous, but apparently Bajawri had to fill in some blank in his inspection report. At that point, I told him of Habib's excellent crosswind landing practice yesterday, which the inspector seemed pleased to hear. Without any further jury-rigged testing procedures, we landed back at Kabul around noon.

On October 3, Habib received DGCA's official blessing as an Ariana DC-3 captain, and all concerned felt the impact of the Afghan proverb, *Yaz roz deedee dost digar roz deedee birawdar*—The first day you meet you are friends, the next day you meet you are brothers.

Over the next few years, soft-spoken competent Habib and I were to become firm friends. During the Soviet occupation of Afghanistan in the 1980s, I was able to help him and his family emigrate to the U.S. where they took up residence in a supportive Afghan community in Los Angeles. He worked 15 years in a warehouse, his wife worked for an electronics company, and they managed to put their four children through college. I visited them several times and attended Habib's son's wedding.

Shortly after my arrival in Kabul, I had been issued Afghan Air Authority airline transport pilot license number 26. Not long after Habib's check rides with the DGCA inspector, I was designated Air Authority Examiner #1, replacing Bajawri. His background and experience had been found inadequate to judge airline pilot qualifications. That was no reflection on Bajawri's character; he himself had become aware of his limitations.

Now came the fruit flights. Pomegranates, a major Afghanistan export, had become a primary Ariana in-season cargo. Each fall, the airline flew pomegranate loads—a lot of them—to Lahore, Pakistan, and Delhi, India. Efficient delivery over the desolate landscape depended heavily upon the pilot's ability to recognize key mountains and valleys. Following the Habib qualification flights in October, 1962, Woodie and I lofted the DC-4, stuffed with pomegranates, out of Kabul and headed south toward the location where we would swing eastward on this first of my India-bound flights. The turning point landmark in the otherwise barren landscape to the south was a lone tree, not always visible during sandstorms. From there we had a straight shot eastward to Lahore. Fortunately, most pomegranate flights originated at Kandahar, a single east leg to Lahore, though that route did traverse the 11,000-foot-high Toba Kakar mountain range.

Despite Pan Am's well-run maintenance base at Kandahar, flight operations were fairly primitive. The American-trained Afghan mechanics did a great job under unusually difficult conditions. The air was frequently hazy with blowing sand extremely rough on engines. Russian refineries supplied Ariana's aviation fuel and its octane ratings did not measure up to the ratings required by Ariana's aircraft. The poor fuel quality and blowing sand led to frequent engine failures, particularly the higher horsepower engines of the DC-4 and DC-6.

On a return flight from a cargo delivery to Lahore that fall of 1962, I was also checking out Ariana pilot Inam-Al-Haq Gran as a DC-4 captain. With little warning, one of our engines abruptly "packed it up" in the vicinity of the landmark tree. Having delivered our cargo, we were flying light so we were able to press on to Kabul on three engines. That was the first of some dozen serious in-flight problems I would encounter during my time with Ariana.

Gran, a well-educated member of a distinguished Afghan family, proved to be a natural pilot. He easily passed my check ride. In fact, I found him the most adept of all Ariana's captains. He qualified on the airline's entire fleet, including the Convair 440 added in 1964. Eventually he would become the airline's chief pilot.

Gran and I had several interesting flights together. Late one winter afternoon we took off from Kabul in the DC-4 bound for Beirut, Lebanon, with an intermediate stop at Teheran, a combined passenger and cargo flight. At 10,000 feet in unsettled weather, we began to pick up ice. Dangerous not only because of the added weight, ice can fatally affect lift by changing the airfoil configuration of a wing. We activated the venerable old DC-4's de-icer "boots" along our wings' leading edges, but they soon malfunctioned. Over mountainous terrain with visibility not good, Gran and I agreed the only way we could get out of the icing area was to go higher.

Then our air-to-ground radio died. Without clearance we began to climb. At 12,000 we weren't picking up any additional ice, but the load we already had stuck with us. Our airspeed dropped off 30 knots. The windscreen was almost entirely iced over. Its feeble anti-icing hot air flow had no impact at all, and the cockpit heating system gasped out no more than a warmish wheeze. Then it quit altogether.

Our only navigational aid was the ADF—the directional loop antenna—but it failed to pick up any directional beacon signal. By now, night had closed in. With the cockpit heat out, Gran and I wrapped ourselves in blankets and grimly pushed on, still an agonizing two and a half hours out of Teheran without a single alternate airport available in the moonscape below. We had enough fuel to reach Teheran, but should anything else go wrong, the possibility of running on empty crossed our minds.

The good news—for a change—came from the engines. All four were operating nicely. Over eastern Iran's flatter terrain we were able to descend to a slightly warmer altitude and the ice sloughed away in the slipstream. But now we flew into heavy rain. Still, if we stayed on course, Teheran should loom out of the murk somewhere ahead.

After interminable and frigid suspense, I craned forward. "Gran, there are the lights of the city."

"Captain Race," Gran said wistfully in his gravelly voice, "I wish it was Paris. *That* is the city of lights."

We managed to revive the inert radio and were given approach clearance. When Gran at the controls called for full flap, the hydraulic pressure suddenly plunged to zero. Luckily Teheran had a two-mile-long runway. With the flaps only partly extended, Gran managed a successful landing. He taxied us to the terminal and we shut down.

"*Enshallah,*" Gran breathed as we stepped down to the parking apron. "God willing, we will get to Beirut tonight."

A Pan Am captain I knew had just landed. He walked over and eyed our decrepit DC-4.

"What are *you* doing in this part of the world? And in *that* thing, Jack? And why are you wearing that funny hat?"

The Ariana uniform was identical to Pan Am's except for the wings badge—and the Afghan karakul fur hat.

"Ed, we've flown that 'thing' all the way from Kabul," I told him, "and we're hoping to leave for Beirut within the hour."

He gave me a blank look. "Where's Kabul?"

"In Afghanistan, Ed."

"Which is in what direction?"

I pointed east.

He wished us well and shaking his head, walked off in the rain toward his gleaming new Pan Am 707 jet.

Our hydraulic leak was soon set right and off we rumbled for Beirut, six hours further west. The weather cleared somewhat—until we passed just north of Damascus, Syria where it socked in again. When we finally reached Beirut, conditions were barely above minimums for the NDB approach to Runway 18. Rain and a healthy crosswind plagued us all the way in.

I had the controls on this leg. On the approach I called for full flap. When the flaps were only halfway down, the hydraulic system died again. But again we were lucky. Beirut International had a lengthy north-south runway. But that was one *long* night.

Illogical as it may seem, in the 1950s a focus of Ariana's development had been Beirut's Neptune Bar. In the Middle East, soldier-of-fortune pilots were very much a part of the aviation scene. Many small companies sprang up, usually flying freight throughout this part of the world. DC-3s and DC-4s were plentiful, and a lot of ex-military pilots were looking for flying slots. The Neptune Bar in Beirut was widely known as a clearing house for job-hungry pilots. At that time, lacking Afghan pilots, Ariana recruited foreign nationals; American, British and Indian pilots plus a scattering of other nationalities. Gradually they were being replaced with the Afghans Pan Am was now training. Pilot recruitment at the Neptune Bar had become a thing of the past.

Not all my traveling in Afghanistan was in the air. The ancient country offered unique auto touring possibilities. My little Volkswagen had been shipped from home by air to Karachi, Pakistan, then by truck to Kabul. It arrived battered but still serviceable. In the Volks, Katherine, David and I drove to many parts of the rugged nation, usually acompanied by at least one additional car of friends. About 100 miles west of Kabul we found the beautiful valley where the two giant Buddhas of Bamian had been carved into a huge cliff. The taller of the pair soared up a full 173 feet. The faces of the Buddhas had been damaged, but the towering figures were still an awesome presence in the silent valley—an impact not pleasing to the coming Taliban regime. In 2001, the rigidly doctrinaire Taliban would dynamite the 1,300-year-old figures into rubble.

We also drove west of Bamian to Badi-Amir, more than 10,000 feet above sea level. Our VW struggled up so-called roads, rutted, rock-strewn and not built for automobiles. We forded streams and detoured around impassable sections, and were finally rewarded with the vision of Bandi-Amir's idyllic dark blue lake. We camped on its shoreline mindful that five feet from water's edge the depth plunged almost straight down at least 100 feet, possibly deeper. The water was so cold only a few of our little group had the nerve to dive in.

Afghanistan's more populated areas offered gas stations with familiar pumps, though they resembled American stations of the 1930s. Far more exotic were the gas "stations" in the country's more remote areas. Few and excruciatingly far between, these rural "stations" were hard to find and totally unreliable. We had to be carefully briefed on their locations, and the dispensing system was a cultural jolt. The customer pulled up to an unmarked but known fuel dispensary, usually a little adobe building with a hole in the roadside wall. The buyer passed the required amount of Afghanis through the hole. Out snaked a hose. The customer inserted the hose in the car's fuel tank and the prepaid gallonage issued forth.

Fairly often we drove to Peshawar in Pakistan through the fabled Khyber Pass. That journey risked attacks by roving bandits, though we never encountered any. The winding road through the pass lacked even the hint of a guardrail—far more of an actual threat, I decided, than the possibility of a brigand surprise. As we jounced, bounced and scrabbled through the Khyber Pass, Rudyard Kipling inevitably came to mind. *For to admire an' for to see/ For to be'old this world so wide . . . .*

One memorable day six of us adults and several youngsters, including David, drove to Salang determined to climb to the top of the Hindu Kush in that area. We parked our cars well below the towering crest and tried to follow the old caravan trail used long before the occupying Russians built the great Salang Tunnel. The climb took several hours, part of it through patches of snow, though this was in August. Determination completed our mission and we descended elated. But before we reached home, I and several other climbers developed absolutely agonizing headaches, apparently the result of all that exertion in the rarified mountain air.

Though our auto tours were eye-opening, flying devoted pilgrims during the annual Haj would be the most unusual experience of my years in Afghanistan.

SECONDS AFTER LIFT-OFF, NUMBER THREE ENGINE DIED

The month-long observation of Ramadan was a major event of each year's Ariana operations. Every devout Muslim is expected to make at least one haj—a pilgrimage to Mecca—during his lifetime, and Ariana conducted haj flights throughout Ramadan.

In earlier times, the DC-3s had been pressed into haj service. During my years in Afghanistan we used the DC-4 and DC-6 exclusively. Many hajis saved for years to afford the flight. For most, the trip by air would be their first. For more than a few, this would be the first time they had even seen an airplane.

Kandahar served as our staging point for departure from Afghanistan. The destination: Jeddah on Saudi Arabia's Red Sea coast, some 50 miles from Mecca, the holiest city of Islam. In the DC-4 the haj involved a nine-hour flight, and not a comfortable one. To meet the demand, we reconfigured the plane's interior to accomodate as many pilgrims as possible.

Haj flights were like no others. The pilgrims brought along their own food for the lengthy non-stop aerial grind. Quite a few of our passengers also carried aboard little Primus stoves on which they intended to brew tea. Firing up the stoves in flight was a definite no, though attempts to do so kept the stewards nervously alert.

Restroom facilities on these all-male flights were limited, especially on the DC-4. It was not unknown for some of our desperate travelers to relieve themselves in places not meant for such activity.

We carried two hard-pressed stewards on each flight, and they had their hands more than full trying to maintain some semblance of basic decorum. This is not to say the passengers were an unruly lot. Flying simply was an event far beyond anything most had ever experienced.

The cabin arrangements were made even more complex when mandatory prayers were said with the participants kneeling on prayer rugs and facing Mecca. Hard to do in a crowded aircraft.

Occasionally I would leave the cockpit to peer into the cabin to see how our mostly elderly passengers were faring. As I began a cabin check on one extremely populated flight, a steward intercepted me at the cockpit door.

"Captain, you would be happier not to go back there."

The volume of cabin noise and a heavy influx of strange aromas convinced me he was right.

The route from Kandahar took us southwestward over the Dasht-e-Margow Desert—the Desert of Death—then over Iran, across the Persian Gulf, over tiny Bahrain, past Riyadh and finally across the Hejaz Mountains to Jeddah on the Red Sea coast. We navigated by dead reckoning and NDB beacons in usually pleasant weather, though over Saudi Arabia we would often encounter the roiling dust and sand of towering siroccos.

In the unpressurized DC-4, we usually cruised at 10,000 feet. Some of those sandstorms loomed even higher. With 10,000 the maximum recommended altitude for flight without oxygen equipment, we were forced to fly right through such airborne grit, a practice hard on engines.

During the haj, Jeddah International Airport was an extremely busy destination for incoming aircraft from all over Asia and Europe. The airport was a total madhouse with aircraft and pilgrims all over the place. We in the flight crew would stay in Jeddah to recuperate from our nine-hour ordeals while our passengers trekked westward on the long road to Mecca. The empty DC-4 would immediately be flown back to Kandahar by a different crew while we recuperated. When the plane returned to Jeddah with another load of eager hajis, we would fly it back to Kandahar empty.

Returning hajis arrived lugging more than their basic belongings. Now they also toted containers of holy water, holy stones and other revered items they had gathered in Mecca. There was absolutely no possibility of our weighing everything they carried. I'm sure we usually lumbered into the air above maximum take-off gross weight.

Fortunately Jeddah's runway was a long one—10,000 feet—parallel to the shoreline. We departed at night when the cooler air was denser. Those overloaded take-offs went well enough, but our rate of climb was sluggish indeed. We struggled for altitude along the Red Sea's shore, turning inland only after we had clawed up to 5,000 feet, the minimum safe altitude to cross Saudi Arabia's western mountains. On some return trips our shoreline climb would grind along for 20 to 30 minutes before we could safely turn inland.

As we made ready to depart Jeddah one evening with a full load of passengers, this time in the DC-6, we heard a great shout of joy from the cabin. An elderly haji had just died. The happy outburst celebrated the ultimate pleasure in one's dying during his haj. Our flight was delayed while the body was removed and another haji was summoned to take his place.

The DC-6 was a far better haj transport than the outmoded DC-4. Pressurized, it could fly at a higher, more comfortable altitude. And it was faster, cutting flight time between Kandahar and Jeddah to seven hours. For both the DC-4 and DC-6, the problem on the return flights lay in the chronic lack of weather reports from Kandahar, plus the fact that Kandahar's NDB beacon was often inoperable due to pilferage of its generator fuel.

As we passed over Zahedan, Iran, on one vividly memorable return flight, Baba, my first officer, did manage to get a weather report from Kandahar Radio. We were told to expect a sandstorm to hit there just as we would be landing. At that point, we were an hour and a half from Kandahar and would arrive there with an hour's fuel reserve. From Kandahar, though, there was no alternate airport within that fuel range.

I was certain the Iranian authorities would not welcome the surprise arrival of a large contingent of Afghans without a single visa among them. We would surely be confined to the airport, maybe even to our aircraft. Who knew what complications would snarl us in Iranian red tape, possibly for days?

Baba and I discussed our two options.

"*Enshallah,* Captain," he shrugged, "it is in Allah's hands. Allah willing, we will land safely at Kandahar."

We pressed on northeastward. As we approached the airport the onrushing sirocco blackened the sky. But Kandahar's usually undependable NDB came in strong. Homing in on the beacon's signal, we finally located the airport in the pre-storm haze. We touched down just minutes before blasts of stinging sand obscured visibility to just about nil.

"*Allah akbar,*" Baba murmured as we shut down the engines.

And I echoed, "*Allah akbar* indeed."

With Ramadan over, we resumed training flights, working them around regular airline scheduling as best we could. Our son, John, joined us during vacations from his boarding school in Massachusetts. I had taught John how to fly and he had soloed when he was 17. Several times I took him along on Ariana DC-3 and DC-6 training flights. On one of the DC-3 trips, I let him fly around a while, then try a landing. He did exceptionally well.

The DC-3s still were the mainstays of our limited fleet, and I had several unusual experiences in those old Gooney Birds. In February, 1963 a photographer from *Life* magazine visited Kabul on an assignment to photograph the towering Hindu Kush mountains in the area of Salang Pass. On this mission, I flew him in an Ariana DC-3. During a day of good weather, we were able to pull in close to the mountains at 12,000 to 14,000 feet. I found that to be an enjoyable assignment, and the story appeared with one of the Hindu Kush aerial photos on the cover.

One extremely hot summer day I was flying a DC-3 passenger trip from Kabul to Kunduz north of the Kush, with Wali Azimi as first officer. The aircraft was fully loaded and we climbed out of 6,000-foot-high Kabul Airport making the usual slow progress upward. Twenty minutes into the flight, our male steward rushed forward to tell us one of the women passengers, traveling with her husband, seemed very ill. We turned back to Kabul, radioing the tower to call for a doctor to meet us at the airport. As we landed, the doctor was waiting with an ambulance. As the ill woman was rushed off to the hospital, the husband decided to continue the flight. While we stood by, he hurried into the terminal then reappeared with another woman—wife number two.

Azimi later flew as captain for Air Malta then Continental Airlines. Wali Azimi and his wife, Martha, are great friends of ours.

Of the engine failures I experienced during my years in the Kingdom, two were in DC-3s. One of them occured during a passenger flight Woodie and I were shepherding to India. Forty minutes from Delhi, engine number two quit. We limped into Safterjung. Built by the British during the days of the Raj, the airport had served Delhi until Palaam Airport was built. Safterjung was a good-sized grass field with capable repair facilities. Our passengers were bussed into Delhi. After Safterjung's mechanics expertly replaced the engine, we made our way back to Kabul.

After a year's miserable incarceration, Rahim Nawroz, the Airana captain jailed on the alleged gun-running charge, was released. John Willard, the American captain on the flight in question, had not been detained. The whole incident had ballooned from a cargo loading mis-whack. In the spring of the previous year, a Pan Am flight had arrived in Frankfurt, Germany with a shipment aboard destined for the Imperial

Iranian Air Force Academy in Teheran. With Pan Am abruptly shut down by a brief strike, the cargo was transferred to an Ariana DC-4 captained by Willard with Nawroz as his first officer. At a subsequent intermediate stop in Zagreb to reload the cargo to correct weight-and-balance, the six IIFA Academy cases had somewhow became 12 cases. Six of them were moved forward. When the cargo was unloaded in Teheran, the six cases forward were mistakenly left on board. Finally unloaded at Kandahar, there on the ramp sat those six cases, not listed on the manifest—and plainly stencilled "Machine Gun Parts."

Off to jail went Nowroz and the entire crew including the cabin attendants—except Willard. He was not charged with anything and contuinued to fly for Ariana until his contract ran out.

Nawroz, on his release, was anxious to put his miserable year in jail behind him. As the most senior of Ariana's Afghan DC-3 captains, he asked to be checked out immediately as a DC-4 captain. Clearly, I felt, he first needed to put in some remedial DC-3 flying and first qualify as a DC-3 captain. Though I did my best to have him accept that decision gracefully, Afghans are a proud people. My putting him back in the DC-3 visibly rankled him. I liked Rahim, though he was not a top-drawer pilot and had the unfortunate impression he was better than he actually proved to be. I worked with him, encouraged him, but I was always concerned about his immodesty regarding his flying skills.

Well-educated with a good command of English, Rahim had an English wife, Valerie, a lovely woman who worked at the British Embassy. A proud man, he took a little longer than usual to qualify as a captain on DC-3s, and unfortunately the Afghan co-pilots were not keen on flying with him as they felt he could be a bit overbearing.

Our master plan for Ariana included acquiring another DC-6 and selling the DC-4. In the latter part of 1963 when I checked out Gran on the DC-6, Rahim asked to be DC-6-rated as a matter of pride. So I worked with them both. Though Rahim was senior, Gran proved to be the superior pilot and promptly passed all checks for DC-6 captaincy. I counseled Rahim to be patient, that when we acquired our second DC-6, he would be ready—I hoped.

Shortly after that, negotiations were completed to purchase a DC-6 from an air charter company in Oakland, California. Captain Gran, an Ariana flight engineer and I flew Pan Am to Oakland. We performed a test and acceptance flight then flew the DC-6 back to Afghanistan by way of Newark, Gander, Shannon, Frankfurt and Beirut.

In March, 1964 Ariana bought a Convair 440 from Allegheny Airlines. The twin piston-engine transport was capable of 300 mph cruising speed carrying up to 52 passengers. I had never flown a

Convair; neither had Woodie. He shoved off for the Allegheny Training Center in Pittsburgh, qualified for his type rating and returned to Kabul. I proceeded to Pittsburgh next, for type training then to ferry our Convair to Afghanistan. Two Ariana DC-3 captains, Rahim and Bismillah, came with me.

The training went well and we ferried the 440 back to Kabul by way of Goose Bay, Labrador; Keflavik, Iceland; Frankfurt; Rome; Beirut; Teheran and Kandahar. That seven-day tour in the 300-mph Convair required 39 flying hours. The aircraft performed nicely all the way—except on one leg when we had to shut down one of its two engines because of low oil pressure.

Over the next few days I route checked Rahim and Bis and began training several co-pilots on the Convair. Soon we had two all-Afghan crews flying the new acquisition.

On a take-off from Kandahar to Kabul a few months later, one of the Ariana pilots, Captain Bismillah, called for gear up a little too soon. The Convair settled. He heard an odd noise, but the engines were running smoothly so he continued on to Kabul. There a careful examination of the Convair revealed that when the plane had settled on take-off, the runway pavement had ground away three inches on all three blades of the right side engine's propeller.

We decided the damaged plane could be safely ferried back to the Kandahar maintenance facility for a replacement prop. I agreed to fly our wounded bird down there, but I needed a volunteer co-pilot. A pleasant young Ariana pilot, Monir Younazai, stepped forward. The son of a fine family, Monir had married the daughter of Afghanistan's ambassador to France, a well-educated woman who spoke French and English very well. Despite the crudely remodeled propeller, volunteer Monir and I enjoyed an uneventful flight.

With our second DC-6 in hand, the time had come to dispose of Ariana's last DC-4. Negotiations with Trans Australian Airlines led to the sale, and I was authorized to complete the transaction upon delivery of the DC-4 to TAA in Cambridge, England. After months parked in the desert at Kandahar, the old crock took quite a bit of refurbishing—especially the radio equipment—to make it airworthy. Even so, the radios, adjusted to European frequencies, were a looming question mark.

In April, 1965 Woodie and I shoved off in the DC-4, for Beirut, a long trip but one without problems. So far, so good. From Beirut one of our DC-6s flew Woodie back to Kandahar. He was replaced on our crew by an Afghan pilot named Akbar. Flight engineer Tom Fiedjeland also joined me in Beirut, and our happy little crew took off for Athens four hours to the west. All went well on that leg and on the next one to Italy.

When we landed at Rome's Fiumicino Airport, Pan Am pilots were on strike and the airline's ground staff was down to a skeleton crew. Our pressing need was radio maintenance, but there was little in the way of replacement parts for our ancient communications system. Because of our inability to operate on many of the radio frequencies required for clearance to fly through France and into England, we replanned our route to avoid all high density air traffic areas.

We overnighted at an airport hotel and shoved off for Cambridge April 5th. The weather forecast was favorable enough, VFR most of the way if we flew at the lower altitudes. European air traffic controllers were helpful in assigning us the limited frequencies our radios were capable of tuning. We managed fairly well, with some complications in the Paris area. There we stayed well clear of the heavy traffic and managed to have our position relayed to Paris control through small outlying airports' control towers. Altering course from time to time to stay in visual flight conditions in unsettled weather, we neared the end of French airspace flying at 3,000 feet.

We tried in vain to contact British air traffic control on an assortment of frequencies. Finally some kind soul in a British aircraft heard us and relayed our position report to London. Air control there relayed back a frequency for low level aircraft in our area and we managed to make direct radio contact. London's signal was feeble and fuzzy, but we were given clearance to fly direct to Cambridge maintaining low level VFR.

We crossed the English Channel and map-read our way to Cambridge over territory still surprisingly familiar to me from 20 years before. We landed at Cambridge in the beautiful spring afternoon. A rain shower had just passed through. The sun was brilliant and a glorious rainbow arched over the rolling green countryside.

"*Allah akbar*," said my copilot as we taxied in.

"*Allah akbar*," Tom and I agreed.

After tea with the TAA representatives, we were given a lift to the train station for the rail journey to London. Over the next two days, I met TAA officials in their London headquarters. Money changed hands and I signed the papers transferring the ownership of that memorable DC-4.

During the course of our London negotiations, I learned TAA maintained a fleet of DC-3s in Australia. Coincidence of coincidences, they owned and still operated the very same DC-3 (C-47) I had flown for Montgomery's 21st Army Group, the second Bluenose B.

After a few days enjoying London, we flew Pan Am back to Beirut, the pilots' strike having ended. From Lebanon, we returned to Kandahar via Ariana.

One of the notable flights I had in the Convair was a charter trip from Kabul to Kandahar and return for His Excellency, King Zahir Shah. The king did not have a personal aircraft. Prior to Ariana's availability, what little flying he did had been in ancient Russian-built military aircraft. Our take-offs and landings with the King aboard the Convair were accompanied by copious pomp and ceremony. His majesty, though gracious and kind, was a real stickler for promptness. Departure and arrival times were to be strictly on the dot. We managed to make split-second arrivals by adjusting our airspeed.

In those days, the king was much respected. With the help of USAID programs and the involvement of other western nations, Afghanistan was visibly moving forward—unfortunately into future cataclysms.

Another flight of political interest—this in one of our DC-6s— returned Afghanistan's Prime Minister Daud to Kabul from a meeting in Beirut. As with King Zahir, the plane was rendered spotless for this jaunt, and again timeliness was of the essence. My first officer was Afghan pilot Maiwandi, a member of an upper echelon Kabul family and a good friend. Katherine and I had attended his wedding reception at the Spinzer Hotel, a great celebration lasting far into the night. Aware that Afghan custom permitted as many as four wives per husband, I had said to him, "You have a lovely bride, Maiwandi. I hope you won't acquire others later on."

"I have no plans for any others" he assured me. Then he added, "But . . . *Enshallah*. If it is Allah's will, who knows?"

Now as we approached Kabul with Prime Minister Daud aboard, Maiwandi informed Kabul control, "We will stop in front of the tower precisely at the designated time."

"But it is almost that time now," came the response, "and you have not even landed."

Having checked with the observatory in Greenwich for international "Zulu" time, Maiwandi was correct with his ETA. The control tower was three minutes fast.

He keyed his mike. "All over the world the time is 1654Z. Only in Afghanistan at Kabul Airport is there a different time. We will never be a great country if you cannot keep the right time. Now please give us landing clearance as we are turning on final approach."

We taxied in precisely on time.

On a flight from Kabul to Iran in the Convair with Habib, we approached Teheran through a classic sand and dust storm. Visibility:

less than a mile. Normally this would have been a DC-6 flight but we'd had to substitute the much shorter-range Convair. With no alternate airport in reach should we fail to land at Teheran, we had no choice but to land at that storm-shrouded airport. Without an up-to-date ILS (Instrument Landing System) in place there, a non-precision NDB beacon approach would have to be it. We let down cautiously but were not in an accurate glide path on our first attempt. We nailed the next one—with the help of Teheran's two-mile-long runway.

I experienced three engine failures on the four-engined DC 6s. Amazingly—and luckily—all three were inboard engines, the best situation if you must have an engine fail. Still, on one take-off from Kabul with a full cargo on a hot summer day, an engine failure had us with our hands full. With Amiri as copilot and flight engineer Asefi, we took off on Runway 29 which required a left turn almost immediately to avoid slamming a ridge of high ground a mile off the runway's end. Just after lift-off, number three engine died. Engines are numbered from the left, the furthest outboard as number one. Our dead number three was the right side inboard engine. Its propeller had auto-feathered to reduce drag, but as we began to retract the landing gear, number four engine started backfiring.

We reduced power on that engine and with about half rated power, struggled to gain some altitude. Number four's cylinder head temperature gauge rose well into the red. We felt that engine, too, could give up completely and we would be in a quite an iffy situation.

With the mountains looming ever closer, I began a shallow left turn. I called for Amiri to retract the flaps—"Just a little." Then the cylinder head temperatures on engines one and two hit red line. We were able to inch upward only about 50 feet per minute. Ever so gently, we managed to gain a mere 200 feet above the ground. Amiri called the tower for emergency landing clearance. Our long 180-degree swing downwind to return to Runway 29 seemed to take forever. We roared over the city close to rooftop level, unavoidably straight over the palace with a plume of black smoke from engine number four billowing behind us.

Opposite the approach end of the runway, I made another sweeping 180 to final. Close to short final, I called for gear down. With rated power on just two engines, we touched down at the beginning of the runway "on the numbers." From me it was, "Praise God!" From Amiri and Asefi, *"Allah Akbar."*

The failure of number three engine and partial failure of number four had been caused by detonation due to poor fuel quality. The detonation—firing out of normal 4-cycle sequence—created temperatures high enough in number three engine to produce "copper runout." The spark plugs' electrodes had melted away. That shut down the engine. If it had not, the engine could have torn itself apart.

That whole sequence from lift-off to touch-down had taken 20 heart-stopping minutes. We weren't finished yet. We had barely stepped down to terra firma when I received a citation for violating the strict no-fly zone over the palace. However, after we explained the situation all was graciously forgiven.

As I was to discover, that tension-filled experience would not be the most harrowing flight of my Afghanistan assignment.

A SKY FULL OF AGGRESSIVE FIGHTER PLANES

Our DC-6s did very well flying on three engines. When one needed an engine change, I ferried it down to Kandahar with that engine dead throughout the flight. Though Kabul was 6,000 feet above sea level and the hot summer made the air even thinner, the DC-6 handled satisfactorily after an understandably sluggish take-off. Though the mountainous terrain put me closer to the ground than would have been "ideal" for the crippled DC-6, I made the flight safely.

The rugged terrain was a concern on all Afghanistan flights. On a scheduled DC-3 hop from Kabul to Kunduz, Gran and I climbed to the minimum 14,500-foot altitude required to cross over the Salang Pass. As we neared the pass, we began to sink. We went into a full-power climb but the altimeter told us we still were losing altitude.

The problem was a strong north wind rushing over the Kush range to pour down the south slope and take us down with it. We turned south out of that strong downflow, climbed to 18,000 feet over Bagram then took another shot at the Salang Pass. As we neared the mountains, we hit the massive downdraft again. And again we began to sink toward the jagged crests. This time, we stayed on course, hoping we would have the 13,500-foot absolute minimum crossing altitude when we reached the pass. Bucking the persistent downdraft at full power we made it across Salang Pass safely.

Two of the airports on the airline's schedule were turf fields—Maimana and Khost. Fortunately the DC-3s were quite happy with turf. Neither airport had a terminal building nor a control tower. From a small adobe structure, each airport's Ariana agents talked to our pilots over hand-held radios. At those stops, we were back to basics.

My absolutely most nerve-jangling experience during three years in Afghanistan occured in 1965 on a DC-6 cargo flight. Two Afghan pilots, Sidiqi and Baba, were flying with me on this non-scheduled trip from Kabul to Lahore then on to New Delhi. At the time, Pakistan and India were embroiled in one of their more serious feuds. Their borders were closed to each other's travel, ground and air, though neither border was closed to Afghanistan.

We cleared the Pakistan border and arrived in Lahore without any problem. We refueled there then visited the control tower as customary to file our flight plan to New Delhi, India's capital, southeast of and adjacent to the ancient city of Delhi. Normally radio traffic between Lahore and Delhi was routine and efficient. But on this day, Delhi was not speaking to Lahore. So the best Lahore could do for us was clear us to the Indian border, a mere 30 miles east. Sidiqi, Baba and I discussed this unexpected clearance glitch and believed once we were airborne, we would be able to contact Delhi Radio ourselves. Indian airspace personnel, who should be willing to speak with an Afghan radio source, then would surely clear us to enter India.

Off we went. A minute or so from the Pakistan-India border, we made contact with Delhi Radio. Yes, we were assured, we were cleared to Palaam Airport at New Delhi—and please change to another frequency they gave us. We switched over, called. No one responded. But having already received clearance, we crossed into India.

Almost immediately we were jolted by the appearance of six Indian Air Force jet fighters, British-made Hawker Hunters. The fighters swung around to flank us left and right, startlingly close.

We continued to call—urgently now—on the new frequency Delhi Radio had given us. Still no response. We tried international emergency frequency 1215. No response there, either. In our desperate efforts to reestablish radio contact, we tried to reach Delhi on the original frequency we'd used but now there was no response on that frequency.

While we held steady on course at the clearance altitude Delhi had advised before shunting us into radio limbo, the fighters persisted in their harassing closeness. Then they all soared back into formation high above us. That was a relief . . . until Baba shouted, "Look!"

One by one, the jets peeled off and swung down toward us in what looked to me suspiciously like an attack. There is nothing to match the apprehension of a pilot and crew in an unarmed aircraft when a flock of aggressive fighter planes appears about to—

Delhi Radio blurted into life. We were directed to change frequency once again, and Delhi added the alarming comment we had no permission to be in Indian airspace.

In train, the fighters raced past us. Guns silent. Then they began circling our still-inbound DC-6.

We switched to the new frequency, and again were told our flight was illegal. We were cleared to land at New Delhi, but we would be met at the airport by the proper authorities. As we neared the city, radio communication improved and I read back our clearance from Delhi Radio, including the frequency we had then been assigned and the time we had received that directive.

The fighters disappeared. Tension aboard eased. Ground control became less belligerent. But now I had become belligerent myself.

"I intend to report this incident to the highest levels of authority," I informed the ground operator. "I am a citizen of the United States of America. Our embassy will hear about this outrageous and dangerous situation!"

With that off my chest, I recalled belatedly the U.S. Secretary of State had recently announced the United States was "tilting toward Pakistan." Great! My threat and two rupees might buy me a cup of tea.

After landing, I regained my captainly aplomb and visited the control tower to discuss the matter gently and without a hint of rancor. The cause of the incident, I was assured, was simply a breakdown in communication between Delhi Radio ond certain Indian authorities enroute.

The cargo was unloaded and our return flight encountered no further international bumbling. But at Kabul Airport, I did feel it appropriate to file an official protest with the Afghan Air Authority.

In mid-June Everett "Woodie" Wood left never-never land, returned to Germany and continued to fly for Pan Am until mandatory retirement at age 60. The most intellectual pilot I have ever known, he could easily have enjoyed a brilliant career as a college professor. A published author, he nevertheless was a devoted man of the air. Old friend "Woodie" made possible three of the most challenging, adventurous and enjoyable years of my flying career.

With Woodie's departure, I became the airline's chief pilot through the next six months of the Pan Am contract. Working with Ariana was a truly exhilarating experience. The Afghan pilots were an excellent group of men—diligent, courteous, not given to taking undue risks and loyal to their employer. The Pan Am maintenance people were of the highest quality and they did an excellent job of transferring their skills to the Afghan mechanics.

December 15, 1965, on a round trip to Delhi via Lahore, I captained my last flight for Ariana. "Bis" Bismillah Hamid, a fine man, flew with me as first officer. Sammi Asefi was flight engineer on the DC-6.

The evening of December 16, Katherine and I were given a wonderful farewell party at Kabul's Spinzer Hotel. Almost all Ariana's pilots attended, plus many other airline employees. Colonel Gul Bahar, head of the Afghan Air Authority offered the first of several touching tributes. I was presented with a turban and a *chapan,* a long richly colored robe and was told I was now an adopted Afghan. For Katherine and me, the evening was an unforgettable experience.

Our departure from Kabul the next morning was quite emotional for me. Many Ariana pilots and American friends from USAID arrived to see us off. I was leaving a country I had come to care for and where I had made firm friendships, many of them lasting to this day.

Katherine, too had made many friends in the kingdom. During almost all our time there, she had worked as a volunteer in Kabul's Abesinia Hospital and at an institution for the blind. She also had assisted the USAID program in showing educational films to Afghan women.

Katherine, David and I boarded Ariana's DC-6 flight to Teheran. Our departing flight over the rugged Afghan countryside held no hint of that country's turmoil to come. From Iran, we flew Pan Am to Berlin where we planned to spend the Christmas holidays.

And then . . . ?

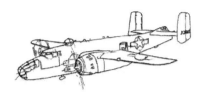

CHAPTER 17

"WHERE DID THAT COME FROM?"

John joined us in Germany, and the four of us celebrated Christmas, 1965 with Woodie and Barbro in their flat near the Kurfurstendam, Berlin's best-known avenue. At the time, Woodie was flying the corridors out of Pan Am's base at Tempelhof. All five of us Afghanistan veterans enjoyed a delightful reunion, then we Races were off to London for several days of leisure, including a New Year's performance of *Peter Pan*. Next, on to New York. And we moved back into our house in Ridgefield, Connecticut. During our three-year Afghanistan sojourn, we had rented the house and had been really long-distance landlords.

Now I began my training for the long-delayed DC-8 type rating. My instructor was Bill Angleman, an impressive veteran pilot who knew the "8" inside out. On my type rating ride March 23, I was accompanied by a demanding FAA inspector known for his intolerance of the merest error. At the end of that nerve-twanging check ride, he said, "That was a good flight," words I'd been told he had never been known to say to anyone. I was so flabbergasted I thought I might be awarded the Distinguished Flying Cross. Alas, though I now had my DC-8 type rating, my seniority number still was not yet strong enough to put me in the left seat. For several months, I flew as first officer.

During the summer of 1966, we stayed at the cottage we owned at Crystal Lake. My friend Nick Meholic, a Pan Am mechanic from Carbondale, owned a classic open-cockpit biplane and based it at a private strip near Crystal Lake. I had the pleasure of flying his Kinner Fleet around the area. That brief return to aviation's Golden Age may have been the major impetus for my noticing a Waco UPF-7 for sale in an issue of *Trade-A-Plane* that fall. On October 15, money changed hands in New Haven, and I became the gleeful owner of NC30130, a 25-year-old open-cockpit biplane built in November, 1940.

That same month, I was asked to serve as a DC-8 training captain, an offer of good duty I readily accepted. Most of the training flights originated either at Riverhead on Great Peconic Bay near the east end of Long Island or at Atlantic City. Since the flight simulators of that day were still quite primitive, almost all training took place in the aircraft. I handled type training and the mandatory six-month flight checks. One of the February flight checks was a stand-out for me when friend Woodie, who was visiting us in Ridgefield, came along for the ride.

After four months of instructing in the DC-8, I was asked by chief pilot Bob Weeks to begin training in the Boeing 707 jetliner. That sent me back to Kennedy (formerly Idlewild) for 707 simulator and ground school classes at Pan Am's training center. In March, 1967 I flew my Waco with sons John and David in the front cockpit to Lehighton, Pennsylvania for a complete fabric recovering job. Floyd "Eggy" Eggenweiler would spearhead the work, assisted by John during his vacations from Syracuse University. The recovering job would take 16 months of off-and-on work, with Eggy highly complimentary of John's aptitude.

Now came something of a career acceleration. In April I journeyed south to Augusta, Georgia, for 707 type training with Ted Roosevelt as my instructor, a fine man. Within a week I flew my 707 transport pilot type rating ride with FAA inspector John Macanulty looking over my shoulder. Macanulty was known for his propensity to give an impressive number of down checks. He was demanding, all right. But all went well, with Ted riding along in the copilot seat.

Back on Long Island, I flew a brief DC-8 requalification ride followed by an international qualification flight with Captain Doug Moody as check pilot and Bernie Lyons as second officer. On a rainy night in early July that was a demanding grind indeed. We flew from New York bound for Boston where the weather was reported at minimums. By the time we reached the Boston area, conditions had deteriorated below minimums—there and all over the Northeast. Since an approach to mimimums was permissible, we decided to give that a shot.

In gusty air and persistent rain, we reached minimum altitude with airspeed, heading and altitude right on—but with visibility just about nil. I was set to execute a missed approach when Doug called out, "Runway in sight!" So we managed to complete the landing—but what a way to begin this flight so important to me.

We departed Boston promptly and flew on to Santa Maria in the Azores. Doug was happy with the ride so far, and he flew the next leg to Lisbon, Portugal. The following day, we flew to Rabat, Morocco. Though I was in the left seat, Bernie flew that leg. He made an excellent landing at Rabat Airport. But as we rolled out, we spotted a wheel bounding down the runway ahead of us.

"Where did *that* come from?" we asked each other.

As we taxied clear of the runway, the tower announced, "Pan Am Clipper, you are missing one wheel on the right side."

We parked the DC-8 and piled out to take a look. Sure enough, one of the four wheels on the right side main gear was not there. Since all four of our landings had been smooth, none of us could have been guilty of knocking a wheel loose. An inspection of our renegade rolling equipmment revealed a mechanical flaw in the wheel itself had resulted in its departing the axle. A new wheel was promptly installed and the next day, we retraced our route back to New York as planned. All in all, that was a pleasant round trip with a congenial crew. And at long last, I was now a line and training captain on the DC-8 and the 707.

That same month, I flew as captain of training flights on 707s in addition to regular line flying. And shortly I was appointed a designated check airman, approved by the FAA.

Pan Am had established a training center at Roswell, New Mexico, and I was sent there intermittently—a couple of weeks at a time—to serve as initial training instructor and type rating instructor in the 707. My first assignment, in September, 1967 was to qualify two recently hired pilots as 707 second officers. Manny Lewis and Don Manthei, both good guys to work with, made the assignment quite enjoyable. Manny, bright and personable, was blessed with a wife who was an expert in the kitchen. Word was out that her lasagne was a culinary triumph.

Another unexpected event in Roswell was the opportunity to renew my friendship with Harry Burkstaller and his wife, "Poogie." In 1941, Harry and I had been students together in Scranton Airport's CPT program. A year later, we both were CPT instructors there. Now Harry managed the Roswell Airport. A former U.S. Air Force base, the airport offered long, wide runways ideal for training in large high performance aircraft.

In about a week, Manny and Don were qualified and we all returned to New York. I then captained several flights to the Caribbean, including a couple to Rock Sound, a tiny island 20 minutes flying time from Nassau.

That remote resort island won its listing on Pan Am's schedule partly because of its seclusion but more likely because Juan Trippe and several other Pan Am executives had estates on Rock Sound. The runway at its small airport seemed to have been paved a little too casually, so no matter how beautifully a pilot "greased on" his landing, it was doomed to be a rough one.

In January, 1968 I returned to Roswell to conduct more initial and type training. This time Katherine came with me, and she accepted my offer to take her along on one of the training flights. These four-hour trips were not standard airline gentle ascents, descents and shallow turns. With all our steep banks, stalls and recoveries, engine cuts and more aerial out-of-the-ordinaries, I noticed my blonde was becoming a bit pale. But she soldiered on. After she had recovered back on Mother Earth, I think she was pleased to have had that first-hand look at what went on during those training sessions.

My candidates for type rating included two good friends. Both were DC-8 captains but had recently been awarded captaincies on the 707. That required, of course, they be type rated on the Boeing. One of them, a handsome Swede with bright yellow hair, made an impact on the ladies sufficient enough to earn him the nickname "The Golden Stallion." Now that he was in training, he devoted himself to a near-monastic regimen—in bed early every night, observing a healthful diet, exercising faithfully and engrossed in the required technical studies.

I had worked with both captains for their FAA oral exams, and soon they were ready for their rating rides. Both did well on the pre-FAA rating flights—but with an exception for one of them. On a V_1 (the airspeed at which a take-off cannot be safely aborted) engine cut on take-off, he controlled the aircraft well but forgot to call for gear-up after he had established climb. "You you did a fine job," I told him as we landed, "but you've got to remember to call for gear-up after the V_1 cut and you've established climb."

From the ground the next day, I watched his departure on his check flight with the FAA inspector. I saw an outboard engine cut out. He maintained excellent control and began climbing. "Now gear-up!" I said aloud. But that was not to be. The landing gear did not make the slightest move.

Since everything else went well, the FAA inspector had him repeat the engine cut-out procedure. This time flawlessly. He had earned his B-707 type rating.

The other candidate, had been a friend since our days together in Frankfurt. We both had flown DC-4s up and down the Berlin corridors in the 1950s, and we both had bought homes in Ridgefield, as had many of Pan Am's returnees from that Germany assignment. At Roswell, his training progressed smoothly and both pilots qualified for his 707 type rating at the same time.

On my return from New Mexico in mid-February, 1968, Katherine, David and I flew Pan Am to Munich where we rented a car and drove to Filzmoos, Austria, for a skiing holiday. We were joined by Bob and Edith Tegeder, the friends who let us in on this little gem of a relatively undiscovered ski resort. Fifty miles south of Salzburg, Austria, Filzmoos was not yet a well-known skiing mecca, though it boasted the longest chair-lift in all of Europe. Crowds had yet to discover its slopes, and we enjoyed great skiing.

Home again for routine Caribbean flights then Middle East trips flying as captain primarily to Beirut, Ankara, Istanbul and Teheran. No problems on any of these largely pleasant trips.

In August my Waco, now wearing gleaming new scarlet fabric, was ready to take to the air again. In murky weather, John drove me to Beltz Field near Lehighton. I flew the Waco back to Crystal Lake in the rain. Visibility was reduced, but the windscreen deflected the rain past the cockpit and I stayed dry. With hangar space at Clifford Airport not immediately available, I put the Waco down on a nearby private airstrip owned by the Malinchak Family. There my venerable flying machine had to stay outdoors anchored with tie-downs for a month or so, flown only when I had an occasional break.

The following month, in addition to periodic route checking of various Pan Am pilots, I flew South American routes. On one, as we taxied from the terminal at Rio de Janeiro, Brazil, the tower ordered us to return immediately to the gate. An emergency? No, the entire field was closed down—for the arrival of Indian Prime Minister Indira Gandhi.

Then back on the check pilot schedule, routine route checks plus something new—instructing pilots in Doppler navigation that had just come into wide use, and in which I had recently been trained. I liked teaching this new system, but I couldn't help feeling a touch of regret. Doppler eliminated the requirement for licensed navigators on transoceanic flights. In that department, I had just become obsolete.

As can be imagined, when a check pilot shows up to conduct a routine route check, he is not always greeted with joy and gladness by the operating crew. I'm aware of absolutely no crew member ever having been elated by the presence of a check pilot on the jump seat. If he seems to be taking a lot of notes, the tension mounts. Pan Am had a few such nitpicking check pilots, but most flight crews were not subjected to such nerve-jangling note-taking. The best check pilots were usually those who'd had experience as flight instructors. They realized a compliment to the crew on some aspect of the flight was always appropriate—and often a performance enhancer.

I was once given a New York to London periodic route check by a newly-appointed check pilot. Heathrow was down to minimums and early morning arrivals were stacked up. For some time we had to fly a holding pattern before receiving approach clearance. At the risk of sounding immodest, the crew and I couldn't have done better. Everything from cabin announcements to planning and executing the approach and landing was of the highest level. As I parked at the gate, elated by the whole sequence of stellar success, the check pilot frowned.

"I can't think of any criticism right now," he muttered. "So I'll give you a . . . satisfactory."

In November I flew an African pattern: New York-Dakar, Senegal-Roberts Field, Liberia-Accra, Ghana then return. I had never met my first officer, "Jake." I had heard of his reputation as a somewhat antagonistic pusher of limits. I'd also been told he would sometimes show up for a flight just a little late. His excuses, though a bit thin, were said to be delivered courteously. He was known to enjoy drawing people into disagreements just for the sake of arguing—as if he were testing others.

True to all these tales preceding him, Jake did not show up for briefing before our take-off. Instead, he phoned the dispatcher to say he was unavoidably detained and would arrive as soon as possible.

By the time I finished all the paperwork, just a half hour remained before crew boarding time. That made Jake already a half hour late. I was about to request a reserve first officer when the dispatcher notified me Jake would be in the terminal in 15 minutes.

"Send him aboard the minute he gets there."

Fifteen minutes before engine start, my copilot bustled into the aircraft laden with snorkeling equipment including a spear gun.

"Sorry I'm late, Captain. Would it be okay if I bring this gear into the cockpit?"

He was really bending the limits, but there was no time left for discussion.

"All right," I agreed reluctantly.

Apparently realizing he had pushed me enough for one day, he performed his duties adequately. I was relieved at that; we would be flying together for almost a week.

On the lay-over at Dakar, though Jake's primary interest was snorkeling, we did manage to spend some time together. His conversation was sprinkled with opinions I deduced were intended to draw me into controversial areas. Such bait did not evoke a rise.

The next day we flew to Liberia's Roberts Field near Monrovia. This was Jake's leg to fly. During let-down at Roberts, he held 300 mph airspeed.

"Jake," I reminded him, "standard practice below 10,000 is to slow to 250, and I'm asking you to do that."

Still descending at 300 mph, he tried to argue the point.

I cut him off. "We'll talk about it after we land."

He then slowed to 250 and made a nice landing. When the subject came up later, he tried to defend his unapproved descent procedure. By then I had decided not to be drawn into a debate that obviously would lead nowhere. And so it went for the rest of the African trip until he gave up his captain-baiting. We then began actually to enjoy our time together.

A year or so later I was in the chief pilot's office when Jake strolled in.

"How have you been keeping yourself, Jake?" I greeted him.

"Not too well apparently. I've been called in here because of negative reports by some of the line captains. I need some *good* reports, Captain."

Then he had an inspiration. "You never reported anything negative about me. How about turning in something positive?"

With me, he had turned out to be erratic in keeping to schedule, but at least he'd been polite about it. His flying skills, I was able to report to the chief pilot, were . . . satisfactory.

Alas, through ensuing years Jake more or less continued his feisty demeanor. He was still making wavelets when I retired.

As I continued giving route checks, initial qualification rides, type training and simulator training, I came into contact with a variety of flying personalities. Some were egoists, others were modestly laid back. Many were excellent pilots. A few perhaps might have been better suited to another profession.

For a reason that had nothing to do with flying, I fondly remember First Officer Al. We flew together just a few times. He was mild-mannered with adequate but not really strong flying skills. Of Italian heritage, Al's greatest strength lay in his deep love of family. His mother, confined to a nursing home, had told Al her sole remaining pleasure in life was his singing Italian songs to her. A truly devoted son, he would go to a phone between flights and sing to her long distance. As I recall, Al's Pan Am career was a brief one, but I always enjoyed our layovers with such a gentle, good-hearted man who truly loved his family.

I always found line flying a pleasant relief from the greater tension of training and checking duties. My line flying was all international—to destinations in Europe, the Middle East, Africa and South America. During times off, I most often hurried back into the Northeastern Pennsylvania sky, reveling in the rush of air in the open cockpit, free from the pressures of schedules, alone in the blue in my Waco.

On one of my 1969 check flights, I was prepared for tension plus. One of the veteran chief pilots, who had spent years on administrative duties, had decided to return to line flying. The man had a reputation for aloofness and lack of charm. I was asked to requalify him on the Boeing 707.

Off we flew on a series of Caribbean hops; lots of take-offs and landings. Interestingly—and to my pleasant surprise—once away from his commanding office environment, he mellowed. His gruffness evaporated. He accepted instruction and correction gracefully. His understandably rusty flying skills improved steadily to the point where I could promptly and confidently turn him loose.

To celebrate New Year's Eve 1970, I met Katherine and David in Miami. On January 2, we were joined by Iman-ul-Haq Gran, our great friend from our days in Afghanistan. Gran, now chief pilot for Ariana, had come to Florida for Boeing 727 jetliner training at Pan Am's Florida training facility. Now he needed a ride to New York.

"I'm about to fly to Kingston, Jamaica, then to Montego Bay then on to New York, Gran. You're welcome to come along on the jump seat."

He was delighted with the offer, and with Katherine and David, he boarded my 707 flight. The two stops in Jamaica were brief and routine, but as we neared Long Island, the weather began to thicken. With that and the usual evening arrivals converging on JFK International, we encountered a long holding pattern. Fortunately I'd taken on extra fuel at Montego Bay. Finally we were cleared to land just before the weather deteriorated below minimums.

My combination of line flying and check flights continued into 1970. On a late February flight to Buenos Aires, Argentina, I was assigned a first officer I had not previously met. He seemed a friendly enough fellow, but immediately after our landing in Argentina for a two-day layover, he disappeared. None of us on the crew caught even a glimpse of him until he showed up in the hotel lobby two days later for departure back to New York. Such isolation was not unheard of but it was unusual among crew members on long layovers.

Before I left on my next flight, the chief pilot asked what I thought of the man.

"His performance was adequate," I told the chief, "but he's a fellow who clearly wanted to be by himself during the layover."

"Word is he's been doing quite a bit of solitary drinking. I think that needs looking into."

Indeed, the man turned out to have a drinking problem and his days with Pan Am soon ended. I felt sad about that. I'd found him a competent enough first officer and good person at heart

In contrast, the next flight—an early March cargo trip—was to be one of the highlights of my flying career.

18
CHAPTER

"YOU'LL HAVE A SPECIAL PASSENGER"

March 5, 1970. I captained a Pan Am cargo flight that originated in San Francisco, bound for New York with a stop in Los Angeles. On this rainy night as I waited in the cargo office for the loading of additional cargo at LAX—Los Angeles International Airport—the Pan Am station manager stuck his head in.

"You'll have a special passenger on the flight to New York, Jack."

"A passenger?" The only passenger seat we had on our 707 cargo jet was the jump seat behind the pilot. This guy must be desperate to get to New York.

"It's General Lindbergh."

"You mean Charles A. Lindbergh?"

"Yep. He's waiting in the ops office upstairs."

Lindbergh, a close friend of Juan Trippe's, had played a vital role in aviation's and Pan American's early days. He was currently a member of Pan Am's board of directors.

"Unless you think he'd rather not be disturbed," I told the station manager, "I'd like to go up and reintroduce myself."

Upstairs I went. The door was open and there sat the man I most admired in the world of aviation.

Writing in a notebook, he looked up with a pleasant smile as I walked into the room. When I'd met him briefly in 1955, he had been 53. Now 68, he was still an imposing figure, almost militarily erect and notably alert.

I mentioned our brief earlier encounter, we exchanged pleasantries and I assured him I would personally let him know when we were ready to board for the flight to New York.

At departure time I walked with him to the 707. Despite his generations-spanning fame, he was pleasantly informal. Aboard, I introduced him to First Officer Wes Bragg and Flight Engineer Jerry Newsinow.

"May I hang up your raincoat, General?" I offered.

"Thank you, no." He rolled up the raincoat and tossed it in a corner. "That will do fine." We stored the small bag he carried, and he settled on the cockpit jump seat behind the captain's seat.

I asked if he was familiar with the 707's emergency equipment.

"Yes, Captain, I am."

One aviator to another, I showed him our flight plan and weather folder. As we taxied out, I took the opportunity to tell Lindbergh how impressed I'd been by his book, *The Spirit of St. Louis*. I have always considered that book and St. Exupery's *Wind, Sand and Stars* the two greatest aviation books ever written. While we waited for take-off clearance, I couldn't resist showing him a photo of my Waco.

"That's a nice looking ship," he said, and I realized I had heard only those from aviation's early days call an airplane a "ship." I didn't know it then, of course, but nineteen years later, my "ship" and I would be linked with Lindbergh coast to coast.

It was my custom to maintain a "sterile" cockpit—no socializing or non-flight-pertinent talk from take-off until we cleared the area and climbed to 10,000 feet. Lindbergh instinctively observed this, silently concentrating on our departure checks and cockpit briefings.

We took off near maximum allowable gross weight and levelled out at an initial 29,000 feet. The night was moonless and black. We flew over a dark carpet dotted here and there with city lights. Now and then, Lindbergh would identify a city below and comment briefly about his barnstorming days and air mail flying, relatively carefree days, I gathered, before international fame intruded on this modest man's life.

Then he asked about the flying I had logged—this from the immortal pilot who had fascinated me with aviation in the first place.

I made certain I did not launch into an unseemly dissertation, but as we passed south of Rockford, Illinois, I did mention I had dusted crops way down there.

Overall, though, Lindbergh's conversation with me was on a more sophisticated level. I was aware of his interest in ecology and his efforts in that area, a subject I, too, felt strongly about. He spoke quite fervently about the need to invest time, energy and resources in the ecological movement, and I was quite impressed with his detailed knowledge.

Then he moved on to space exploration. "I'm all for it and I recognize its inevitability. But we must not support it at the expense of limiting our attention to the problems on earth—education, medical advances and the problems of racial prejudice."

He also touched on the frequent distortions by the press and its compulsion for sensationalism. I couldn't help but think of the way the press had besieged him and his wife following the tragic kidnapping then murder of their first child in the early 1930s. The media of that day had been so intrusive the Lindberghs were forced to move temporarily to England for some degree of privacy.

I told him I had once taken a course in journalism and found it so superficial I came away rather disillusioned.

As we neared Kennedy International, I asked if I could call Pan American Operations to arrange ground transportation for him at the cargo area. At 5:00 a.m., that was going to be a desolate spot.

"No thank you," he said quite emphatically.

Low clouds hung over Long Island. At 10,000 feet rain began to pelt the windows and we hit fairly heavy turbulence. We were cleared for an ILS instrument approach to Runway 4R. We let down through the murk and at 400 feet broke out of the clouds with Lindbergh peering over my shoulder. On short final, I held a 10-degree crab into the crosswind and prayed I could bring the big jet down in an especially good landing. Over the threshold I began flare-out, straightened from the crab . . . and the landing gear rumbled smoothly on the runway.

As we turned to clear, Lindbergh said, "Very nice landing, Captain." For me that was like getting the Victoria Cross.

In dawn's first light, Charles Lindbergh and I said our goodbyes.

"See you around the campus," Wes Bragg quipped.

Lindbergh smiled, then he walked aft. Steps were rolled up to the exit door, and from the cockpit window I watched Charles A. Lindbergh, living legend, stride off through a maze of crates and loading equipment, his rumpled raincoat clamped under his arm, travel bag and ever-present notebook in his hand. Still a heroic figure to me.

When I heard of his death on Maui four and a half years later, I was profoundly saddened and felt a degree of personal loss.

In early April, our chief pilot asked me to go to England on a special Pan Am assignment. My job was to qualify Lloyd International pilots on the Boeing 707. The Lloyd operation had just acquired a 707 for use in the company's charter work. All the pilots had their British air transport pilot certifications but lacked long distance flying experience, especially on oceanic routes.

Lloyd was based north of London at Stanstead Airport. I arrived there April 16 and spent a week familiarizing myself with the company's activities and qualifying for my British ATP certificate. Without it, I could not have flown in command of a British air transport.

Lloyd's pilots were mainly British plus a few Aussies. Some were soldier of fortune types, having flown with other charter companies. After evaluating the situation, I took a room over a pub in Bishop-Stortford near Stanstead. The pub was a pleasant homey establishment as so many British pubs are—and so unlike often boisterous American bars.

The five captains and five copilots assigned to the 707 were a good bunch and I enjoyed being with them. We flew east as far as Singapore and Kuala Lumpur, Malaysia, and west to Canada and Los Angeles. All the pilots did well. Since they were a small group, we became good friends. Some of them were aware that whenever I could, I attended a nearby church for vesper services. Several of the pilots began to share their personal problems with me and, I felt, looked upon me as something of a "confessor." That unexpected role was one I felt comfortable with and complimented by.

While with Lloyd, I occasionally journeyed to London to visit a friend of ours from Ridgefield, Ruth Kirby. She and her husband had lived near us until they decided to move to London, a city they both loved. Her husband had since died.

I called Ruth one fine day in May and asked her to lunch. She agreed, and I took a bus to her flat in Richmond. There we called a cab to take us to her favorite restaurant in Kensington. Off we rode, taking a longer route than necessary, I thought. The cabbie seemed to be hesitant, deliberating over something. Then he stopped short of the restaurant, shut off the meter, slid open the glass panel between him and the passenger compartment and turned to face me.

The man was ashen-faced. A strong sense of premonition had just taken hold of him, he explained. "I'm awfully sorry about this," he apologized and he appeared to get hold of himself. We set out again and soon arrived at the restaurant. As I reached to pay him, he said in an emotional voice, "I must speak to you privately, sir."

The doorman escorted Ruth into the restaurant while I waited to hear . . . Lord knew what. The cab driver—whom I had never before met—said in a shaky voice that his vivid premonition concerned me.

"You travel long distances, sir." That much I thought he could have assumed from my American accent. "But you must not go on the third trip you are scheduled for. It will be tragic, sir."

I was astonished. The man appeared absolutely serious, but I felt his warning had to be some well-meaning fantasy. Too many years driving in London traffic? I joined Ruth and we had a pleasant lunch.

My next scheduled flight with Lloyd would be Stanstead to Prestwick, then on to Canada. From Ottawa Airport, we were to take a limo to the city. Another crew would fly our 707 back to England and we would have three days in Ottawa before flying back to England ourselves.

On the spur of the moment, I decided I would rather spend those free days with my family in Pennsylvania. Then I would fly commercial back to Ottawa in time for the scheduled return flight to London.

I hopped an Air Canada flight to New York then drove home from there. My free time at Crystal Lake passed pleasantly, but I couldn't get that London cabbie's warning out of my mind. Ridiculous. It had to be a bored taxi driver's idea of a joke.

After two enjoyable days, I boarded an Air Canada flight back to Ottawa and rejoined the crew—a shaken crew. During their limo ride from Ottawa Airport to the city the day we had arrived, a car had darted from a crossroad and crashed into the limo's right side. The impact demolished the unoccupied passenger seat next to the driver. All aboard were severely jarred but unhurt.

When the crew traveled by limo, the front passenger seat was customarily mine. If I hadn't decided to skip that ride, I would have been sitting in that seat. I was shocked to realize the limo ride would have been the "third scheduled trip" the London cab driver had warned me about. I've been a believer in premonitions ever since.

During my month and a half with Lloyd, Boeing 707 "G-AYAG" had no major glitches. The cabin staff was definitely top drawer and the company was well thought of as a charter airline. But alas, a few years later it lost out to the majors. In days to come, I would occasionally meet some of the old Lloyd chaps flying for other airline companies, usually in the Middle East.

In early June, I returned to Kennedy, flight checking, instructing and flying the line—plus time off to put in some Waco hours back in Pennsylvania. I also instructed son David in an Aeronca Champion owned by friend Nick Meholic. On August 12, David's 16th birthday, we rose early, drove the three miles to Clifford Airport's undulating sod field, and David soloed—three take-offs and landings, each worthy of an "atta boy." A born pilot.

Through the rest of 1970, I continued route checking and line flying. At a layover in Dakar, Senegal, the copilot and I looked into the possible purchase of a Belgian-built Stampe, a replica of the open-cockpit British Tiger Moth biplane. It hadn't been flown for quite a while but looked quite sound. We were told it had been owned by a local flying club, now disbanded, but we were unable to track down the current owners. The idea of two Pan Am pilots owing a Belgian plane in Dakar had exotic appeal but the venture ran into so many obstacles we dropped it.

At the turn of the year, I was offered a remarkable assignment. Would I be interested in flying as captain of a luxury round-the-world charter in a specially reconfigured 707? The Boeing's seating had been altered from its normal 180 seats to an 80-seat all-first-class arrangement. The Olson Travel Agency in Chicago had offered the world tour at $10,000 per person, and all 80 seats were sold. Each layover would include luxury accomodations and escorted local touring. The select Pan Am cockpit and cabin crews would participate equally in all this lavishness. What pilot in his right mind would turn that down?

On January 16, 1971, with Buck Clippard as copilot, Ed Wolak as flight engineer and a cabin crew of eight headed by Ray Ladour, we departed Kennedy for Rabat, the capital of Morocco. Each day was carefully programmed for touring and side trips by bus. Passengers and crew alike were treated to special events every evening.

In Casablanca we visited the site of the 1943 Roosevelt-Churchill Conference, the King's Palace, Green Mosque and the centuries-old landmark for the Barbary Pirates—the El Hauk Lighthouse. In Marrakech we toured the Palace of Dar el Beida, the Casbah, the Tombs of the Saiadlay Princes and the Menora Gardens. Back in Rabat, some of us golfed on King Hassan's course.

January 20 we took off on a seven-and-a-half hour flight to Nairobi. We landed just after sunset, a fairly late arrival for the tour. Darkness fell just after we touched down. In Africa there seemed to be almost no twilight. Tour take-offs were never to be made before 10 a.m., and arrivals were almost always in the late afternoon.

Nairobi's highlight for all of us was a visit to the Mount Kenya Game Ranch. The ranch had been founded by two Americans: TV personality Don Hunt and film actor William Holden. Under their guidance and with their continuing support, the Ranch would remain "Timeless Africa" and would become one of the world's significant conservation organizations.

Another high point of our Nairobi stop was an overnight stay at Mountain Lodge in the African jungle. The lodge was elevated on stilts near a natural watering hole in easy view. We were treated to the regular evening observation of incoming thirsty wildlife.

We on the crew were expected to be an integral part of the group. That unusual requirement was no burden, but any group of people constantly together can develop some, well, isolations. I tried to be alert to that sort of reaction among crew members and to speak a word about it during our daily briefings. All went well—except with one of the flight attendants who insisted her time on the ground was her own—and was not consistently gracious with our passengers. We had to arrange for her replacement, and she was not unhappy to return to New York.

We left Nairobi January 23 for Addis Ababa, Ethiopia, an hour and 15 minutes north. Addis was not part of the Pan American route system and we were the first Pan Am aircraft to land there. Before touchdown, we made a slow fly-by past the airport. That put us on the front pages of the next day's newspapers. With Addis 7,000 feet above sea level and the air further thinned by the day's high temperature, we met the runway at a dramatically high speed. Fortunately the runway was almost two miles long.

Trevor, the Pan Am station agent from Dar-es-Salaam, Tanganyika, had come to Addis to handle our tour requirements. With a genuine appreciation for the Ethiopian people, he did an excellent job for us— and for the community. A high point was his arranging a tour of our 707 for groups of local school children. One of the flight attendants and I spent most of that day showing the thrilled children around the big airplane. The event was such an enjoyable success for us as well as the youngsters, we decided to conduct similar tours through the aircraft at other ports of call on our globe-circling itinerary.

While in Ethiopia, the ancient region of Solomon and Sheba, we visited Menelik Palace and Jubilee Palace, home of Emperor Haile Selassie, the famed "Lion of Judah." We stayed in a thoroughly modern Hilton Hotel, and that was indeed "Well done, Conrad!"

The morning of January 25, we lifted off for Bombay, India, a five-hour flight. The tour arranger had tried to avoid our encountering the depressing poverty there. We were treated to snake charmers and street entertainers of all descriptions but the poor were everywhere. I found the Bombay experience heartbreaking.

The morning we were to leave for Delhi—a brief 90-minute hop— our destination reported dense fog. It was expected to burn off by noon, but in case it didn't, I decided to take on extra fuel.

"No need," said Vijay, the pleasant and accomodating Pan Am rep at Bombay. "I am from Delhi, and in all my years there, the fog was always gone by noon."

Despite that assurance, I elected to take on enough extra fuel to enable us to hold over Delhi for an hour and still return to Bombay, plus a 45-minute reserve.

"You won't need it," Vijay insisted. But by the time everyone was aboard and we taxied out for take-off around 11:00 a.m., Delhi was still socked in. I was beginning to wish we had taken on even more fuel.

"Ten thousand more pounds of it might have been a good idea," I said to Vijay, who was flying back to Delhi with us.

"No, no, Captain," he said in his wonderfully soft voice, "I assure you the fog will lift before we arrive."

Despite his confidence, when we arrived overhead at 12:30 p.m., Delhi remained solidly fogbound. We entered a holding pattern. After a few minutes, Delhi Radio reported, "Due to unforeseen elements, we do not expect improvement for some time."

With that, I headed back to Bombay.

"Captain," said Vijay, "Delhi will be clear in one half hour."

"Sorry, Vijay. We're going back to Bombay, refuel then return."

On the retreating flight, a nice onboard lunch was served to the passengers, who were all quite understanding about our back-and-forth shuttle. Not until we landed at Bombay an hour and a half after we left Delhi airspace, did Delhi finally go above minimums. We refueled quickly and took off once again for Delhi, arriving at tea time, all in all a scheduled 90-minute trip accomplished in three 90-minute legs plus the holding time over Delhi—but all of it with passenger safety foremost.

Our five-day stay in Delhi was a high point for me. I had arranged for Katherine to fly over from New York and spend the time in Delhi with us. Together we enjoyed all the events laid on by the tour directors, including a visit to the truly impressive Taj Mahal in Agra. By now, through all our shared experiences, the passengers and crew were . . . buddies.

Katherine returned to New York, and the tour departed Delhi February 1 for three days in Bangkok then we moved on to Hong Kong, my first visit there. Depending on the wind direction, the approach to Hong Kong International airport could be attention-riveting. Usually wind conditions were such that Runway 31 was approached through the Lei Tu Mun Gap heading northwestward straight for Hong Kong Island and the mountains to the north. That was not difficult, but should wind and weather require landing southeastward on Runway 13 (Runway 31 in the opposite direction), an unusual and intricate procedure was required—as I was to experience three years later.

Fortunately on this first trip to Hong Kong—though the weather was cloudy with persistent rain—conditions permitted the easier Runway 31 approach.

Hong Kong, at that time still independent of China, was to me the most fascinating area of the Orient. Vibrant and progressive Hong Kong Island was a continuous bustle, its harbor teeming with picturesque sampans and junks. Everyone on the tour had a grand time.

From Hong Kong we "set sail" for Singapore, a flight just over three hours. Again we experienced the best of accomodations, food and local sightseeing. Next we flew to the fabled island paradise of Bali. There we toured the entire island, enjoyed the centers of Indonesian art and culture, especially the exotic Balinese temple dancing. We on the crew were hugely enjoying an elite world tour—and were being paid for it.

Our itinerary next took us to Sydney, Australia, where the harbors and the great botanical gardens were unforgettable. Next stop, Aukland. The pace of life there seemed so comfortably laid back, New Zealand quickly became one of my favorite countries.

On to Tahiti, our final stay before the homeward flight to Los Angeles. The idyllic tropical island was an appropriate last stop on this grand aerial cruise, a fitting locale for rest and relaxation.

After more than a month of mutual experiences, the tour ended at Los Angeles International Airport in a flurry of warm farewells. We were no longer passengers and crew but simply friends. The crew and I returned to New York—and reality.

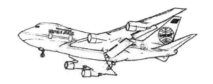

19
CHAPTER

"QUARANTINE OR LEAVE!"

Following a few free weeks in February, 1971, I was one of three check captains asked to return to England on a six-week contract to qualify Dan-Air pilots on the Boeing 707. The assignment was much the same as my work with Lloyd International the previous year.

Dan-Air, a major British airline based at Gatwick Airport about 30 miles from London, provided domestic service and tours to Europe and the U.S. Dan-Air's pilots had qualified for their 707 type ratings but they had no 707 route experience.

My British air transport pilot rating was promptly renewed, but the British Board of Trade required that we American instructor pilots complete a transatlantic "proving flight" from Gatwick to Gander, Newfoundland, and return. That flight, involving oceanic clearances, flight planning and doppler navigation, was accomplished March 23 and 24. Then came three weeks of documentation and related paper-pushing before route checking could begin.

I was given those three weeks off and returned to Pennsylvania and the center of my universe, Crystal Lake. We had moved there from Ridgefield, Connecticut in 1970. Our son John, by now a Syracuse University grad, had been building flying time as a flight instructor. Holding instrument and multi-engine ratings, he had landed a flying job with Buckeye "airline." Buckeye operated a small fleet of twin-engine Beech Model 18s. The little cargo and night mail service required no copilots—nor cargo handlers. The pilots themselves loaded and unloaded the aircraft. The pay was meager and almost all the flying was at night.

Katherine and I visited John at Huntington, West Virginia, and for several nights I flew with him on his scheduled trips. The Beech 18 he was flying seemed barely airworthy, not a comforting realization in the poor weather during the nights I flew with him. Visibility was limited, and frequent thunderstorms churned over the mountainous terrain. The night we arrived over Louisville with weather deteriorating to minimums, the directional gyro on the left side instrument panel failed, forcing John to refer to the gyro in front of the copilot seat. That instrument seemed to be expiring as well. In spite of—in fact because of—the difficulties John encountered on this tough job, the experience was invaluable. And he would move on to bigger and better days.

When I returned to England, two of us, Bill Roberts and I, found lodging in an ancient thatched-roof home. Our proprietress had been an RAF WAAF during the big war. Her RAF pilot boyfriend at the time, she told us, had managed somehow to take her for a ride in his Spitfire, no mean feat in the cramped single seat cockpit. She had sat on his lap.

Dan-Air's pilots were fine chaps. One of them, Arthur, was a proper English gentleman, not losing a degree of his cool on the night we flew into Benina International Airport at Benghazi, Libya, an airport neither of us had before experienced. Ours was a cargo flight, so the tower directed us to taxi to the cargo area. The directions did not include instructions on where we were to park. A flagman showed up to signal parking instructions but he seemed as uncertain as we were. He gave us a stop signal. Then a come ahead. Turn here. No, don't turn. I watched this bewildering display from the copilot seat as Arthur, in the left seat, calmly followed the man's confused flurry of hand signals.

"What's wrong with this guy?" the flight engineer muttered behind me.

I made some comment about the confusion seeming to prevail.

Arthur said nothing.

Finally we perceived what seemed to be the final signal to stop and shut down engines. Our engineer shut down numbers 1, 2 and 4, leaving number 3 idling, customary until external electrical power was connected.

The flagman trotted back into view and signalled us forward. With three engines out? An absurd climax to a comedy of errors.

Arthur finally broke his above-it-all silence. He looked over at me and in his grandly cultured English voice said, "Extrawdinary, wot?"

When my mission with Dan-Air was completed, I returned to my New York-based routine—flight and simulator checks with the welcome relaxation of flying the Waco during times off.

Pilots with suspected drinking problems were monitored with extreme care. Pan Am enforced a 24-hour rule: Drink nothing alcoholic within 24 hours of a flight. A violation could mean dismissal forthwith. But if the violation wasn't a flagrant one, the company had available a rehabilitation program including a year off flying status and an in-depth evaluation.

For one of the simulator checks, I was scheduled one evening to evaluate "Bill," a fine pilot with a lovely family. I'd known him for several years. The late hour and just one pilot scheduled with no one else around should have alerted me. Something was afoot that I wasn't privy to. When Bill showed up he was, as always, pleasant. We moved into the briefing room for the oral examination segment. I asked him to go to the chalkboard to illustrate instrument landing procedures. He said he would first like to demonstrate his ideas concerning holding patterns.

"Okay, Bill," I told him, "go right ahead."

With chalk in hand, he scrawled several weird-looking holding pattern entries. I let him go on a while, but I soon realized he had been drinking.

Not at all eager to write an unfavorable report, I suggested we cancel the session. Bill insisted we continue. I was sure this wasn't going to come to a positive conclusion, but, all right, we moved into the simulator room. I set up the device, and Bill took the left seat.

As we went through the check list, his responses bordered on the incoherent but finally we were ready to begin the simulated flight.

"Bill, take off and climb straight ahead to one thousand."

"Right. Climb straight ahead to . . . uh, what altitude?"

"Just take off, Bill."

He rammed the thrust levers forward and yanked the controls back to the point of almost spinning us in. I shut down the simulator.

"We'll reschedule for another time," I said.

As we left the simulator, I wrote "incomplete" on the report form. Bill now knew that I knew. I locked up and went home.

The next morning, my phone rang. "How did the check go?" asked the chief of flight training.

"I gave him an incomplete, but I'm afraid he has a real problem."

"I thought that might be the case."

Bill was given the option of entering rehab, which he accepted. When he returned months later, he soon relapsed. So ended his flying career. I found that very depressing, but there had been no alternative.

In 1972, I was again asked to fly an Olson round-the-world luxury air cruise, an offer that I didn't even think of refusing. I had the same great cockpit crew, the same excellent flight service people in the cabin—eight flight attendants for 80 first class passengers—and the same three fine Olson on-board tour guides. And some of the customers were repeats from last year.

We left Kennedy International on January 21 for essentially the same ports of call as in 1971. After a week of glorious days in Rabat, Nairobi and Addis Ababa, we landed at Delhi the night of the 30th. Passengers and crew were required to present personal immunization records to local health authorities at the airport. We all had our proper inoculation records—but some lacked up-to-date entries of yellow fever immunizations. Only a few countries required yellow fever shots and our itinerary did not include any of them. Millie, one of the flight attendants, and I, plus some 10 of our passengers, did not have records of yellow fever shots within the required five-year period.

Yellow fever shots weren't required in India unless the arrival had come from—or through—a country that did require the shots. We hadn't been through any of those countries.

"Ah," said the health official, "but you have been on the *continent* of Africa. That is reason enough to put you in quarantine until your planned departure date. Or you can leave now."

I tried to reason with the man, quite a pleasant chap despite his officiousness.

"No one in all of India has yellow fever," I pointed out.

"Precisely. It is the only disease we do not have. And we do not want to get it." He repeated his two options: "Quarantine or leave! But," he added, "the quarantine accomodations here at Palaam Airport are quite comfortable."

Our Delhi departure was scheduled five days from now. Immediate departure would bollix up the rest of the tour's plans and reservations. Quarantine seemed our only choice. While the rest of the crew and passengers were taken to the Intercontinental Hotel, off the dozen or so of us went to the airport's quarantine quarters. To our surprise, quarantine facilities did turn out to be quite decent. But for five days?

From our enforced isolation, I contacted Frank Gurney, the Delhi Pan Am agent, and a good friend of mine from my Afghanistan days. Frank believed since we were a VIP group, he could spring all of us by next morning. "And I have something that might interest you, Jack," he added. "How would you like to go to Kathmandu in Nepal? I can get you and Millie comp tickets on the Nepalese Airline. There's a flight leaving in the morning."

In the morning, Frank had prevailed. Quarantine was ended, and off Millie and I went to Nepal. While on leaves from Pan Am, flight attendant Millie had been in Nepal several times as a volunteer nurse with the Tom Dooley Foundation. On this trip, she spent her time in Kathmandu with her Dooley Foundation friends. I logged most of my couple days there in my hotel room nursing a cold, though I did get around a bit—in persistent rain. We returned to Delhi several hours before our planned February 4 departure time for Bangkok. The group with whom I had spent the night in quarantine had also been sprung the next morning and were able to join the planned Delhi itinerary. They looked upon their night in isolation as a pleasant experience with all kinds of adult beverages and excellent food aplenty.

The rest of this second luxury tour went off very well. Katherine joined me in Hong Kong for several days, an exotic experience for both of us. On February 23, the tour came to its scheduled end in San Francisco.

Air Line Pilots Association rules at that point afforded me a month free of duty. I had just completed a top notch world tour and had an entire month to recover from it. Another pilot asked if I was embarrassed to cash my paycheck.

Then, inevitably, I was back to route checks, regular line flying and—during times off, flying the Waco. I gave family and friends dozens of rides and on one bitter winter day, David and I landed on and took off from Crystal Lake's ice with remarkable ease. Katherine, though, watching this unusual performance, slipped on the ice, fell flat and banged her head.

In January, 1973, Olson organized a third round-the-world luxury charter. This time I would have a different cockpit crew, and the selection was to be mine. As first officer, I recommended Dick Laumeyer, a former Navy pilot before he joined Pan Am. As flight engineer, I opted for Manny Manioudakis. Greek through and through, Manny had flown pre-Pan Am as a pilot with the Presidential VIP helicopter group in Washington, at one time flying President Lyndon Johnson himself. Manny, his wife Anna and their two children all spoke Greek. He loved Greece and he loved America. I had known Dick and Manny as companionable men who would fit in well with the tour group. Our cabin staff would be virtually the same as on the previous tour, all well chosen by our director of flight service, Ray Le Dour.

On this junket, Katherine and Dick's wife, whom he had nicknamed "Loopy," were to join us for our four-day stay in Nairobi. Their Pan Am flight to Lebanon went well, but at Beirut International Airport they missed their outgoing plane and somehow were put on a flight they later told us was going "only God knew where." Fortunately, the Pan Am station manager, a kind and conscientious fellow, sorted things out just before they were whisked off to limbo. He found them seats on another airline to Nairobi.

Our days in Nairobi were great fun. We visited the great Serengeti Plain and game preserve—flying there in a twin Beech. And we toured world famous coffee plantations then spent a night at Treetops, the jungle lodge built on stilts. There we enjoyed superb views of wild animals making their evening visits to the nearby water hole.

On the evening before we left for Addis Ababa, Dick and I saw Katherine and Loopy off, making sure they were on the right flight to New York. The rest of the tour: Addis Ababa, Delhi—with no yellow fever complexity this time—Bangkok, Hong Kong, Singapore, Bali, Sydney, Aukland, Tahiti then Los Angeles—all went precisely as planned. Again, passengers and crew were just superb. Though all the Olson charters were great experiences, I believe this third one was the most enjoyable of all.

We returned to New York March 3 and again I had earned three weeks off. And again, I tried not to feel embarrassed when I cashed the paycheck. Then it was, as ever, back to route checks, OECs (original equipment checks) and more line flying as captain.

Not all these OECs and flight checks reached pinnacles of enjoyment. Shortly after my return from the third Olson tour, I was scheduled to give an OEC to a pilot I had not previously met. My first impression was not an inspiring one. "Bud's" uniform looked shabby and his attitude seemed more than a little know-it-all.

We had an FAA inspector aboard who was not a favorite of many, though he and I got along well enough. I sat in the right seat handling copilot duties. In the left seat Bud flew the 707, not smoothly but he managed. Destination: Paris.

As we entered the Paris control area, Bud seemed critical of the French controller, mostly because of his accent. Our night landing at Orly was . . . firm, to charitably understate the impact. In fact, I got on the controls to prevent a truly embarrassing outcome. Bud didn't appear very repentent. After we deplaned, I had to tell him he had just flown an unsatisfactory OEC. The FAA inspector agreed. Bud did not agree and told us he could hack the OEC on our return to New York the next day.

I told him honestly, "You need more training. You can fly the left seat on the way back, but you simply aren't ready for command."

Though his return flight was somewhat better, I wasn't about to give him an "up." The FAA man flew back with us, and after we landed at Kennedy, he told me now he thought Bud would be okay.

I took my checkee with me to the chief training pilot, who happened to be a friend of Bud's. After I gave the chief my report, Bud was scheduled for another check ride with a different check pilot. I heard later he had qualified for captain on that ride—but I don't recall ever seeing him again.

In June, I was asked to fly to Dallas, pick up Liberia's President Tolbert and his entourage and fly them to Haiti. The 707, chartered by the U.S. State Department, had been specially converted to provide the president and his wife a private compartment.

Our send-off from Dallas was spiffy. A band played amid an aura of high pomp. During the hour-long flight to Haiti, one of his aides asked me to go aft and greet the president and his first lady. I was happy to do so and found them both pleasantly informal. Mrs. Tolbert had been reading her Bible. When I mentioned I was familiar with the Scriptures, we became instant buddies; the Tolberts had been in Dallas to attend a high-level Baptist gathering.

I had been briefed to arrive in Haiti at a precise time and impressed with how important it was that I taxi to the terminal and stop at exactly the programmed minute. As we approached Duvalier International Airport at Port au Prince, several aircraft of the Haitian Air Force flew out to greet us then pulled alongside in a ragged formation. I hoped they wouldn't try to close in tight and breathed easier when they stayed clear.

As we landed, we could see a great crowd assembled to greet the Liberian president. I taxied to the tarmac at the terminal and stopped precisely when and where and I'd been told. A lengthy red carpet dramatically unrolled toward us—and didn't line up with the debarking steps. An awkward moment. The band played on as the carpet was yanked into alignment.

The uniforms of the Haitian honor guard were resplendent, a glorious sight. And here strutting toward the plane came infamous "Papa Doc" Duvalier himself, appearing as splendid as did the honor guard. But one had only to peer beyond the airport to be appalled by Haiti's abject and enduring poverty.

After the formalities were completed and the limousines departed, we ferried the plane to Miami. Three days later, we returned to Haiti to fly the Tolberts and their group on to New York. When we neared Kennedy in "down" weather conditions, airplanes were stacked up in holding patterns all over the place. We held as long as we could, trying to get a priority clearance. With fuel diminishing and with most of the East Coast in "down" weather, I headed for Dulles Airport in Virginia. There the weather was much improved and the facilities would be convenient to Tolbert's party. When we were well on our way there, Kennedy landing clearance came through at last—and too late. We landed at Dulles. There we waited two hours, took on fuel and finally arrived at Kennedy three hours past our originally planned ETA. So much for split second timing.

Later I was told some low level State Department employee was in hot water for not having prearranged a priority clearance for us at Kennedy. Some of the Liberian aides had been disturbed by the lengthy delay, but President and Mrs. Tolbert endured it with presidential grace. They returned to Liberia and continued to preside over that troubled nation until Tolbert was assassinated in 1980.

My flight instructor rating expired in June. In July I made an appointment for a flight check at Pennsylvania's Allentown-Bethlehem Airport where the FAA had a general aviation office. David and I lifted off Clifford Airport one calm summer morning and flew the Waco down there. In the FAA office we met Inspector Norman Johnson who was to give me the check ride. He turned out to be a fine fellow indeed. When I told him my Waco had no communication between the cockpits and suggested he tell me beforehand what maneuvers he would require, he shrugged. "No need to do anything. Just let me fly it."

Let *him* fly it?

"I haven't flown a Waco UPF-7 since I was a CPT instructor," he said wistfully.

"Well, sir, I will be pleased to have you fly this one. "

He climbed into the rear cockpit. I sat up front in the cockpit usually assigned to passengers. Bemused by this unique flight check procedure, I was suddenly struck with a disquieting thought. Would he fly well enough so I wouldn't embarrass him by having to take over the dual controls?

He flew the Waco beautifully! Smooth as polished glass. A half hour of excellence, including two superb landings.

We walked back to his office with him smiling all the way. As he renewed my instructor rating, he grinned again. "You did a good job."

David joined us for lunch and at my urging, the inspector told us of his aviation experience. Just another pilot—and the nicest FAA inspector I ever met.

20

CHAPTER

A COLOSSAL SWINDLE
AFOOT?

David passed his private pilot flight check in July, 1973, a proud accomplishment for both of us. Now the family had three pilots. In the fall, David and I flew the Waco to State College in central Pennsylvania where he applied for acceptance to Penn State the following year. Surely he was the only applicant to arrive in an open-cockpit biplane.

I finished out the year route flying mostly to European destinations, but also to the Caribbean and Central America. Then I kicked off 1974 by taking Katherine with me on a flight to Brussels. We stayed at the fashionable Metropole, enjoyed the hotel's New Year's Eve dinner and special entertainment program.

Just weeks after we returned, I was to captain a fourth Olson luxury charter, not around the world this time, but a quality tour of South America, Africa and part of the Middle East. The cockpit crew was the same as on the previous tour: First Officer Dick Loumeyer and Flight Engineer Manny Manioudakis. By now, the three of us were great friends. The cabin staff was much the same, and many of the passengers were Olson tour regulars.

On January 26, we took off from Kennedy bound for Caracas and a two-day layover there. Next stop, Buenos Aires, Argentina. I had bought flight tickets for David to meet me there. Together we joined the tour group, which included two young "hippie"-styled girls. Their parents had obviously thought sending their daughters on this month-long trip would benefit them culturally—perhaps environmentally as well, considering the tour's tight scheduling and escorted group activities. Those parents were right. The girls were well-behaved, quite demure in fact, and they joined most of the excursions. David befriended both of them in Buenos Aires and our next layover, a five-day stop in Rio de Janeiro, was great fun for all three. Rio was a happy whirl for everyone: Sugar Loaf Mountain, Copacabana's crescent beach, sumptuous dinners with entertainment every night—elegance all around us. But within a mile of the world-famous beach, I noticed that people lived in depressing poverty.

David boarded a flight home, and on February 4, we lifted off for Cape Town, South Africa. Our Atlantic crossing was blessed with fine weather all the way—and through our three days in Cape Town. On to Durban, then to Johannesburg where we visited one of the famed gold mines. I sensed the disturbing impact of apartheid most strongly in that area.

During our stay in Johannesburg, one of the most pleasant couples on the tour received the tragic word their daughter had been killed in an automobile accident. They left immediately for home, and we all felt for them.

Our next stop, Tananarive on the island of Madagascar off Africa's southeast coast, was something of a pioneering event since no Pan Am flight had ever landed there. In fact, I wasn't aware any major airline had. We arranged with the local air services for parking, aircraft security and refueling—50,000 pounds of jet fuel for our flight three days hence to Lusaka, the capital of Zambia in Central Africa.

"It will be done," the air service agent assured me. Having no inkling of the major dilemma I was about to face, I joined the tour activities.

Madagascar's people were warm and hospitable. The entire country-side was scented with vanilla, an important export of that isolated island country.

On the morning of February 15, our passengers and crew assembled at the airport. With our departure formalities completed, Dick and I filed our flight plan and were about to board. The agent for fuel supply handed me the loading sheet. Fifty thousand pounds had been piped aboard as I had requested, and all was in order.

"Now," the agent said, "I need the payment of eleven thousand dollars."

"Pan Am will pay," I assured him. "Just send them the bill." That was standard operating procedure at Pan Am stations all over the world.

"No," said the agent. "That will not do."

I turned to our flight engineer. "Manny, go on out to the aircraft, open the cockpit locker and bring in the Pan Am credit card."

Manny trotted out and returned with the card.

The agent glanced at it and shrugged. "That will not do."

By now, the passengers had become aware of the problem and several offered to have the fuel charge applied to their credit card accounts.

The agent insisted even that would not do. "Only cash in U.S. dollars will do."

"We don't have that kind of cash available," I told the man. Then, in desperation, I took a long shot. "The only possible way to resolve this," I told him as convincingly as I could manage, "is for me to write you my personal check."

He looked at me, deliberated, then announced, "Yes, that will do."

And so it was that Captain Race, check kiter *par excellence* with nothing even close to $11,000 in his checking account, scrawled a bogus check, hustled his crew and passengers aboard, rushed out of Madagascar and set course for Lusaka.

Was a colossal swindle afoot? Only for as long as it took us to radio the Pan Am station in Nairobi and request that $11,000 be immediately transferred to my personal account to cover the check I had just written. That was done forthwith. The check did not bounce. As Arthur, my friend at Dan-Air might have put it, "Extrawdinary, wot?"

Three hours later, we landed at Lusaka, where the tour indulged in a mini-safari complete with hippos, rhinos and elephants in profusion on the plains.

On to Nairobi. Again we journeyed to Bill Holden's magnificent spread in the foothills of Mt. Kenya. After five days in Nairobi, we were off again, this time bound for Iran's capital, Teheran, in an area completely familiar to me from my years with Ariana. The shah was still in power, and the city's impressive museums and beautiful gardens were much visited. In addition, arrangements had been made for our group to tour several Islamic holy places.

Three days later, we landed in Athens. Flight Engineer Manny was in his element. He spoke Greek every bit as well as English and he really knew the city. On an evening our tour group was hosted at a Greek restaurant, a troupe of male dancers trotted on stage to launch into traditional dances. Manny was not impressed.

"They're doing it all wrong," he told us—and with that, he leaped onstage with them. Shortly he was leading the dancing himself—to powerful applause. Manny turned out to be the much-appreciated star of the show and of our stay in Greece.

From Athens we flew to Lisbon, Portugal, the pre-arranged terminus of this Olson charter tour. Which, except for the fuel finagle in Madagascar, had gone smoothly in mostly good weather.

After the customary three weeks off, I completed my annual simulator check and conducted a couple of routine route check flights. Then I was asked to return to Afghanistan for a month to qualify some of Ariana Airline's pilots on the Boeing 707-720. That model was a slightly smaller version of the standard 707. Ariana had just acquired two 707-720s from Pan Am. The pilots involved had already completed their ground school and simulator work at the Pan Am Training Center in Miami.

I had left the Kingdom 10 years ago; it was good to return and renew old friendships. My first mission was to qualify my special friend, Inam-Al-Haq Gran on the 707. Gran, Ariana's top captain, was now the airline's chief pilot. Ariana had expanded through the past decade and currently flew to European destinations as well as serving airports in Turkey, Iran and India. Gran and I proceeded to fly all Ariana's routes in the 707.

We promptly completed Gran's qualifications on the jet then I began qualifying copilots. All of them had low flying time logged and needed quite a lot of training. They were diligent men, a quality of all the Afghan pilots I worked with. Since the copilots I was training had never flown outside Afghanistan, they were unfamiliar with communication requirements in more sophisticated areas. They were also unfamiliar with 707 check list formalities. I spent a lot of time coaching these eager young men in those techniques.

Since the early flights with the copilot trainees required much concentration on check lists and communication formalities, I handled most the flying. One such flight was from Kabul to Istanbul with a copilot trainee, we were at 31,000 feet preparing to descend into Istanbul's Yesilkoy Airport. Our top-of-descent procedure called for the captain to brief the copilot on the coordinated plan for descent, approach and landing. As I carefully called out each duty he was to perform, he was super attentive and eager to please.

I reached the point in the check list concerning the landing gear activation. "And then I'll call for gear down," I said.

With that, he grasped the landing gear handle and shoved it to the "Down" position.

No!" I shouted. We were still at 31,000 feet barreling along at .82 mach.

"But I thought you called for gear down, Captain!"

The slipstream slamming the extended gear produced the standard roar—but a noise never expected at 30,000 feet. In considerable embarrassment, he quickly retracted the wheels. The only damage was to his pride. There had been no undue stress on the aircraft. In fact, lowering the gear was standard procedure for a fast emergency descent in the event of cabin depressurization.

All the training was completed in six weeks. Again I said farewell to my Afghan friends. At the time, Afghanistan was progressing nicely in education, agriculture and light industry, and medical services were improving. Russian occupation then the terror of the Taliban were yet to come,

I especially wished Gran well, a man of true integrity and sincere friendship. I regarded him as a brother.

Back in New York in early June, 1974, I returned to my check piloting routine and line flying, including several African flights. One in particular stands out as an example of confusion in the air traffic control department. I was flying a passenger trip from Nairobi to Lagos, Nigeria. As we were descending from cruising altitude for landing at Lagos, I heard a KLM Royal Dutch Airlines flight report its arrival from a different direction. Our ETAs were identical.

The air traffic controller cleared both of us to let down to the same altitude over the same outer marker. I had found some air traffic controllers to be not overly trustworthy on occasion—and this was one of those occasions.

Both we and the KLM crew informed Lagos ATC our clearances were not acceptable. The controller's flustered reaction told me he probably had never before been involved in such a situation.

In self defense, the KLM captain and I agreed to eliminate the controller from our proceedings. Ignoring ground control, we coordinated our approaches directly with each other. Then we informed the befuddled controller what each of us would do in terms of clearing ourselves for final approach and landing. To his credit, he was quite amenable to our taking over traffic control ourselves, As we landed in turn with no conflict, he stayed silent.

Then it was back to the Waco for an August vacation. Son John flew a Helio Courier seaplane to Crystal Lake and moored it to our dock for several days. I made a few flights in it, then John gave me a check ride. Now I had a single-engine sea rating.

The turn of the year brought yet another Olson tour around the world—this one with innovations. Eric Friedrichsen served as my first officer, with the incomparable Manny Manioudakis again with me as flight engineer. The cabin crew, headed by capable Ray LeDour, was virtually the same.

But the intinerary wasn't. We took off January 9 headed for Abidjan on the west African republic of Ivory Coast. None of the crew had ever been there. Why, we wondered, would any luxury tour group hanker to go to Abidjan, so far off the beaten path?

After a nine-hour flight, we landed late at night and, to our surprise, were treated to a luxury hotel. The next morning, we discovered we were in a truly lovely modern city with a distinctly French atmosphere. In fact, the official language was French.

Our stay in Abidjan was intended only as a comfortable rest stop before we pressed on to more notable places, but I found the city well worth more than our casual visit.

Next came our now-standard Nairobi appearance and trip to Holden's lodge at the base of Mt. Kenya. For me, the most memorable moment of this trip's Nairobi experience took place just after our departure. I called for gear up. Eric raised the lever, but when the wheels were only party retracted, the hydraulic pressure plunged toward zero. Manny acted instantly and with an alternate system, we managed to raise the gear the rest of the way without losing too much fluid. Since we would next be in the Seychelles for several days, we would have ample time for repairs.

In the Indian Ocean 700 miles northeast of Madagascar, the 86 coral and granite Seychelles Islands had the most beautiful beaches I had ever seen—miles and miles of sugar sand edging crystal clear ocean. We landed at the airport on Mahe Island and stayed near the beach in Victoria, an aging capital city with noticeably British architecture. The Seychelles then were a British possession—slated to gain independence the next year—and there was a small American presence in the city. We noticed a group of impressively large antennas there, perhaps some sort of government-operated listening post.

Next stop, now-familiar Delhi. Katherine flew over to meet me there and together we joined the tour folks during our full week's stay. At all the notable sites poverty persisted in the backgrounds, a visual demonstration of the clear division between haves and have-nots.

January 23 we lifted off for Colombo, the capital of Sri Lanka, formerly Ceylon. I found this West Virginia-sized island off India's southeast coast notable for the kindness of its people and the impressive numbers of elephants. The ponderous pachyderms were the nation's hardest workers. Since they were incapable of perspiring, they were frequently taken to the rivers for cooling baths. Their rapport with their masters was remarkable, a true bonding.

Bangkok, Thailand, was our next port-of-call, a highly colorful city with temples everywhere. Of particular interest were the Great Buddha, the Emerald Buddha, richly clad court dancers, floating markets—altogether an almost overwhelming feast for the eyes.

Then on to Hong Kong where the weather turned sour for our arrival. This time the wind direction required us to conform to the infamous, attention-compelling "checkerboard" approach to Runway 13. We descended to 1,000 feet over Stonecutter beacon, turned straight toward the 1,500-foot mountain just north of Kowloon City, held that heading until a huge checkerboard appeared. In 1973, The big orange and white pattern had been painted on a concrete-faced slope as visual aid to airmen negotiating this tricky landing approach. Sighting the checkerboard, we swung into an immediate right turn to the runway, bled off the 1,000 feet in a steep descent and touched down at sea level on Kai Tak Airport's infamous and not exactly world class Runway 13. Normal braking stopped us well short of Kowloon Bay. Twenty-three years later, in 1998, Hong Kong finally opened a new international airport nine times larger than Kai Tak and with better approaches. The legendary checkerboard approach passed into aviation history.

Hong Kong's Kowloon Island—insistently called "Calhoun Island" by one of our tour members—was surrounded by floating restaurants, ferry boats and picturesque sampans. And it was a great place to buy high quality tailormade suits for $50 to $60. I bought one that I wore for years. Many of the men on the tour bought several. One tour member was so carried away by the bargain pricing, he visited an area ship builder and bought a yacht.

A few days later we flew on to Singapore on the tip of the Malay Peninsula for a few days' layover. Our next destination was Bali, the island just off the eastern tip of Java. Known as the "Jewel of the East," the exotic island was recommended as an excellent place to relax. Eric, Manny and I rented motor bikes and spent a day "relaxing" in the rain by putting up the slithery approach road to an active volcano.

February 6, Eric's turn to fly, we headed east-southeast, flew over Australia's Great Barrier Reef then south to land at Sydney's Kingsford Smith International Airport. We enjoyed a great tour-filled visit there, with the Aussies living up to their gregarious reputation. Then we took off eastward for Tahiti.

There, Eric, Manny and I and one of the passengers named Meade rented motor bikes with the idea of making a full circuit of the island. No rain this time; the challenge was fuel consumption. The only gas station enroute was near the end of our projected round trip. Captain, first officer and flight engineer—veteran fuel consumption experts all—conferred. We determined a full tank for each bike would, with proper fuel conservation effort, take us the full course.

Each with a tour passenger on his bike's pillion seat, the four of us confidently blapped off. We were doing excellently until just a few miles short of completing the trip, Meade's bike stalled and quit. Out of gas. Eric and his passenger went on ahead to look for that lone gas station. Manny and I waited with Meade. Waited . . . and waited. Until I decided to conduct a search mission while Manny stayed put with Meade.

A mile further on, I found Eric—out of gas. I forged ahead and just as my bike's engine conked out, there stood the gas station. I coasted in, filled my tank, bought a gallon in a can, putted back to Eric, gave him half, moved on to Meade for most of the rest, plus a dash of fuel for Manny just in case. We fuel consumption experts then rendevoused at the gas station to ride en masse and triumphantly back into Papeete.

The tour ended in Los Angeles, an eight-hour flight from Tahiti. I was off to Crystal Lake for the customary three weeks, during which I rented Duane Johnson's single-engine, low-wing Piper Cherokee and flew to State College for a brief visit with Penn State student David.

Then I returned to Kennedy for routine route check rides. On a trip to Norway, my checkee was Joe Hazelwood, a man of notable dry wit—and father of oil tanker Captain Joe Hazelwood who in 1989 would be embroiled in the *Exxon Valdez* oil spill. As we flew over Norway's scenic fiords, Joe announced to our passengers in a serious and believable voice, "We are now passing directly over Edsel Fiord." No one questioned the pilot's geographical acumen.

I also gave a route check to former Pan Am chief pilot Kim Scribner. A former national aerobatic sailplane champion, he was noted for having attempted to slow roll a sailplane while on aerial tow. He didn't quite make it and suffered multiple broken bones.

I joined him in Lisbon. The route check was to be flown from there back to Boston then New York. We had known each other for some time. In fact, shortly before our route check flight I had filled in as his first officer, due to the sudden unavailability of his scheduled first officer. We had flown a two-day pattern and I had been impressed by his competence.

Now, after our exchanging hellos, he said, "Jack, I know from my own days of check flying you don't get to handle the controls much. Why don't you do the flying? I'll just go back and sit in first class."

"Well, I'd love to, Kim. Thank you."

After I landed in Boston, I thought he would like to take over for the short leg to New York.

"No" he said, "You stay with it. I'm enjoying the ride."

So I flew us on to Kennedy, filled out the appropriate route check forms and in the remarks section, wrote, "Well done!"

At midyear, David and I flew the Waco to Traverse City, Michigan, where our older son John now owned and operated Loon Aviation at Bowers Harbor. Enroute we dodged several thunderstorms, then as we flew over a broad stretch of Lake Erie in my 35-year-old airplane well beyond gliding distance to land, I thought I heard an intermittent arrhythmic noise from the aged engine. Not a confidence builder. Splashing into the Great Lakes would be no fun at all. Then the engine seemed to smooth out, but on the return trip I avoided flying back over the lake. I now believe that unusual engine "tic" was imaginary. In potentially dangerous situations, a pilot's ears become ultrasensitive to any odd sound, including a phantom one.

On my annual time-out in August, I finally succeeded in taking my father—never an aviation enthusiast—aloft in the Waco for his first airplane ride ever. The flight was my present to him on his 80th birthday. A naturally stoic man, he showed no discernable emotion when we returned to Mother Earth.

Halfway through that vacation, I received a call from Pan Am. I was to report to Amman, Jordan, to investigate a serious situation at Royal Jordanian Airline.

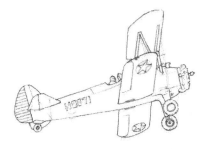

Jack Race's
favorite photographs
1942-2000

Civil Pilot Training Program class at Scranton Municipal Airport, 1942. Standing, L to R: student Tony Koveleski, instructor Jack Race, students Jim Pedrick and Le Roy Craig. Kneeling, L to R: students Tommy Davis and Donald Barkley. (1942)

2nd Lieutenant Race, newly transferred from civilian ferry pilot to active service in the U.S. Army Air Forces. (1943)

Katherine Race, nee Adams, the "avid dancer" who married Race despite his "two left feet." (1942)

Lt. Race with North American P-51 Mustang, one of many types he flew as a USAAF pilot. (1944)

The first crew of <u>Bluenose "B"</u> L to R: Deacon Galbraith, co-pilot; Joe Aaronson, radio operator; Jack Race, pilot; Emerson "Gene" Autry, flight engineer. (1944)

<u>Bluenose "B"</u> the C-47 Race flew for British General de Guingand, Field Marshal Montgomery's chief-of-staff. (1945)

Nazi Colonel General Alfred Jodl walks past <u>Bluenose "B"</u> upon his arrival at Rheims, France, to surrender the Third Reich. (May 1945)

NSA's Schweizer 2-22 utility glider poised for an airplane-towed take-off. (1947)

NSA's 1931 Kinner Bird towplane.

Co-author Bill Hallstead bids farewell to the windstorm-wrecked Bird about to be towed west by Ohio collector. (1947)

Scranton Municipal Airport in the mid-1940s G.I. Bill boom. (1947)

Pecatonica-based Stearman crop duster. (1949)

Piper J-3 Cub duster, flown by Gordon Wills, after crash near Beaver Dam, Wisconsin. (1949)

Atwood's Grumman Goose showing fabric damage during the 1949 flight from Ontario to Detroit. (1949)

Modified piper J-3 low down and dusting in Illinois. (1948)

Captain Race in Pan Am uniform. (1960s)

Pam Am Captains Everett "Woodie" Wood (left) and Jack Race ride to work on local transport in Afghanistan. (1962)

L to R: Jack Race with sons David (left) and John in Kabul. (early 1960s)

Race and Afghan Copilot Inam-Al-Haq Gran in the cockpit of Ariana's DC-6. (early 1960s)

Guests Jack and Katherine Race are intent on indigenous refreshments at an Afghan wedding reception in Kabul. (early 1960s)

Passengers on Olson around-the-world tours were assured first class attention from select Boeing 707 crews such as this one: L to R: Manny Manioudakis, flight engineer; Dick Laumeyer, first officer; Millie Adams, senior flight attendant; Jack Race, Captain; Andrea Jan; Ray Ladour, chief purser; Julie Sinkey; John Stolle, purser; Marianne Schoemacher; Mike Acre, purser; Tony Volpe, purser. (1970s)

Captain Race hosts a visit to Boeing 707's cockpit by children in Addis Ababa, Ethiopia's capital city. (1971)

Son John Race after his Fleet check ride. (1971)

David and Jack Race after a flight to Traverse City, MI. (1974)

Pastor John T. Race and Katherine stand proudly at the entrance to Jack's first pastoral assignment, Clifford Baptist Church. (1982)

The ORBIS flying eye hospital
DC-8 in flight. (1980s)

The operating room aboard
the ORBIS flying eye hospital.
(mid-1980s)

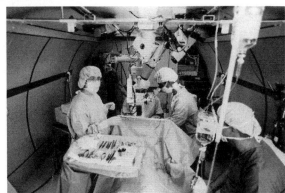

Captain Race and Viktor, the
Soviet-provided navigator,
debarking the ORBIS flying eye
hospital DC-8 after the Moscow-
Sarajevo flight. ORBIS
Executive Director Oliver Foot
descends exit step. (mid 1980s)

The collapse of Clifford Airport's
hangar. Race's damaged cessna is
pinned by a beam at left; his
prized Waco UPF is crushed
beneath roof at right. (1986)

Jack and restorer Hugo Bartel discuss progress during the Waco's extensive rebuilt. (1987)

Race, with Soviet interpreter at microphone, and ORBIS Executive Director Oliver Foot, second from right, make a 1987 public appearance in Leningrad. (1987)

Jack, in rear cockpit, and friend Milt Massey, are about to enjoy a hop in the just-rebuilt Waco. (1988)

Set to go, Race flashes a smile from the Waco's cockpit just before take-off from Clifford Airport on his 1989 recreation of Lindbergh's famous 1927 Guggenheim Tour. (1989)

Off at last. Well-wishers at Clifford Airport watch the Waco out of sight on its way to re-create Lindbergh 1927 Guggenheim. (1989)

Heading eastward over the mountains of southern California, September 11, with one third of the tour still to go. (September, 1989)

Race and his Waco, temporarily designated <u>Spirit of Orbis</u>, on the Lindbergh tour re-creation. (1989)

A quiet moment along the way. Jack and Katherine meet at Cincinnati's Lunken Airport before jack greets the waiting crowd. (August, 1989)

The return to Clifford after 18,900 miles with 96 take-offs and landings in 180 flying hours. (October, 1989)

Larry Ross's museum in the Spirit of St. Louis's crate, Canaan, Maine. (1944)

Pastor Race in the pulpit as guest speaker at First Presbyterian Church, Carbondale. (1999)

Race and the Waco fly a low pass during the two-decades-delayed "last plane out" ceremony at former Scranton Municipal Airport. (September, 2000)

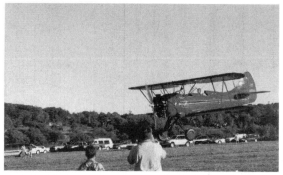

CHAPTER

21

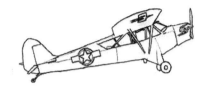

STARING AT ME FROM MY RICE PILE WAS AN EYE

In the mid-1970s, the Royal Jordanian Airline had suffered a rash of air-craft accidents. The persistent mishaps had prompted King Hussein to ask Pan Am to send in a two-man team to investigate, evaluate then submit a report with recommendations for corrective actions. I was to conduct the operations portion of this probe-and-report. The mainte-nance investigation fell to Manny Manioudakis, an excellent choice.

Before leaving New York, Manny and I were briefed by Pan Am's vice-president of flight operations on the current status of the Royal Jordanian Airline—currently known as "Alia" in honor of the King's wife.

We arrived in Amman, Jordan's capital city, August 28, 1975. We were met at Amman Airport by a Pan Am rep who had arranged for our stay at the Intercontinental Hotel. He told us we had been given free rein to fly on any Alia flights we wished, an arrangement that did not overjoy many of the airline's pilots. Only a couple of them were Jordanian 707 pilots. Most of the 707-qualified pilots were British, other Europeans and one American.

The airline also operated a fleet of Boeing 727s, a jetliner with a shorter range than the 707s. That part of the line was operating well. One of the 727 captains was Haqiqi, the very same Afghan pilot I had trained in the Kingdom a decade earlier. Renewing our old friendship, I was delighted to be able to spend some time in Amman with Haqiqi and his Danish wife.

The first Royal Jordanian pilot Manny and I met was the airline's chief pilot, the only American pilot there. All flight crews had been ordered to be cooperative, but he greeted us coolly though he did invite us to his home to "have a beer." All alcoholic beverages were banned in Islamic Jordan, of course, but non-Islamics did have access to alcohol, I believe, via the American Embassy's commissary. We arrived at the chief pilot's house one afternoon and shortly realized he was trying to inveigle us into having more than one beer, which we managed to resist.

Soon after our arrival in Jordan, Manny and I were invited to a dinner hosted by the Jordanian Air Authority. As many as 50 pilots were in attendance, and we were the guests of honor. As senior honoree, I was escorted to an impressively long table laden with great platters of pilau— mounds of rice, raisins and pieces of lamb and chicken. The building was plain, and so was the table. No eating utensils. The procedure was to plunge your hand into the pilau pile, form the mixture into a ball then pop it into your mouth.

The host escorted me to the largest pile of rice where I stood trying to maintain my composure. That was a difficult challenge because staring at me from the apex of my rice pile was an eye. A local delicacy, I was told. A lamb's eyeball, but in appearance it could have been just about any eyeball.

"That," our host confided, "is reserved for the guest of honor." And, he assured me, he himself would be highly honored by my tossing it down.

The dinner went on and on, everyone plunging in with gusto. After a time, the table and the partipants were well festooned with rice fallout. Partakers would adjourn frequently to a nearby washroom for a rinse-off.

As with all great affairs, this one eventually wound to a close. I felt Manny and I had comported ourselves well, and we warmly thanked all for inviting us. With the 707 pilots not exactly thrilled by our arrival, the party had been, in fact, a generous invitation and event.

Did I eat the eye? I'll never tell.

Manny set about checking the maintenance department, and I, over the next few weeks, closely examined the cockpits of every aircraft in the 707 fleet. I discovered the 707s had been purchased from various airlines in the Middle East and Europe. Check lists were different in each airplane, a serious lack of standardization. Also, instrument panel dials were in varying locations from aircraft to aircraft, a sure invitation to confusion among interchangeable pilots. Moreover, when I flew as observer on several flights, I found the crews to be undisciplined to varying degrees with a lack of smooth in-flight performances.

Manny and I also accompanied several training flights. One such flight at night turned out to be a hair-raiser. On a V_1 cut off of an outboard engine, the trainee failed to apply enough rudder pressure to offset the resulting yaw. The training captain called for more rudder. The trainee didn't react. Apparently to emphasize the need for more rudder, the captain himself shoved in far too much counteracting rudder. We swung into an alarming yaw in the opposite direction. All this marginally controlled weaving about on three engines took place in the dark a mere 100 feet above the ground.

Manny and I both shouted, *"Bring in the down engine!"* I began to shove the engine's thrust lever forward before the training captain grabbed it. The aircraft stabilized and we resumed normal climb. That was not a happy experience.

As we moved ahead on our assignments, Manny was able to rate aircraft maintenance as satisfactory. I found the 707 pilots capable but they needed to conform to standard operating procedures.

From time to time, we met with the airline's director, Ali Ghandour, a knowledgeable man who asked all the right questions. Also present at these meetings were all the upper echelons of airline management and the Jordanian Air Authority. I was much impressed with the overall demeanor and expertise of this forward-thinking group.

After four weeks "on location," Manny and I were summoned to meet King Hussein himself. A royal limousine delivered us to the designated palace. We were escorted from the ornate entrance to a room where King Hussein, Queen Alia and a burly bodyguard received us.

A stocky man of middling height, casually dressed as was the more regal-appearing queen, the 40-year-old king greeted us graciously. The conversation was general, then the king, himself an accomplished pilot, talked of some recent aerobatic flying he had enjoyed. He asked me about my experience, then the subject turned to the matter at hand, the problems with Royal Jordanian Airline. I summarized our findings, and to my surprise, he did not press us with any specific questions.

I did speak positively about several of the pilots and thanked the king for the cooperation of airline personnel and for the high quality of service Manny and I had experienced.

"It has been a great pleasure to be in your country," I assured him, "and we believe the airline has fine leadership."

Tea was then served and the atmosphere became quite relaxed. We were there for an hour, and I found King Hussein to be a kind, compassionate man with the qualities of a conscientious leader.

Now came the time to write our final evaluation reports—Manny's on the maintenance aspect, mine concerning operations. At our final meeting with Ali Ghandour, we went through the reports in detail.

A day or two later, Ghandour asked me to return to his office. What now? To my surprise, he said, "Might you consider moving to Amman and accepting the position of director of flight operations for Royal Jordanian Airline?"

"I'm honored," I told him, "but I have family commitments back in the U.S."

"You will be provided a home and considerable additional benefits, Captain. Think about my offer for day or so, then let me know of your final decision."

He clearly did not want no for an answer, and I avoided a discussion of salary because I was not at all inclined to accept his offer.

Ghandour also offered Manny a leadership position in engineering and maintenance. In the end, we both declined. "I'm honored by your confidence in me," I assured Ali Ghandour, "but for personal reasons, my answer has to be no."

Before we left Jordan, Katherine and Manny's wife, Anna, flew over to join us for a week of exploring the Red City of Aquba, the shore of the Dead Sea, Galilee in Northern Israel and Jordan's many Roman ruins. We left with a positive impression of Jordan, the king and his people. Sometime later, I was told the airline had enacted our suggested changes and had avoided further major accidents.

In the late 1970s, a major improvement of Amman's airport was commissioned to an American firm. The design team included Lisa Halaby, daughter of Najeeb Halaby, the FAA's administator in the 1960s and now a Pan Am director. A Princeton graduate, Lisa Halaby held a degree in urban plannning and architecture. Queen Alia had been killed in a 1977 helicopter crash, and King Hussein began dating Lisa Halaby. In 1978—three years after Manny's and my sojourn in Jordan—they married and she took the title Queen Noor ("Light"). She and Hussein were married for 21 years, the longest of his four marriages, until he died in 1999.

Returning home in the fall of 1975, I resumed my vacation, flew the Waco frequently, then reported to New York—and I was back in the check pilot routine.

I had given Ali Ghandour only general reasons for my reluctance to become a Royal Jordanian Airline executive. A specific one would have been the fact that as the airline's flight operations director, I would have been flying a desk more than an airplane—and at Pan Am, I expected soon to be moved up to the huge Boeing 747.

CHAPTER

22

A VISIT TO THE TWILIGHT ZONE

Following the Jordan adventure, 1975 wound down with my required periodic simulator check, this one administered by sim training and check airman Rod Jocelyn. Rod had been national aerobatics champion in the 1950s. Some time ago, when he was junior on Pan Am's seniority list, a pellet from a careless hunter's shotgun had cost him the sight of one eye. A fine man, modest and unassuming, he was now assigned to the simulator.

In February, I conducted flights to the Middle East. One night after lift-off from Teheran's Mehrabad Airport, the 707's landing gear refused to retract. We were certain the gear locks had been properly removed; I had seen the disengaged locks during the pre-flight check. Hydraulic pressure? The reading was normal. Our prompt trouble-shooting revealed nothing out of whack, but the gear stubbornly stayed down.

An immediate return to Mehrabad was in order. The murky weather called for an instrument approach. We landed and taxied back to the terminal where the maintenance department corrected the problem in a few hours. Then we were again on our way to Ankara, Istanbul then Rome, where we "slipped"—as the British term laying over—for 24 hours.

Age 60 was—and is—the mandatory retirement age for airline pilots. On February 11, my good friend Woodie reached that bittersweet milestone. On the 10th, a retirement party was organized in Berlin where he would land on his final Pan Am flight. I flew there to be on hand when Woodie arrived from Frankfurt.

The party was a smashing success, an appropriate tribute to the man who had made such a profound impact on my own flying career.

In April, I flew a round trip charter from New York to Freeport International Airport in the Bahamas. Not a luxury cruise, this one was a gambling junket. A Freeport casino had chartered the Pan Am 707 for the ride, a two-and-a-half hour flight from Kennedy. In the early evening, I landed 150 optimistic gamblers on Grand Bahama Island. They were promptly driven to the casino. Six hours later, 150 mostly morose gamblers returned for our wee hours flight back to Kennedy. I assumed the casino had gambled that the gamblers would lose enough to pay for the charter plus a tidy profit for the casino.

The following month, I flew a charter trip to Moscow, something of a pioneering flight in that it led to Pan Am's establishing scheduled service to the Soviet capital.

In mid-year, I rented Duane Johnson's Cherokee and flew our daughter, Jackie, to Traverse City to visit John at his Loon Aviation seaplane operation. Our younger son, David, a junior at Penn State, was a summer employee at Loon, generally helping out—including phone answering.

"Good afternoon. Loon Aviation. May I help you?" Then I saw him turn to John. "Is all this formality necessary? A lot of the calls are from your buddies."

"Yes, it's necessary, David. Just keep at it."

"Good afternoon. Loon Aviation . . . ."

Charter, scenic flights and instructing made the season a busy time for Loon Aviation. Aside from the phone etiquette stand-off, John and David were spending a happy summer together.

Jackie and I flew homeward July 1—with a brief visit to the *Twilight Zone*. I planned a fuel stop at Ohio's Wadsworth Airport, about 10 miles west of Akron. As we circled the field, we spotted at least 30 lightplanes down there, a real beehive of an airport. We glided in and landed on the long paved runway.

Taxiing toward the terminal building, I peered along the flight line and the ramp. "Strange, Jackie. All those planes, but I don't see anybody anywhere."

We pulled up to one of the gas pumps. No one appeared. I cut the engine. We climbed out and walked to the small neatly-kept terminal. Inside we found no one at the counter nor beyond the open office door.

"Hello? Hello?"

Silence.

The day was cheerfully sunny, but we both felt an eerie chill. The whole airport looked as if everyone had suddenly disappeared into another dimension.

We walked back out to the ramp and returned to the gas pump. It was unlocked and operable, but I just didn't feel right about filling the Cherokee's tank on our own at this weirdly deserted airport.

We waited 20 minutes. Still nobody anywhere. Not a sound broke the dead silence.

"We have enough gas to reach Akron/Canton Airport," I assured Jackie. "Let's go there."

We boarded the Cherokee, taxied out. Still no sign of life. We took off utterly mystified. A few minutes later, we landed at Akron/Canton, a reassuringly bustling airfield. As we gassed up there, I asked one of the locals what he knew about Wadsworth.

"Oh, that's a pretty busy place."

But not today.

Years later, when I happened to fly over Wadsworth Airport, I saw lots of activity down there. I never did hear any explanation of our strange experience there July 1, 1976.

As I had hoped, after several weeks of mid-summer line flying, I was awarded a bid for captaincy on the Boeing 747—the huge four-engined jet liner easily identified by the elongated "hump" on top of the fuselage. In late August I reported to 747 ground school in San Francisco, a four-week course. Though it wasn't required, I visited the Pan Am hangars at San Francisco International Airport to climb aboard a 747. The first time I sat in the cockpit of this giant aircraft, logic told me it should be impossible for any pilot to land a 300+-ton aircraft while perched up here in the hump, 32 feet above the ground.

To increase passenger capacity in the late 1960s, the 747 was designed with the cockpit placed above the nose area, enabling the passenger space to extend all the way forward beneath the cockpit. This unusual design would also permit the installation of a hinged nose as a loading door in 747 cargo versions.

In the initial 747 design, the cockpit was housed in a simple round bump up there. That produced so much air resistance it was extended into a long teardrop shape. Major customer Pan Am asked Boeing to use the resulting space behind the cockpit for a lounge and bar, a delightful luxury for first class passengers—until the fuel crisis of 1973. The non-revenue-producing lounge was converted into seats for fare-paying passengers. Thus the famous elongated hump made the 747 into a passenger double-decker.

After the month of ground school with most of my free time spent studying, I began 747 simulator training. The first five sim sessions were preparation for the pre-rating sim check followed by the simulator portion of the FAA type rating check. Each sim session was usually four hours—two trainees for two hours each. I had an excellent instructor and soon was scheduled for the FAA oral exam preceding the FAA simulator check ride.

Of the several FAA inspectors who conducted these examinations at the training center, all but one were considered "comfortable" to work with. Fate insisted that I be assigned that hard-nosed chap to administer my oral exam and sim flight check.

The oral usually lasted an hour, but the "one" was known to exceed that time by a goodly amount and delve deeply. I was acutely aware that failures on the oral were not uncommon. With all that trepidation nagging at me through the barrage of questions, I was greatly relieved when I passed that part of the procedure.

Next came the check ride in the simulator. I sat in the captain's seat. Training Captain Fred Slightam manned the copilot position. As with many Pan Am training captains, Fred was not on the seniority list. He—and they—were hired exclusively as instructors with the title "training captain."

The FAA inspector perched on the jump seat behind us. From there he could program in all sorts of compelling emergency conditions.

The "ride" was more or less standard—until the final landing event. During a simulated non-directional beacon approach in rough air at night, Fred inflicted an emergency: two engines out on the same side, no less. No go-around would be possible with two dead same-side engines. The landing had to be completed on the first and only approach. This was a truly unrealistic set-up, but I managed—and sighed with relief as we rolled to a safe simulated stop.

Relief was premature. The diabolical inspector now programmed a brake fire. I whipped through the check list to deal with that, then went posthaste through the evacuation procedure.

Now came the debriefing, mercifully short. Because I hadn't been asked to repeat any simulator maneuver, I suspected I had passed the check ride. The inspector logged his blessings on his report form. We shook hands. Then the dreaded FAA man said cheerfully, "So, how about a cup of coffee?"

Next in order were two pre-rating flights in an actual 747. In nine-abreast seating across two aisles plus the seating in the upstairs hump, the massive aircraft could carry up to 450 all-economy class passengers. In mixed-class seating, 360 to 380 was the norm. The swept-back wings stretched 195 feet from tip to tip. The 20-foot-wide fuselage measured 231 feet, nose to tail cone. This mighty flying machine could cruise almost 6,000 miles at 600+ mph before refueling.

Despite all the massiveness, the pre-rating flight checks turned out to be the easier parts of the rating requirements. On both of those flights out of Sacramento Metropolitan Airport, I discovered to my surprise that landing a 747 while perched three stories above the runway was not difficult at all. I then took my FAA rating ride with an inspector of remarkably pleasant disposition. After our 30-minute flight, I had my Boeing 747 type rating in hand, my eighth type rating in airline aircraft.

Before I left San Francisco, Katherine joined me and we spent some time with Paul Gillette, a long-time writer friend from Carbondale. Paul had published several books, fiction and non-fiction, and had written screen plays, including "Play Misty for Me," the first movie directed by Clint Eastwood. A wine connoisseur, Paul took us on a tour of the Napa Valley vineyards. We were delighted to have another wine expert in our little party. Old friend Woodie and his wife, Barbro, had joined us in San Francisco.

On my return to New York I passed the required international 747 command check flight then was scheduled for my international FAA check ride as captain of a passenger flight from Kennedy to London then Amsterdam and return. Check Captain "Frank L." flew as copilot.

The flights to London then on to Amsterdam were routine. For the return leg to New York, FAA Inspector Warren Harris came aboard to take over the checking responsibility. This was not a routine flight. We were carrying a fifth pod, a jet engine we were transporting to New York for overhaul. The extra pod was slung beneath the right wing, so some non-standard operating procedures applied. Fuel consumption would be greater and air speed slower: Mach .80 instead of Mach .84.

Weight and balance figuring fell to Frank as part of his copilot duties. Then I as captain would review and approve or disapprove his result. When he handed over his calculation, I realized he had gotten it wrong. I didn't want to embarrass him in front of Inspector Harris, so I quietly made the corrections then handed the paperwork back to Frank.

The observant FAA man noticed I'd made the changes. Frank knew he had been found in error and was considerably chagrined. We both realized we were unlikely ever to become bosom buddies.

Despite that sticky start, the flight back to Kennedy went smoothly. Harris was quite complimentary; check pilot Frank simply approved.

At last a fully qualified transoceanic 747 captain, I finished out the year flying European and South American routes, with one Middle Eastern jaunt. And I came to be very fond of the Boeing 747.

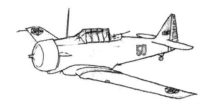

THE WORST NEWS ANY PARENT COULD EVER HEAR

For a year to be marked with almost overwhelming tragedy, 1977 began with routine line flying in 747s. While David was home between semesters at Penn State, I prepped him for his instrument rating.

In March, Katherine and I flew in Duane Johnson's new Cherokee Arrow to Ohio to visit son John at New Knoxville. He was flying as chief pilot for The Way International, a nondenominational Christian teaching ministry headquartered in that rural town. During summer seasons, John continued to operate Loon Aviation in Michigan.

The next month, during his Penn State junior year, David returned to Kabul for a practicum as part of his human development major. Our close friend, Inam-Al-Haq Gran, gratiously became David's guide and counselor during his six weeks in Afghanistan. When David returned and his spring semester ended in June, he went off to Traverse City where John's Loon Aviation was back in summer operation. David regularly flew Loon's Cessna floatplane on charter hops and scenic flights from the many lake resorts in that part of Michigan.

On my days off in May and June, I gave Duane Johnson a hand instructing at Clifford Airport. In July, Pan Am asked me to serve as a 747 check pilot. I was glad to accept and went through the required syllabus that included a right seat checkout. That same month, Katherine and I flew to Traverse City to spend a few days with our sons at John's seaplane operation. Watching David in action, I was really impressed with his mastery of floatplane flying.

After we flew back to Pennsylvania, I conducted check rides on the 747 then returned to Crystal Lake for a few days off in August.

On the night of August 18, Katherine and I were awakened by urgent knocking on our cottage door. Two Fell Township police officers whom we knew slightly stood there, faces grim. In as kindly a manner as they could manage, they relayed the worst news any parent could ever hear. Late that afternoon at Lake Leelanau north of Traverse City, a Loon Aviation seaplane had crashed. David and his three passengers had not survived.

A few minutes later that appalling news was confirmed by a phone call from John.

The days that followed were dismal. Duane Johnson flew to Traverse City to bring David home to us. After the funeral service, Katherine and I flew to Traverse City on the 24th. We were taken to Lake Leelanau where we checked into the same resort from which David had made his final flight. Al Lawicki, the resort's owner, and his wife were as devastated as we. Their two sons had been aboard the fatal flight, and Al had watched the whole tragedy unfold.

David's regularly assigned Cessna 180 was out of service for a repair on its starter. He had been flying a "loaner," a 1940 four-place Fairchild 24 on floats. He had made a normal take off from the lake. As he circled back over the resort at about 800 feet, Al was horrified to see fabric peel back from the top of the left wing and trail in the slipstream. Then the left wing's fuel tank popped upward, acting as a giant spoiler before it broke free. With so much lift thus destroyed, the Fairchild banked sharply left and plunged into the lake.

David had often flown from the lakeside lodge, and Al thought the world of him. We talked with several people at the resort who had known and admired David. One man told us he had never seen David happier than he had been the day of the crash. "There was a kind of glow about him." I felt as if God had made our son's last hours on earth truly fine ones.

The National Transportation Safety Board investigation revealed the Fairchild had been rebuilt by an unlicensed mechanic, though a licensed aircraft mechanic had signed off on the work. Faulty installation of the left wing's fabric had led to its failure and the loss of the airplane and those aboard. The owner's insurance company settled, but there was absolutely no joy in that for our devastated family.

That miserable time for all of us was made even blacker two weeks later. Shortly after take-off from White Plains, New York, our long-time friend Duane Johnson apparently flew into a layer of dense fog. The White Plains Airport tower heard Duane radio, "We're in the soup!" Then he lost control and the Piper Cherokee crashed, killing Duane and his passenger.

Two weeks after that second trauma, yet another tragedy hit us—this one in Kabul. In Afghanistan, our dear friend Gran was assassinated. Some believe his death was the outcome of his outspoken criticism of the then-current regime. Others have said he may have been the victim of mistaken identity. Whatever the motive, one evening as Gran entered his apartment, he was shot in the back. What a tragic loss to Afghanistan and a heartfelt loss to our family.

The sorrow we felt that tragic autumn was made bearable only by God's grace. Our memories of the joy David had brought us and others during his short life were comforting. Clearly a part of our healing was our awareness this life is not the end. I found solace in Lindbergh's words: "I have seen enough decency, goodness and beauty to be ready to affirm that the world and all of us in it are not flying blind in mean-ingless chase. The universe bespeaks purpose and direction . . . ."

In the spring of 1978, three years from mandatory retirement, I began to think seriously about what I would do following such a profound change in my and Katherine's lives. Whenever possible during the irreg-ular schedule of an airline pilot, I had been active in church matters. During our stay in Germany in the 1950s, I had found my work with the congregation in Wiesbaden quite an inspiring experience. I had also felt complimented by the number of fellow crewmembers who, over the years, had come to me for consultation on personal problems.

I've always felt an affinity with the Scriptures. I had been baptised, raised and confirmed in the Episcopal Church and until I began my flying career, regularly attended Trinity Episcopal in Carbondale. After Katherine and I married, we attended her Presbyterian Church for a while, but we were really ecumenical. Doctrinal differences among the various denominations, I have always felt, are diversions from the real meaning of Christianity.

In view of all that, I decided to study for the ministry with the goal of completing my studies just before mandatory retirement from Pan Am. A good friend of mine, area minister Reverend Leland Pease, encouraged me to enroll in the Southern Baptist Seminary in Louisville, Kentucky. All my studies would be through the seminary's off-campus program and they could be worked on during Pan Am layovers and off times. By retirement date, I planned to be a licensed American Baptist lay pastor.

Among my 747 flights, mainly to European, Middle East and African destinations, were 13- to 14-hour flights to Bahrain and Dharan. The usual layovers there were three days, good opportunities to study my seminary courses. These flights were in the 747SP, a shorter and slightly faster version of the standard 747. On such unusually long hauls, we carried an extra copilot and flight engineer.

Most of our passengers were oil field workers who had put in a half year or so in Bahrain or Dharan then were given a break at home. Since both sites were Islamic and non-alcoholic, our flight attendants on the New York-bound trips could be considerably challenged. Many of our passengers, eager to make up for lost elbow-bending time, had to be restricted from overdoing it. In one instance, I found it necessary to leave the cockpit and hustle into the cabin to intervene. The overzealous drinker had refused to listen to the flight attendant. But he did listen to me and no drastic action was needed.

In late April and early May, 1979, I gave an annual route check to a very senior captain whom I'd known for years. Way back, I had flown once or twice as his copilot. He was still a good pilot, but a couple of times on this ride, had not his first officer alerted him, he would have gone right on through cleared altitudes, a serious violation. I felt the veteran captain had blown it big time.

"What was the problem?" I asked him during our layover in Frankfurt.

He told me he was preoccupied with serious family problems, then assured me that was not meant as an excuse. I could see he was a fatigued, strung-out man. Yet he had a clean record with Pan Am. I understood his concerns and did my best to get him back on track. On the return flight to New York, I gave him a recheck. This time his performance was excellent. A year later, he reached age 60 and retired in good standing.

Though some pilots found flying many long trips each month a boring routine, it was never so with me. Every flight was different, an opportunity to learn something new about aviation and the people involved. I could not understand incidents of pilots falling asleep at the controls. One night as we reached cruising altitude after take-off from Rio de Janeiro enroute Caracas, Venezuela, the first officer asked, "Do you mind if I close my eyes and sleep a while?" That, after a two-day rest stop in Rio. After we landed in Caracas, I had a serious talk with him, but I could see he wasn't listening. Unfortunately, that had to go into my flight report.

One of the drawbacks of flying for an airline employing more than 3,000 pilots was that crewmembers aboard would most often be strangers to each other. Real friendships usually were not formed aboard, but in the communities where crewmembers lived. A case in point was Ridgefield, Connecticut, something of a pilots' town. I had made many friends there, but our flying together was rare.

My last full year as a Pan Am captain—1980—began with flights to London and Frankfurt, followed by a couple of Houston-Mexico City excursions. Next came Pan Am's recently established non-stop flights from New York to Tokyo. We flew 747SPs on a great circle route over Canada then along the Aleutian Islands chain, not exactly a comfortable distance from Russian territory. We knew we were scanned by Soviet radar. This was around the time a Korean Airlines passenger flight strayed into forbidden Soviet territory and was shot down. With three navigation systems on board, we consistently and closely checked our position.

I enjoyed Tokyo, that earthquake-prone city of extreme courtesy. In my 20th-floor hotel room one day, the entire building began to move. I decided that was a good time to leave and joined several like-minded people in the hallway. With the building swaying alarmingly, we hurried into an elevator and headed down to emerge into the crowded, chatter-filled lobby. The hotel manager assured all of us the hotel—and other tall Tokyo buildings—had been designed to withstand earthquake shocks by controlled swaying, and we were perfectly safe. On a subsequent visit during another quake, I did indeed see the largest buildings in noticeable sway mode.

I was scheduled in June for a New York-Caracas-Miami pattern. After take-off from Caracas on a night flight to Miami, Pan Am Operations radioed, "Clipper, you may have stowaways aboard." As we received that message, our purser rushed to the cockpit to report he had just found two boys hiding in one of the cloak areas. He told us they appeared to be about 14 years old, had no weapons of any kind—and seemed thoroughly frightened. He had put them in empty seats in the rear of the plane and assigned one of the flight attendants to watch over them.

By now Traffic Control was aware of the situation. Standard procedure called for our return to Caracas, but since the boys were obviously no threat, I suggested we continue to Miami to be met there by the proper authorities. Since we would be returning to Caracas almost immediately, we could easily return our young stowaways. While this discussion was going on, each boy's background was checked in Caracas. That investigation determined the boys' action had been no more than a misguided prank. U.S. Immigration reps met us at Miami

International and agreed to our flying the boys back to Caracas on our soon-departing return trip. Back in Venezuela, the shaky young international hitchhikers were turned over to their waiting parents. If they faced punishment, I found myself hoping it would be light.

I continued my seminary studies, and on a 14-hour Tokyo flight, the first officer and I fell into a discussion of Christianity. One of the flight attendants overheard us and she turned out to know some Scripture herself. I asked if she had a favorite Bible verse.

"One Corinthians 13:13," she said with no hesitation. "So faith, hope, love abide, these three; but the greatest of these is love."

A marvelous passage indeed, I thought. It had been part of the impetus in my studying for the pastoral ministry—not because I was drawn to preaching; because I would be able to serve others.

I wasn't attracted to any particular denomination. I felt at home in most churches, though I did not find extreme narrow fundamentalism acceptable. I also felt comfortable with other religions, again excepting the fundamentalism that so often becomes a part of all religions. I find it deplorable that while every major religion preaches love of one's fellow man, so much of the violence in the world has been brought about in the name of religion.

During the summer of 1980, I continued to fly the Waco, giving rides to many in our community. Often I visited the Carbondale Nursing Home. When I was away on Pan Am flights, I sent postcards to the many friends I made at the home. Back again at Crystal Lake, I took several of the more mobile nursing home guests on rides in Clifford Airport's Citabria.

In November, I flew the faithful Waco to Wurtsboro, New York for fabric recovering and an engine overhaul. While she was undergoing those lengthy procedures, I flew my final six months with Pan Am.

FLOWERS, BOWLS OF FRUIT AND CHAMPAGNE

Toward the end of January, 1981 I captained a 13-hour non-stop flight from Kennedy to Saudi Arabia. Pan Am had recently established service there, primarily for American oil workers. During baggage inspection at Dharan Airport, a Saudi customs official pawed through a bag carried by our second officer.

"What's this!"

He had discovered an item of forbidden literature. He immediately confiscated the offending publication and Saudi authorities detained our crewmember. Sending him out of the country on the next flight became a real possibility.

As captain of the aircraft that had transported this nefarious publication, I was questioned concerning how I could have let such a violation occur. This was a very serious matter, the Saudi officials informed me when they finally released our man several hours later. "No such incident will be tolerated in the future," I was solemnly warned, and I believe the second officer's name was placed on some sort of watch list. Was the offending publication a tract on overthrowing the Saudi monarchy? A condemnation of things Islamic? No, it was a copy of *Playboy* magazine.

During times off, I frequently visited the Christian Bookstore in Scranton, a few miles "down the valley" from Carbondale. There I became acquainted with a kind and gentle woman of about 60, Lorna Line, who worked as a salesperson. Lorna had served as a missionary in Africa, and as some Christians might put it, she was still "on fire for the Lord." For some time she had been planning a missionary trip to Liberia, and she wondered if she might fly there on one of my scheduled runs to Monrovia's Roberts Field.

I helped her with ticketing and had myself scheduled on the Pan Am Nigerian flight to fly her there. But we had a problem. Lorna's ticket was a standby. Worse, her status was somewhere around #12 on the standby list.

The day before the flight, I checked with Pan Am Ticketing. The news was not good. "Lorna," I told her reluctantly, "it's very doubtful you will be able to get on the flight."

"Oh, there will be a seat for me. The Lord will provide."

The next morning she rode with me to Kennedy Airport. I took her directly to the passenger agent handling the flight. The agent was close to overwhelmed with checking in some 400 passengers, but Lorna's lovely smile and attitude of complete confidence got him to pause. I explained how important it was to her to get on this flight.

He pointed at his lengthy list. "I'm very sorry," he told Lorna, "but I have to tell you it will be a miracle if you get on."

"I believe in miracles," she said pleasantly.

At that point I had to leave her to attend to weather reports, clearances and all the other preflight paperwork. When I finished, I returned to the departure gate.

"Any cancellations?"

"None," the agent said.

"Any change in the standby list?"

"Not so far."

Forty-five minutes before boarding time, I spotted Lorna sitting primly in the waiting area, reading her Bible.

"It doesn't look good," I had to tell her. "If you don't get aboard, one of the passenger agents will arrange for a motel for you for the night. Now I'm afraid I have to board the plane myself."

She was absolutely imperturbable. "Jack, don't worry so about me. I will be on the flight."

The crew and I boarded and proceeded through the check lists. With all passengers in place, the operations rep brought the final weight and balance data to the cockpit. I noted every seat was taken.

"Did any standbys make it?" I asked.

The ops rep nodded. "A few, I think."

When he left, the purser came to the cockpit to report all doors closed and all flight service ready.

"Might you recall among the last few to board a pleasant lady about 60?" I asked him.

"The lady with the Bible? Yes, she was the very last one."

Seven-and-a-half-hours later, we made an intermediate stop at Dakar. I brought Lorna to the cockpit, and first officer Bernie Woesner and Second Officer Vince Calamia were captivated by this plainly-dressed gentle soul.

Then we were off to Monrovia where Lorna was met by friends from the missionary station. The following morning, Bernie and I drove out there a few miles from Liberia's capital city in a rented car along an extremely bumpy road. We spent most of the day at the mission with truly dedicated people. They were devoting their lives to answering some of life's basic needs of the very poor, primarily through teaching and medical care. The mission operated Radio Station ELWA, Eternal Love Winning Africa, a message unfortunately forgotten in that country during its later turn-of-the-century chaos.

The next morning we took off on the return flight to New York while Lorna stayed on in Liberia. Not until several months later did I see her again, back at her sales clerk job in Scranton.

After that Liberia run, I flew several New York-Tokyo and New York-Dhahran non-stoppers. During layovers, I was determined to complete my studies before my retirement at the end of May. Clifford Baptist Church had already asked me to serve as associate pastor, beginning June 1.

Retiring pilots were given super seniority for their last month. I would be 60 May 30, so I chose my flights for that month without any chance of being outbid. For the most part, I opted for the New York-London route.

On May 17, a beautifully clear day, we pushed back from our gate at London's Heathrow Airport. We had our taxi clearance to Runway 28R, but not far from the terminal with the First Officer handling communications, Pan Am Operations abruptly radioed, "Clipper, return to the gate."

"Ask them why," I told the F.O.

The response: Pan Am Ops had just received a phone call that a bomb was aboard.

A bomb?

Something's strange here, I thought. A serious bomb threat should have been relayed by Heathrow Ground Control. And the voice from Pan Am Ops had not seemed particularly stressed. Even more puzzling, no plane was ever returned to the gate to unload a potential bomb. The word "hoax" crossed my mind, but no captain would disregard the possibility that a bomb threat could be real.

If scant time to detonation was not part of the threat, standard procedure called for taxiing to a designated dispersal area. Heathrow Ground Control directed us to the dispersal area, a long, *long* roll to that remote site near the end of Runway 10L.

Our passengers deserved some kind of explanation for this lengthy taxi trip well away from other traffic. I asked Pan Am for any additional information they might have. I was told the call had come from a phone inside the terminal, a male voice with an Indian or Pakistani accent. At the same time, ticketing agents had noticed one of our passengers in transit from Delhi had failed to reappear for departure to New York. But his luggage was aboard.

"Apparently we have an unauthorized bag aboard," I announced over the cabin speakers. "We are proceding to an area where we will all disembark."

Then word came that airport security had managed to track down and arrest the perpetrator right in the terminal. Yet it was prudent for us to go ahead with the evacuation of the airplane. At the dispersal area, I felt no need to deploy the emergency chutes. I called for stairs and buses. When they arrived, we shut down the engines and conducted an orderly egress of some 350 passengers and crew.

We all climbed aboard the buses and reassembled back in the terminal. Over a public address system, I spoke with our passengers in more detail. They were quite understanding, and after a two-hour delay, we finally lifted off for New York.

The miscreant without a conscience turned out to be a passenger who had lingered too long in the duty-free shop. When he realized he had missed the plane, he concocted the bomb threat in an attempt to get us back to the gate so he could board. For that, he had created a fearful mess for hundreds of passengers, crewmembers and airport personnel. I assume his actual destination that day had become a London police station.

On May 25, I began my final Pan Am round trip as captain, London-bound out of Kennedy. The airline had given me first class accomodations for my family. Since John was a professional pilot—now chief pilot for The Way—he would ride jump seat in the cockpit with me. Eric

Friedrichsen, my good friend since our Olson Tour days, was my first officer.

For our two-day layover in London, Pan Am provided our Intercontinental Hotel rooms, replete with flowers, bowls of fruit and champagne. The airline also picked up the check for a dinner. Eric and his wife, Verna, hosted another. In remarkably good weather, we spent two days touring London's highlights, a special time for all of us.

On the 28th, we departed on the return trip to New York. Busy as Heathrow was, as we were cleared for take-off a bonus message came from the control tower: "Congratulations and bon voyage"

During the flight, a surprise arrived in the cockpit from the galley. A birthday cake! An hour out of Kennedy, Eric pulled out a paper he had written and asked if he could make an announcement to the passengers. As I was guarding the Air Traffic Control frequency, I had no idea he was announcing my retirement. When he showed me the tribute he had written, I found it quite touching, including his mention that I was to be assistant pastor at Clifford Baptist Church.

Ten minutes later a flight attendant brought me an envelope from one of the passengers. Inside were a kind note and a check for $100 made out to the church.

At Kennedy in fine weather, I felt a touch emotional as I concentrated on making my last airline landing an ultra smooth "squeaker." In light wind straight down Runway 13R, we touched down with no discernible jolt.

As we turned to clear, Eric grinned. "Not bad—for an old man."

Two days later we celebrated at Crystal Lake; a retirement party attended by many long-time friends including Woodie and Barbro. In his comments to the hushed guests, Woodie fondly recalled in amusing detail our Afghanistan days together. Then he added, "Jack is not really retiring. As a Pan Am pilot he's retiring—that is true. But retiring as a pilot, never!"

Little did any of us realize how accurate Woodie's comment would turn out to be.

CHAPTER 25

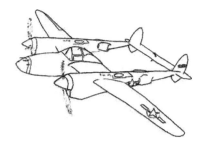

THREE MILES WEST OF WURTSBORO THE ENGINE STUTTERED

Pan Am offered its retired pilots the option to continue flying as second officers—flight engineers. Some pilots welcomed the opportunity to stay in the air, if not at the controls. But it held no appeal for me. I had my Waco.

So on June 1, 1981 I embarked on an entirely new career. Now a licensed lay pastor in the American Baptist Church of Pennsylvania and Delaware, I began my duties at the Clifford Baptist Church as assistant pastor to Dick Olmstead. Dick, five years older than I, had been an Army Air Forces pilot flying the "Hump" in China. But after the war, flying held no real attraction for him. He became a successful sales rep while he took the same route to the ministry as I had. He, his wife and four children lived in Brielle, New Jersey, not Pennsylvania. He drove to Clifford every Friday and returned to Brielle Monday. I was asked to cover for him during the week, my first pastoral assignment.

I felt I had experienced the reality of the Holy Spirit and I felt a real drive to do something for others. I had faith in the Lord, but I believe faith without work in His behalf is not true faith. One need not be a pastor to do good works, of course, but for the present, the church provided me the avenue.

Clifford, a farming community of about 500 people in open country six miles northwest of Carbondale, was noted mostly as the location of its isolated but active airport. The 175-year-old church also served widespread Clifford Township's several other small villages including Royal and Lenoxville.

Clifford Baptist was an easy five-mile drive for me from Crystal Lake for Sunday services that attracted some 60 of the faithful and a weekly Bible study class I conducted. I also visited the sick and those needful of counsel. Though I preached only a third of the Sundays, I conducted most of the Sunday School teaching to youth groups and adults.

The Waco, left at Wurtsboro, New York, for its engine overhaul and new fabric, would not be ready until March next year. In its absence, I flew only occasionally, usually in Clifford Airport's 115-hp single engine Bellanca Citabria ("airbatic" reversed), a two-place, high-wing monoplane of 1970s vintage.

Church work took up a good part of my time—but not all of it. I was able to put in a substantial amount of work on our 52-acre property, including 25 acres of hay to mow and a new shed to be built. My father had died in April the previous year. My mother lived just across the road from our home, and I handled her heavier chores as well. She was in her mid-80s, in fair health, and she still drove her ancient Chrysler. In all, this was a constantly busy time for me, and I yearned to get my Waco back in the air.

January and February, 1982, were cold, grey typical Northeastern Pennsylvania winter months. On a chilly day of sleet showers I conducted my first funeral service. On a brighter note, I did manage to drive to Wurtsboro Airport a couple of times to check progress on the Waco. She was undergoing major surgery, but the rate of repair buoyed my spirits. On March 20, the old ship finally was ready for a test hop.

As I circled around the airport, the engine cut out then restarted a heart-constricting moment later. Several times. I took her back down for a carburetor adjustment. That done, I took off for Clifford, about 60 miles almost due west, a 45-minute flight, mountainous at each end.

Just past the New York-Pennsylvania border, the engine cut out again. Then picked up again. I was closer to Clifford than Wurtsboro, so I stayed on course and landed none too confidently at Clifford.

The persistent engine hiccoughing absolutely would not do. The next morning, I set out on a return flight over the northern Poconos, then the southern Catskills to Wurtsboro. Usually I flew that brief hop at 3,000 feet over those rolling mountains. This morning, considering the engine's quirky behavior, I took the Waco up to 4,500.

Three miles west of Wurtsboro Airport, over the highest ridge in the area, the engine stuttered. I waited for it to pick up. The propellor's disc dwindled to slow windmilling as the engine quit altogether. The only sound now was the sigh of slipstream through the struts and bracing wires.

I tried to coax the engine back to life. No response. I concentrated on reaching the airport in what was now an alarmingly inefficient glider. Drag from the windmilling propeller made our sink rate a lot greater than it would have been in a glide with the propeller simply idling under reduced power. I realized this was turning into what could be a near thing.

Wurtsboro was an uncontrolled airport—no radio communication. Traffic was on its own. As the field came into sight in the valley beyond the ridge, I spotted aircraft landing to the southwest on the main 3,000-foot paved runway. A shorter southeast-northwest runway was not well marked and hardly ever used. Wurtsboro, also a glider port, was quite busy. I noted a sailplane on final approach to the long runway and a towplane on its downwind leg preparing to land. Both were potential conflicts with my emergency approach. That convinced me to forget about trying for the long runway.

By now I was almost over the end of the short runway. I peeled off in a steep 180° slip to the left. The propeller stopped its useless windmilling and stood still. Now it no doubt dawned on the people below that my unusual approach was for a forced landing. As I touched down, I realized if I'd been flying at my usual 3,000 feet when the engine cut out, I never would have made it to the airport.

From the hangar area, a car raced toward me. Among those piling out of the "rescue" sedan was the airport owner's daughter. She told me she had known from my unusual approach to the field that I had a problem, and now she gave me a big hug. All hands helped push my stricken bird to the hangar.

What had caused the engine failure? I'd had plenty of fuel. But its flow had stopped at the carburetor. The carb was pulled and we discovered the fuel flow had been cut off by a blocked jet. Also we found dirt in the carburetor's float chamber and a bent needle valve. So much for alleged attention to the carburetor during the recent prolonged engine overhaul. Now I insisted the carb be minutely overhauled. I returned home by bus.

Two weeks were to elapse before a new needle valve for the 40-year-old engine was found and installed. On April 29 I revisited Wurtsboro by air, courtesy of a kind Clifford soul, and flew my ship back to Clifford, this time with the engine purring all the way.

Through the next several weeks I took many church folk and almost all the Sunday School children on Waco rides. Then in early June, the engine began intermittently cutting out again. Back to Wurtsboro. This time the problem was a defective magneto. The airport mechanics readjusted the magneto. I made a couple of test flights at Wurtsboro and all appeared well, so I flew back to Clifford to enjoy more local "barnstorming."

Ruth Hasbrouck, a Clifford Baptist member, had been 14 years old when the Wright Brothers made the world's first successful powered flight in 1903. Now aged 93, she had never been up in an airplane. She attended church every Sunday and never missed mid-week Bible study. At my invitation, Ruth arrived at Clifford Airport one fine Sunday afternoon with a group of friends to see her off on her first flight ever. Also on hand was a reporter from the newspaper in fairly distant Montrose.

Ruth needed some help climbing into the Waco's front cockpit. Then we took off, flew around gently for 15 minutes, and glided back down. As I helped her dismount, she gave me a wonderful smile.

"Mrs. Hasbrouck," the reporter asked, "what is your impression of flying?"

"I enjoyed the flight very much," she said in her rather droll manner. Then she quoted, "The Heavens and earth proclaim the glory of God."

A month later as I was taking two of our grandchildren for a hop, I felt a roughness and slight loss of power on climb just after take-off. The right magneto had failed completely. Bob Seamans, one of my fellow instructors at Scranton Airport in the 1940s, had built his own airport on family acreage near Factoryville about 12 miles southwest of Clifford. One of his mechanics had told me could easily handle magneto problems. I flew the Waco down there and let him have at it. A couple weeks later, I was back in the air.

In September, Katherine and I decided to visit John at Neil Armstrong Airport in New Knoxville, where we would leave the Waco with him through the coming winter. He and his mechanics would do a careful and complete engine check. On the 17th, with Katherine properly helmeted and goggled in the front cockpit, we took off from Clifford on a course for Clarion in Western Pennsylvania, the first leg of our westbound route. This leg would take us over high, unpopulated terrain, not really a good idea given the engine's recent history of persistent arrhythmia.

About 15 minutes into the flight, the left magneto quit operating. I made a 180 and retreated to Seaman's Airport. The fix was an easy one—a loose wire. After a brief test flight, I decided all systems were "go," but I did put off our departure until the next day.

This time I decided we would avoid any desolate terrain, so we made our first stop Lock Haven. From there, we flew northwest to Clarion, thus avoiding much of Central Pennsylvania's Allegheny Mountain range, known to the air mail flyers of the 1920s and 1930s as "The Pilots' Graveyard." Then we cruised on to Philadelphia, Ohio, and finally arrived at New Knoxville near that state's western border, landing in the late afternoon.

The flight had turned out to be trouble-free, especially enjoyable after all the engine balks of the previous months. We spent a few days with John, turned the Waco over to his care, then flew home via commercial airline out of Dayton.

In January, 1983, Reverend Lee Pease, area minister for the American Baptist Churches of Pennsylvania and Delaware, phoned me.

"Jack, the minister of the First Baptist Church in Waverly is moving on to another parish. I think you would be just right for the Waverly church. If you're willing to consider that possibility, I'll be glad to set up a meeting for you with their search committee."

I gave the opportunity some prayerful thought. Clifford Baptist could carry on with just one pastor, Dick Olmstead. I spoke with the Clifford Baptist Diaconate who were agreeable to the suggested change but hoped I would continue to conduct the mid-week Bible study at Clifford. I was glad to agree to that, and off I went to a meeting with the Waverly church's search committee.

I proposed to the committee that I be considered as an interim pastor for a maximum of one year. And the committee would have the option to replace me at any time while they continued to search for a permanent pastor. Such an arrangement was agreeable to the committee, and on February 1, I became interim pastor of Waverly's First Baptist Church of Abington, the oldest Protestant church in Lackawanna County.

Before taking up my new duties, Katherine and I made a vacation trip to Ketchum, Idaho, to visit with Woodie and Barbro at Sun Valley. On the way, we spent a day in Salt Lake City, visiting the great Mormon Genealogical Library and attending a truly inspirational performance of the famed Mormon Tabernacle Choir.

In Sun Valley's winter paradise, the four of us skiied the neatly groomed cross-country trails, and we were bemused by Ketcham's sole movie theater's fare. The 1941 movie, *Sun Valley Serenade,* starring Sonja Henie, John Payne and Glenn Miller's music, seemed to be the only film shown. I was told it was featured every weekend—and had been for years.

Then back to Pennsylvania and to work. Waverly, a small residential community nestled in the Abington Hills, lay about 15 miles south of Crystal Lake, an easy open country commute. The town had something of a New England look with a large "town square" as the location of its impressive brick Community House, Waverly's focal point.

The church, on the corner of Waverly's Main Street and Carbondale Road, was an historic wooden structure built in 1803 and reconditioned several times since. A large parsonage stood next door, and a wide lawn with a stand of maple trees fronted both buildings. First Baptist was noted for the excellence of its choir and Choir Director Cindy Pratt. Sunday attendance was in the 50 to 60 range. Mid-week Bible study class drew about a dozen. I also continued the weekly Bible class in Clifford, as agreed.

The pastors of the town's other two churches—United Methodist and Free Methodist—and I met frequently, and all three churches joined to conduct many local events. I soon came to love the people of First Baptist, among them Anne Lewis, who was most supportive. Her late husband, Bill, had been pastor of First Baptist for several years.

By May, the Waco overhaul was completed. I hadn't flown since September, and I was eager to become airborne again. I flew commercial to Dayton. John picked me up there for the Dayton-New Knoxville leg, and I flew the Waco back to Pennsylvania with a refueling stop in Clarion. The old Continental never missed a beat.

About that time, I discovered a four-place, single-engine Cessna 172 for sale by a fellow who occasionally flew it to Clifford Airport, though he kept it at the big Wilkes-Barre/Scranton Airport "down the valley." The 15-year-old Cessna was in excellent shape. With its enclosed cabin, it would be a fine cross-country machine. The price was right; the deal was made.

The 43-year-old, open-cockpit Waco continued to be an attraction, and during good weather I was kept busy giving rides to many friends, including new ones from Waverly's First Baptist.

In the spring, I took up studies under Dr. Rudolph Leibeck, an unpretentious man with an unusual background. Caught up in the turmoil of the late 1930s, he had made his way from his native Estonia to England with just one possession, his precious violin. A gifted musician with a brilliant mind, he completed his education in England with a doctorate in psychology. Emigrating to the U.S. in the 1950s, he became an American Baptist pastor. Married to a school teacher, Rudy now lived in the small Borough of Dalton two miles west of Waverly. He had established a psychology practice in his home and served as pastor of the Dalton Baptist Church. Since Dalton and Waverly Baptist were sister churches, I came to know Rudy well.

He was a counselor for Scranton's Salvation Army Center and asked me to consider becoming a part-time lay counselor for the "Sally." I found that possibility an irresistible challenge. After a course of study with Rudy, I began conducting one or two counseling sessions a week at the Sally Center in Scranton. That was not in-depth psychological work, but it was an effort to help homeless, beaten-down men make a new start in life.

As many as 50 men, mostly young and usually straight off the streets, stayed in the Center's dormitories. They were required to work at the Center sorting incoming truckloads of donated goods and reconditioning items suitable for sale in the store there and at other Sally locations in the region. I found many of these men had lacked stable home lives and frequently had suffered parental abuse.

One young fellow I counseled turned out to have been well-educated, was unusually adept, and shortly he was hired as a full-time employee at the Center. There he fell in love with a fellow employee and he asked me to officiate at their wedding. Thus it came about that this Baptist pastor, raised as an Episcopalian, joined in wedlock the Jewish groom and the divorced Catholic bride at Clifford Baptist Church. That was my first wedding, a blessed ceremony of true ecumenicalism.

In August, a trip to New Hampshire in the Cessna: Katherine and I visited Woodie and Barbro, now living in Hanover. Woodie had often told me for ultimate happiness he would have to live in sight of his beloved Dartmouth's Baker Tower. Now here he was, at last in the center of his revered universe.

My next flight was not in the Waco or Cessna, but in an early model ultralight on invitation from the owner—an inviation I could not gracefully refuse. The flimsy contrivance was powered by a two-cylinder pusher engine of perhaps 25 hp. The wings and tail surfaces were covered with fabric that had a disturbing baggy look. There was no fuselage to speak of. I sat forward on a boom. The exposed seat had no sides. The instrument "panel" offered only an airspeed indicator and an altimeter.

I strapped in, fed in the gas, and the contraption leisurely became airborne. The controls were rudder and elevator only; no ailerons. As I putted aloft, I felt as if I were miraculously suspended by nothing. The controls were so slack I felt they were barely fuunctioning.

I skidded around a circuit of Clifford Airport and in a state of some anxiety, brought the vibrating dragonfly safely back to earth. A few months later, the owner did not fare as well. He crashed his delicate ultralight and was fortunate to incur only a broken bone or two.

Among the flights that summer, one was not a happy one. Katherine and I flew to Syracuse to see her brother, Robert, who was hospitalized with a terminal illness. Bob, my boyhood model-making friend whose sister had become my wife, had taken early retirement from the Air Force as a lieutenant colonel. He then had served as FAA tower chief at Syracuse Airport. When he died a few months after our visit, I conducted his funeral service. As I attempted to read the poem, "High Flight," I completely broke down.

In October I took a week off from church duties. This time Katherine and I flew, not in the Waco or Cessna, but via Pan Am to London. Then we journeyed on to Malta in an Air Malta Boeing 737 commanded by Wali Azimi. We stayed with Wall, his wife Martha and their two lovely daughters in their spacious flat in Valletta, and toured almost every mile of that fascinating island. I had given Wali most of his flight training in Afghanistan. When I left, he had been a junior copilot with Ariana. Well-educated, Wali spoke excellent English and several Arabic and Indian tongues. Before the chaotic Russian occupation of his native country, he'd had the foresight to emigrate to the U.S. We had seen him frequently thereafter, including his visiting Crystal Lake several times before beginning his career with Air Malta.

For me, the island held considerable Christian interest. Biblical lore tells us Paul was shipwrecked here on one of his missionary journeys. As he and the others who had survived the wreck built a fire, Paul grasped what he thought was a stick to add to the flames. But it turned out to be a snake. When it bit him, he threw it in the fire. From that time on, tradition has it, no snakes have been found on Malta.

Back home, on my last flight of the year—in chilly November—I took 91-year-old Jean Ross aloft in the Cessna, her first flight ever. That one, too, was covered by a reporter for his story in an area newspaper.

Through my time at First Baptist, the search committee been active and had finally found a pastor who would serve full-time and live in the parsonage. I felt the church deserved more than an interim pastor and considered my mission there completed. I decided that to serve as a full-time, on-location pastor was not my calling though I would be glad to fill in as interim pastor when needed.

During my close to a year with the church in Waverly, I began to give some thought to what course I might follow next, a means of "pay back" for all the positive things that had happened in my life. Somehow, I sensed such an opportunity would soon evolve.

In December my old Pan Am friend Don Rice called me from Africa. Don was now director of flight operations for Project ORBIS, a non-profit flying eye hospital operating worldwide to help combat blindness. The hospital was a specially configured and equipped DC-8 jet. Don proposed that I sign on as one of ORBIS's volunteer pilots.

"Can you come over here and take a first-hand look at what we're doing?"

To Africa? Not possible with my current schedule.

"Then let's get together in the ORBIS office in New York early next month."

That I was eager to do. A new and unique flying experience was about to take off.

26
CHAPTER

ALOFT WITH ORBIS

In early January, 1984, I drove to New York City. The offices of Project ORBIS, Inc., turned out to be in the old McGraw-Hill Building at 42nd Street and 8th Avenue in what now appeared to be a "low rent" district.

The offices were not impressive. The ORBIS people were. I was immediately struck by the lively enthusiasm of these mostly young, well-educated staffers for the benevolent purpose of their organization.

I was promptly introduced to Executive Director Oliver Foot, a tall, distinguished-looking Britisher in his late 30s. Oliver was the son of Lord Cardamon, who had served as Britain's ambassador to the U.N. Oliver was a charming fellow who had done a bit of acting and was known in theatrical circles. His warmth, sincerity and insistence on quality performance made him the perfect leader for this organization. I would find him an inspiring motivator who expected top performance from everyone on the ORBIS crew.

The group had been organized in 1982 as a non-profit, non-political operation under a major grant from the United States Agency for International Development (USAID), the same agency that had funded Pan Am's 1960s operations in Afghanistan—and hundreds of other altruistic projects throughout the world. The USAID grant to ORBIS had been augmented by continuing additional support from corporations, foundations and individuals on an international scale

The objective, Foot explained, was to help combat blindness worldwide—and to foster peaceful cooperation among nations. To undertake this admirable effort, ORBIS operated a Douglas DC-8, donated by United Airlines. The four-engined jet transport had been reconfigured into a suite of examination and operating rooms equipped with advanced microscopy and laser technology. A section of the cabin served as a classroom during missions. It was equipped with TV monitors where special procedures could be observed via live camera coverage in the operating rooms. In transit, its 18 seats were augmented by two more seats in the cockpit. Twenty-five doctors, nurses, technicians and administrators were required for each three-week stay on location. Most of them traveled on their own using donated airline tickets. The ORBIS group was joined at each stay by local eye specialists, and the organization's leading ophthalmologists donated their time and skill to demonstrate techniques to the doctors of the host nations. To ferry the DC-8 to and from its three-week missions, ORBIS required a half dozen volunteer DC-8 pilots.

"Jack," Oliver said, "we would like you to join us as one of our volunteer jet captains."

What recently retired, public-spirited jet captain would refuse an offer like that? I was only 62 and certain I had a lot of flying left in me.

But I hadn't flown a DC-8 in 17 years.

"Not a problem," Oliver assured me. "We'll make arrangements for your requalification."

Back in Pennsylvania while waiting for the requalifying to get underway, I continued pastoral work part-time for Clifford Baptist—Bible study, visitations and occasional preaching. I also flew the Waco and Cessna out of Clifford Airport, including instructing our 19-year-old grandson, Chad, Jackie's son. He had an obvious aptitude for flying. After the several hours of instruction I gave him, Chad enrolled in a flight school in Allentown and received his private license. Over the next few years he earned his commercial, instrument and instructor ratings and instructed at Seamans Airport while also working as a carpenter and electrician.

In March, DC-8 ground school was scheduled, courtesy of the Flying Tiger Line, the world's largest all-cargo air carrier. I journeyed to Los Angeles International and completed that part of the requalification program in two weeks.

Two months later, DC-8 simulator time was made available by Flying Tiger. Don Rice, ORBIS's director of operations, traveled with me to LAX and "rode shotgun" with me in the simulator. Flight simulators had become so sophisticated that the FAA had certified them for requalifying without actual flight time. I never thought that was a particularly good idea. At least pilots who had never flown an unfamiliar type still had to acomplish three take-offs and landings in the actual aircraft. As a former DC-8 pilot, I was requalified as a captain after a half dozen sessions only in the flight simulator.

Shortly after my return from Los Angeles, I was asked to fly "ORBIS ONE," the DC-8, from Sharjah on the Persian Gulf in the United Arab Emirates to Larnaca on the south shore of the Island of Cyprus. I made my way to Sharjah courtesy of a Flying Tiger cargo jet, not exactly first class accomodations, but the price was right: no charge. Don Rice was already there, busy with what we termed "front work"—organizing ground transportation and accomodations for the ORBIS crew in Cyprus, arranging for fuel for the DC-8, obtaining the rash of permits that were—and are—a major part of bureaucratic life in so many parts of the world.

I arrived in the United Arab Emirates a few days before our planned departure. Don and Flight Engineer Pat Healy met me at the isolated airport in the desert. The 10,000-foot runway was a good one, but the terminal was less than inspiring.

We drove down the coast to the International Hotel near Abu Dhabi. Pat, a pleasant and knowledgeable fellow in his early 30s, had been working for small non-scheduled airlines in the Mideast and South America. Now he was with ORBIS full-time as a mechanic and flight engineer. An impressively bright man, he spoke fluent Spanish and could get by nicely in French and German.

In the morning, we returned to the airport where the DC-8 had been parked for at least six weeks in support of a regional program in Abu Dhabi. Blowing desert sand had infiltrated everywhere. For two days we washed down the entire airplane, inside and out. Because the big jet had been in place so long, we fired up the engines and moved it a short distance just to rotate the wheels.

This was not scheduled airline flying. We handled our own flight planning, weather forecasting and checking of the permits to be sure we were cleared to overfly the countries we would cross in transit. With all preparations completed, we were ready for departure June 20. Several nurses and technicians would travel with us. Doctors and additional personnel were to meet us in Larnaca.

In fine weather, we made the 1,200-mile flight to the 140-mile-long island in three hours and 24 minutes. Everyone aboard was aware this was my first DC-8 flight in nearly two decades, and I worked hard to make a really good landing. We touched down smoothly enough to prompt a round of applause from all on board.

Larnaca and its fine airport bordered the Mediterranean. Lodged in a pleasant hotel, I stayed on for a couple of days to help the ORBIS group prepare for their three-week stint. Since our organization was not an entity of any government, political barriers went down and we enjoyed an aura of goodwill on that island, despite its turbulent undercurrents. Fairly recently, Cyprus had been divided by "The Green Line," with Greeks on one side and Turks on the other in an uneasy detente. But the arrival of ORBIS brought Turkish and Greek doctors and nurses together to work side-by-side.

With the Cyprus mission well underway, I returned to the U.S. via Lufthansa and Pan Am. All such travel to and from missions was through ORBIS's arranging for complimentary tickets from various airlines. Flying Tiger routinely let us travel on their cargo flights. Pan Am was especially good to us. As a Pan Am alumnus, I already had travel benefits on that airline. From time to time, Pan Am would provide blocks of tickets for ORBIS doctors, nurses and technicians. Additional generous support was given by United and several foreign airlines.

Home from my first ORBIS mission, I was soon back aloft in Waco and Cessna, now with two of my colleagues in ministry, Lee Pease and Foster Williams, as students. In July Katherine and I cruised in the Cessna along the now-familiar route to Traverse City, Michigan, to spend a few days with son John.

The next call from New York came in October. The DC-8 was about to complete its three-week stay in Nairobi, Kenya. My assignment was to fly it to Dakar on Senegal's Atlantic coast with a refueling stop in Lagos, Nigeria. Since FAA regulations required pilots to maintain aircraft type ratings by making three take-offs and landings within 90 days before flying passengers, I again flew to Los Angeles to fulfill that requirement in the simulator. This time, I invited Katherine to go along. We spent a few days there visiting friends, including Dan Sjoberg in Santa Paula northwest of LA. Dan had been a USAAF ferry pilot with me 'way back in World War II. We also met daughter Jackie's sister-in-law, Jan Dennis, former mayor of Manhattan Beach just south of Santa Monica. Then, with my required three brief simulator flights completed, we returned east.

On October 25, I departed New York bound for Nairobi via Pan Am. A few days earlier, Carl Prentiss, retired from the Flying Tiger

Line, had arrived in Nairobi. Since Carl was also a qualified DC-8 captain, we agreed we would each fly as aircraft commander on one of the two legs of the Nairobi-Dakar flight.

Don Rice had flown the airborne eye hospital to Nairobi from its prior three-week stay in Botswana. While there, Don had met and fallen in love with a lovely South African woman. When the time came to fly the DC-8 to Nairobi, Don intended to take her with him on the ORBIS jet. She was happy to accompany him, but a problem arose. Every seat was already spoken for. Might you, uh, take a seat in the lavatory for take-off and landing, he asked one of the staff. Don realized there was no seat belt in there, but he could rig up a rope . . . A *rope?* The answer was: No. Don was a flight operations director of noted tenacity, but the answer remained No. He was chastened by the medical staff, but forgiven. And ropeless but not hopeless, love won out. Though Don's fiancee was denied the Nairobi trip via ORBIS, she and Don ultimately married.

On October 28, Carl and I flew the DC-8 out of Nairobi International. Our flight engineer was Ken LaPointe, a likeable man in his 70s who hadn't even begun to slow down. Five and a half hours later, we made our fuel stop at Lagos on Nigeria's coast. Pan Am was our capable handling agent there, and shortly we were off on our three-hour, 45-minute final leg to Dakar's Yoff Airport. The flight went smoothly despite protests from our radio equipment, cranky after its recent three-week stays in humid areas.

After a day's layover in Dakar, Carl and I returned home. I would be assigned another African mission shortly, but not before I was surprised by a promotion offer. Soon after the Nairobi-Dakar flight, Oliver Foot called to tell me Don Rice was leaving to join the World Health Organization in its African work. Might I be interested in replacing Don in a salaried position as director of operations?

I drove to New York to discuss the offer with Oliver. The $50,000-$60,000 job promised much more involvement in ORBIS activities, but accepting would require my being away from home and family some 80% of the time. In the end, I respectfully declined.

Oliver understood my decision, but he wasn't through.

"Might you consider accepting the position of chief pilot for ORBIS?"

That would require my reporting to ORBIS once a week—usually driving to New York on Thursdays and returning home on Fridays. Since some of the volunteer pilots stayed with ORBIS only a short time, reruiting replacements was a key part of the job, and I already knew a few former Pan Am pilots who were interested.

I was glad to accept Oliver's second offer. No longer on volunteer status, I would receive a monthly $700 stipend to cover non-donated travel, meals and other personal expenses.

Along with this personnel change, Oliver told me of a technical step forward. United Airlines had just agreed to the use of their flight simulater in Denver for our training and periodic checks.

And I faced a change of my own at home. The pastor who had replaced me at First Baptist of the Abingtons in Waverly was departing. Might I return as interim pastor?

I was glad to accept—provided the church was aware my ORBIS commitment would require me to be absent from time to time. Agreed. While the committee continued to search for a full-time pastor, I would take over the Waverly pastorate January 1.

When on November 12 I returned to Dakar, I brought Katherine with me. I was to fly the DC-8 from Dakar to its next 21-day stop-over at Ouagadougou, the capital city of Burkina Faso, the Colorado-sized West African country known as Upper Volta until its name had been changed just three months before. No one was asked to be safety-roped in the DC-8's lav this time; I had already arranged for Katherine's seat, available because several of the Orbis group were already in Ouagadugou.

On the 16th, we took off for Ouagadougou with Vic Matloff, a pleasant still-active United pilot, as first officer. Vic, in addition to flying as a volunteer pilot, was instrumental in acquiring free United Airline tickets for ORBIS use. Our flight engineer was the durable and admirable Ken LaPointe.

Our two-hour, 30-minute flight went well in fine weather, but in virtual radio silence. Communications with the ground were non-existent for the entire 1,000-mile trek until we were in radio range of Ouagadougou Airport's tower. Lacking an air traffic control clearance to descend, we overheaded the field at 10,000 feet and simply notified the tower we were on our way down. Losing altitude in a huge orbit with all eyes peeled for possible similarly uncontrolled air traffic, we touched down on the airport's long runway.

The runway was up-to-date, but just about everything else here was primitive. The terminal was dominated by a host of well-armed military folk who didn't seem concerned about where their weapons were pointing. A number of ORBIS medical people and supporting personnel were already on the scene. For all missions, in fact, we needed medical people on location well before the aircraft arrived. They greeted local ophthalmologists and screened assembling patients, including selection of those best suited for the teaching program. Here though, because of pressing needs elsewhere, only a handful of welcomers from the government and local medical community were on hand for our appearance.

Before the plane would arrive for a mission, an advance team of several doctors and nurses routinely set up a screening process with local opthalmologists. Patients with conditions offering the greatest potential for teaching the local medical people would be seen by ORBIS. Though literally hundreds would press forward hopeful for treatment, only a maximum of seven operations a day could be completed aboard the flying hospital. With part of staff's time spent teaching in local hospitals, and with one day a week reserved for staff rest, about 70 patients were treated through a typical three-week stay. Of course, many eye problems could be treated without operations required.

As a political necessity, high-ranking government officials would often have priority, whatever their eye ailments.

At Ouagadougou Airport, the public need was made even more emphatic by the disturbing fact that this remote country with a multimillion population had only *one* fully accredited, practicing ophthamologist. So pressing was the need for medical assistance, we were told, missionary nurses were conducting cataract operations on their own. In that part of the world with cataracts treated by knife, the introduction of laser surgery was a huge benefit. ORBIS trained local opthalmologists in its use and arranged for the donation of laser equipment.

Vic, Katherine and I left that night to return to Dakar. The terminal was overflowing with unusually noisy people and the obvious military presence was unsettling. We seemed to be the only western people in the place, and I'm afraid we were treated quite curtly.

During the departure "formalities," one of the soldiers with a rifle carelessly slung over his shoulder stood close beside us. I noticed the muzzle of his weapon pointed directly at Katherine. Not deliberately, I preferred to assume, but the potential trajectory was disconcerting enough for me to look the soldier in the eye—with a smile—then gently push the rifle barrel away from my wife's head. Bracing myself for just about any kind of reaction, I was relieved that he took no offense whatever.

Eventually we were cleared as passengers to leave for Dakar, a three-hour, 30-minute flight on a small twin-engined prop-driven plane—a Convair if memory serves. It was operated by . . . who knew? Fortunately the long grind west was far less disconcerting than our pre-flight time in that well-armed terminal crowd.

My next ORBIS flight took me to a more pronounceable and less carelessly armed port of call. Since 90 days had elapsed since the Ouagadougu flight, I flew commercial to Denver in January, 1986, for those three required take-offs and landings in the United Airlines simulator. The next month, United co-pilot Bill Bradford and I flew via Pan Am and Turkish Airlines to Izmir, Turkey. There the ORBIS three-week mission was winding up. In Izmir, Bill and I were joined by Pat Healy. In addition to serving as a mechanic and flight engineer, Pat was now the organization's director of operations, the position I had recently turned down.

We spent a few days in Izmir, a manufacturing center on the eastern shore of the Aegean Sea with quite an historical past. One of history's first cities in Asia, Izmir (then known as Smyrna) is one of several claiming to be the birthplace of Homer—and is one of the "Seven Cities" included by St. John the Divine in his writings. The Biblical city of Ephesus lay a mere 40 miles south of Izmir. There St. Paul had ministered and established churches, and I surmised he could have visited ancient flourishing Izmir as well.

The stay in Turkey ended February 17, and we took off for Karachi, Pakistan, with Director of Operations Healy as my second officer and Bill Bradford, the only ORBIS pilot not certified as captain, as my first officer. With my concurrance, Bill was at the controls for the five-hour flight.

We landed in late afternoon to a warm reception from Pakistan's Ministry of Health and various additional government officials. Then we taxied the DC-8 to a less inhabited part of Karachi International Airport and readied our flying hospital for its scheduled three weeks of healing and teaching. Through all that, we took our usual care to conduct ourselves as dedicated ambassadors of good will.

The day after that, we flew gratis commercial back to New York. On my first Sunday in the pulpit following my return, I suggested ORBIS be considered as the Aviation Division of First Baptist Church of the Abingtons. This light-hearted proposal was warmly accepted by the congregation.

As chief pilot, I could arrange my schedule to avoid too many Sunday absences from the church. I was also able to be available for most other pastoral needs.

As part of my duties, I received frequent calls and visits from pilots offering to volunteer their flying time. During one of my weekly New York appearances in early April, a recently retired DC-8 cargo pilot appeared at the ORBIS office. Since he was up on the "8" and seemed a compatible chap, I invited him to go with me on the scheduled flight April 20 from Bangkok to Hong Kong.

One of the organization's most stringent requirements—in addition to technical proficiency—was that personnel be entirely free of dissention, unwarranted complaints or any other negative character traits. We were constantly in the public eye, and ORBIS's success as a non-profit, privately-supported enterprise depended heavily on its excellent reputation. Any pilot, nurse or technician who slipped beyond Executive Director Oliver Foot's strict requirements was promptly replaced.

In Bangkok, another new ORBIS recruit served as reviewer of passports, expediter of visas and arranger of Hong Kong accomodations. Before take-off on any mission, we held a crew briefing attended by everyone who would be on the flight. The new member had done some preliminary work in Hong Kong. During her time to speak, she went way beyond her scope to launch into details of the Hong Kong airport and its famous "checkerboard" approach. "It's scary," she told the crowd, "and you all should know that."

Not good. The new co-pilot and I immediately broke in to assure the group we both knew this approach well, had flown it many times and had found it to be perfectly safe.

We all reassembled at the airport for the two-hour, 45-minute flight. Weeks before, ORBIS had applied for overfly permits from the countries we would cross enroute. All were in hand, except the permit from Vietnam. To overfly Vietnam without permission would be . . . bad politics. To say the least.

We were assured by teletype from ORBIS's overfly permit requesters that the Vietnam permit had been granted. But we needed its number so we could radio it to Vietnam Control before entering that airspace.

With our plane's radios not exactly state-of-the-art, we decided to take off and—with luck—have the permit number radioed to us before crossing the Vietnam border. Crossing a country without an overfly permit would have been a serious infraction. We probably would not have been shot down, but substantial fines would have been levied against ORBIS—which was never in a condition of affluency.

"Plan B," if no number was forthcoming from Vietnam, was to swing south of that country, adding an unwanted hour to our flight time.

We gambled that the number would reach us in time so we stuck to our routing. As we neared Vietnam's western border, suspense built. Then, a mere 10 minutes from that unpredictable nation, our radio finally grated forth the permit number. A few minutes later, we crossed Vietnam in the area of Da Nang where it was no more than 70 to 80 miles wide and emerged over the South China Sea.

We neared Hong Kong on schedule, and sure enough, the wind direction required our flying the checkerboard approach. Though cloud cover was down to 1,000 feet, our approach came nowhere near "scary." Our new person no doubt had inspired some aboard to expect something different. In fact, she herself faced something different a short time later. She was no longer with ORBIS.

Returning to Pennsylvania, I attended to my churchly duties, gave flight instruction in the Cessna to Rev. Lee Pease and Rev. Foster Williams, colleagues and friends in ministry, and spent Thursdays and Fridays at ORBIS's New York office. Amazing the energy one has at the youthful age of 64.

In July, I scheduled myself for an ORBIS flight on the 7th from Shanghai to Cebu City on densely populated Cebu Island in the central Philippines. When space was available, I often invited Katherine to go along. She always accepted with enthusiasm, purposely maintained a low profile and was well-liked by the crew. I arranged to take Katherine on this jaunt. My fellow pilot would be an active United Airlines pilot. A Californian, Vic left from there. Katherine's and my projected non-stop flight from New York to Tokyo turned out to be fully booked. I talked with the Pan Am people I thought might be helpful in getting us aboard. Hearing I worked for ORBIS, an organization she highly respected, one of the flight attendants generously offered to give up her rest seat for the 14-hour flight. Then, miraculously, two seats were suddenly available. We were on our way. From Tokyo, we made connections to Shanghai on United.

There a complication arose. Since all ORBIS pilots—except Bill Bradford—were captains, we customarily rotated command. For this flight, Vic would fly the left seat; I would serve as first officer/co-pilot. That was not the complication. ORBIS Executive Director Oliver Foot happened to be in Shanghai and he and his two children were to fly with us to Cebu. As boarding began, Oliver came forward with his son and daughter and asked the captain if his two, well-mannered, pre-teen children could sit in the cockpit during take-off.

Two jump seats were available and the kids' being there would be perfectly legal, but the pilot's response was, one youngster, yes; both, no. I had an impulse to intercede, but he was the aircraft commander. My intervention would have been bad form.

Leaving just one of his children to ride in the cockpit as the pilot insisted, Oliver said no more. But I could see he was not happy with the pilot's decision.

Other than that little departing set-to, the flight went smoothly. After a day in teeming Cebu, Katherine and I hopped aboard a

Philippine Airline flight to Manila, overnighted there, then returned to
the U.S.

Two weeks later I was back in Cebu, this time with Eric
Friedrichsen, now an ORBIS volunteer pilot, as my first officer. This
was quite an aerial reunion; Eric had been my first officer on my final
flight for Pan Am four years ago. Our assignment now: ferry the DC-
8, with several doctors and nurses aboard, to Singapore for its scheduled
three-week visit there.

During ORBIS's medical stays, fuel, lodging and airport facilities
were usually gratis, courtesy of the host country. At the time of our
invitation to the Philippines, President Ferdinand Marcos was still
viewed favorably by the U.S. As our departure date neared, though, the
political climate was changing and American support for Marcos had
begun to wane. The following year, he would be out of office and flee
the country with his wife, Imelda.

When we called for the fuel truck the day before our scheduled
departure, the fuel company representative told us no fuel would be
delivered without payment in advance—and in cash.

Stunned by this turn of events, Flight Engineer/Director of Operations
Pat Healy and I wangled a car and drove to the home of the person we were
told was the highest-ranking government representative in Cebu. This official turned out to be a relative of Marcos, and quite a lady. Over tea, she
was the soul of courtesy and expressed sympathy for our impasse. She
promptly made several phone calls in our behalf. All seemed to be going
swimmingly, but I detected a mannerly run-around, and in the end,
progress was nil.

Returning to the airport, we contacted the oil company that supplied
the airport's aviation fuel, and we offered to arrange payment from
ORBIS's New York office. Unfortunately, we then learned the funds
transfer could not be completed before our fast-approaching departure
time. And our prompt arrival in Singapore the next morning was of
prime importance in the complex ORBIS schedule.

Through all this, we kept the doctors and nurses fully informed.
Without immediate payment, the entire ORBIS schedule was about to
fall into complicated shambles. The funds needed? Ten thousand dollars, just about the same amount, I realized with jarring déjà vu, I had
been asked to pay to ransom that Olson flight out of Madagascar in
1974. There I had kited a personal check—promptly made good by Pan
Am—but I knew ORBIS would not look kindly upon such a questionable ploy. Nor would the worldly Cebu Airport fuel supplier be
amenable to accepting my personal check for ten grand.

How were we going to get out of here?

"HELP HIM, LORD, HELP HIM."

When word of our dilemma reached Dr. Simon Holland, the doctor in charge of the ORBIS stay in the Philippines, he volunteered to request a $10,000 cash advance on his American Express card. He rushed off to the Cebu Amex office—where he was told only $1,000 in cash could be advanced on any Amex card, including his. The office manager did tell him that if there were 10 American Express card holders among our group, then the office would advance $10,000 total.

Time was fleeting, and the bank—the Amex office's source of cash—was going to close tight at 4:00 p.m., just a couple of hours away.

We gathered in Dr. Holland's hotel room and prayed at least 10 of us held American Express credit cards. I did not. Those who did began to speak up. Incredibly, there were precisely 10. All those card holders raced to the Cebu American Express office where the sympathetic manager dashed to the bank to burst through the door just minutes before closing time.

With the cash in hand, Pat and I hurried to the airport. In the early evening's fading light, the fuel truck rolled up to the plane and fueling was completed at last.

But our troubles were not over. As rain began to pelt down, the conveyor belt loading our supplies and other cargo quit moving. All attempts at repair failed, and a replacement was not available. In desperation, Pat gathered a gaggle of willing airport workers, and they manhandled the remainder of the cargo aboard.

Now another mechanical balk bedeviled us. The DC-8 had been modified to carry a self-contained power unit to supply energy for all the electrical needs of the hospital plane while it was on the ground during its mission. The unit was extremely heavy. For use, we lowered it from its fuselage storage receptacle by activating a built-in powered cable system. When the three-week stay was completed, the cable system would raise the unit back in place.

But not tonight. The cable system refused to budge the bulky power unit. Lifting it by hand was impossible. Our determined flight engineer set to work. Conscientious pilots do not take refuge in the dry terminal while their flight engineer labors in a downpour. Eric and I helped as best we could. An hour later, 10:00 p.m., with all three of us sopped to the skin, we held our collective breath as Pat flipped the cable system switch. Amid Eric's and my congratulations on Pat's wizardry, the unit rose slowly into place. Pat and I agreed that prayer could have been a major factor.

Shortly after daybreak, we lifted off on schedule. Aside from the departure complications, the mission had been a good one with vision restored for many Philippine patients, and local eye doctors and nurses now had upgraded skills. Three hours and 15 minutes later, we landed to an enthusiastic welcome at Singapore International Airport on the Malay Peninsula's southern tip.

Returning to Pennsylvania, I resumed my work at First Baptist; the flying lessons for Foster Williams, Lee Pease and grandson Chad; and the commutes to New York for my weekly two days at the ORBIS office.

In September, I flew the Cessna to Allentown. Leaving my plane there, I flew as passenger via United to Denver for required simulator updating. On my return leg from Allentown to Clifford in the Cessna, the weather over the Pocono Mountains deteriorated to instrument conditions. There was no instrument landing system at Clifford. I decided to use the ILS at Wilkes-Barre/Scranton Airport and land there, some 25 miles short of Clifford. During the instrument descent, I broke out of the overcast at about 1,000 feet—good enough to push on to Clifford VFR.

In early October, Mike Lyon and Eric Friedrichsen, both of them not-yet-retired Pan Am captains, Katherine and I made our way to Kathmandu, Nepal. Katherine enjoyed her trips to exotic locales, and I had invited her on this one to the "mountain kingdom" astride the

Himalayas between southwest China and northeast India. Surrounded by mountains, the airport required a meticulous approach. The Nepalese pilot was impressively skillful at this. When we debarked, we marvelled at the beauty of mountains on all sides, their peaks towering into the clouds.

I was in better shape than during my 1972 previous appearance here when I was mostly hotel-bound with a cold. This time Katherine and I visited a Christian Mission 45 minutes by car east of the city in fairly flat terrain. The mission was directed by a Reverend Barclay, though he told us he never used that title. Nepal law had permitted activation of the mission but prohibited efforts to convert any Nepalese to Christianity. Both those attempting conversion and those inclined to listen were subject to severe penalties. To meet this restriction, the mission had adjusted its agenda to concentrate on non-religious teaching, agricultural aid and medical assistance. The overall objective was to update local skills. I considered the work here to be missionary devotion at the highest level, a non-denominational effort with support from churches everywhere.

Flying the DC-8 out of Kathmandu required a take-off to the southwest where the mountains were just a bit lower. We held maximum rate of climb right through 10,000 feet, headed for Karachi, Pakistan for a brief refueling stop, then flew on to Ankara, Turkey. The trip offered me the opportunity to qualify Mike and Eric as captains on the ORBIS DC-8. While I served as co-pilot, Eric flew the three-hour Nepal-Pakistan leg and Mike entertained our ORBIS passengers, expertly whirling a pair of Buddist prayer wheels.

Mike took over the left seat for the six-hour sector to Ankara—where the weather turned out to be not the best with a skimpy 600-foot ceiling. As he set up for an ILS approach, the system's outer marker abruptly went off the air. With no DME—distance measuring equipment—to indicate our distance from the visual omni range beacon, and with a disturbingly unpredictable instrument landing system and hilly terrain, Mike proved himself a top-notch airman with a fine approach and a glass-smooth landing at the ancient city's Esenbogan Airport. We stayed overnight in Ankara, then Mike, Eric, Katherine and I headed home via Turkish Airlines to Istanbul where we caught a Pan Am flight to New York.

Two weeks later, I returned to Ankara to begin preparations to ferry the DC-8 to Istanbul for its next mission. Former Flying Tiger Line Captain Carl Prentiss joined me for this flight. Good natured and well liked by the ORBIS staff, Carl was noted for an incident during his

Flying Tiger days. The aircraft he was flying—a surplus twin-engined Curtiss C-46, I believe—completed a landing by flipping over on its back. Since this was a cargo flight, only Captain Prentiss and his first officer were aboard. The first priority of any pilot finding himself on the ground upside down would be to GET OUT FAST. Carl wasn't "any pilot."

"Fill out the logbook," he told his first officer as they hung on their seatbelts, "with our landing time." Then they scrambled out.

Our flight November 2 from Ankara to Istanbul, only an hour east, ended routinely and right side up, depriving Carl of an opportunity to augment his legend.

The next ORBIS flight, three weeks later, would be to Baghdad. Though he wasn't scheduled for that flight, one of our pilots questioned Oliver's accepting the invitation. The bitter war between Iraq and Iran, now in its fifth year, showed no signs of winding down. Oliver had carefully researched the situation. He decided the seemingly endless battle beyond Iraq's distant border would not be a threat to the mission in Baghdad and he did not appreciate his judgement being questioned. Shortly that pilot's services to ORBIS were no longer required.

For me, the highlight of 1985 was my officiating at son John's wedding in East Granby, Connecticut. The pastor of the Congregational Church John and his bride-to-be regularly attended had graciously consented to my performing the ceremony, a truly marvelous occasion November 30.

At the time, John was flying as a DC-9 jet captain for a short-lived airline called Best. It soon collapsed, but not before I had the pleasure of riding jump seat on one of his flights. John then flew as a demonstrator pilot for the Montreal-based Canadair company, flying their Challenger, a Canadian-built corporate jet. In 2001, piloting a Bombardier Global Express, a jet roughly comparable to the Grumman Gulfstream but a bit faster, John set the still-standing New York-to-Paris world speed record for corporate aircraft. His six-hour, two-minute flight was less than a fifth of Lindbergh's 33 hour, 33-minute time 74 years earlier.

Based at Bradley International Airport near Hartford, John at this writing is director of flight operations for Bombardier/Canadair, U.S. Division. He and Carolyn, a sign language interpreter, live in Longmeadow, Massachusetts, with daughters Emily and Jenna.

Despite the uneasy pilot's career-changing forebodings back in New York, the flight to Baghdad and the mission went smoothly. On February 23, 1986 Mike and I arrived in Baghdad, courtesy of Alia, the

Royal Jordanian Airline, to fly the DC-8 to its next mission in Amman, Jordan.

At the time, the U.S. was quietly assisting Saddam Hussein to prevent Iraq from being defeated by none-too-U.S.-friendly Iran. I found the Baghdad Airport's terminal magnificent, and the airport's customs and immigration officials welcomed us pleasantly. Our accomodations at the Al-Mansour Melia Hotel were fine. The war did not seem to be affecting Baghdad at all. Mike and I roamed a bit of the sprawling city. The bazaars were booming, and we encountered many friendly and courteous Iraqis.

The evening before our departure, the Ministry of Health hosted all the ORBIS people at a reception in its Baghdad headquarters building. During the festivities, I distinctly heard the distant thunder of cannon fire.

"That is not what our lives are about," one of the Ministry's doctors assured me. "This—teaching and healing—is what our lives are about."

In the morning, Mike flew left seat for the Baghdad-Amman trip, doing his usual fine job, landing with grace in pouring rain. He and I then hopped aboard a Royal Jordanian flight to Rome and there boarded a Pan Am flight to New York.

In April, Lou LeClere and I flew commercial to Alexandria, Egypt to pilot the DC-8 on to Kingston, Jamaica. Oliver and Pat Healy, already in Egypt, would fly with us. A consistent flying ambassador of good will, ORBIS had been warmly welcomed in the turbulent Middle East. Local newspapers had praised the organization's work, emphasizing the fact that we represented no political entity.

We lifted off the Alexandria airport April 17. This was to be a long two-day pull, 17 hours in the air with three refueling stops. The first was at Malta's Luga Airport near the port city of Valletta, a two-hour, 30-minute leg. Then we were off for Santa Maria, one of the nine islands in the Azores, some 1,000 miles west of Portugal, a five-hour, 45-minute flight from Malta. Santa Maria, one of the smaller of the isolated Azores group, offered a major airfield built by the U.S. Army Air Forces during World War II, then purchased by the Portuguese in 1946. There we were driven to a "guest house." With Santa Maria no tourist destination, accomodations were on the modest side. We rested about 10 hours, then well before sunrise, we took off for Puerto Rico.

Seven hours later at San Juan's Isla Verde International Airport we refueled and immediately shoved off on the two-hour hop to our final destination, Kingston, Jamaica.

There Lou left immediately for California. Oliver, who had lived in Jamaica as a youngster when his father served as governor general, stayed on several days. The day after our arrival, Pat and I hired a taxi at the Wyndham Hotel to return to the airport for a check on a few minor problems with the aircraft, primarily the obstinate radio equipment. During the taxi ride, our conversation drifted into some spiritual area. The driver, most politely, joined in. Introducing himself as Leonard Harris, he told us he, too, was active in his Baptist church. On the return trip to the hotel, he heard I was a pastor, and he invited me to go with him to his church that afternoon.

I agreed, and a few hours later, he picked me up again in his taxi. At the church in Kingston's outskirts, I met his pastor, a kindly man, who invited me to speak to his congregation the next day, a Sunday.

On the way back to the hotel, Leonard told me he had been born to very poor parents and worked at a lot of menial jobs, always with the dream of someday owning a taxi. In time, his determination made his dream come true. He married and had four daughters. Working long hours, day and night, he saved enough money to send his daughters, one at a time, to New York. Each had earned a college degree and eventually married.

I realized I was hearing a stunning success story. Leonard Harris, Jamaican taxi driver, was an impressive man.

Sunday morning he picked me up as scheduled, and off we drove to the church. There I met Leonard's wife, a gentle and genial lady.

I asked the pastor if I could speak about five minutes. He amiably agreed. When I got rolling with my brief message, I would hear an occasional, "Preach, Brother, preach!" from the congregation. And "Amens" here and there. But when I hesitated, I would hear, "Help him, Lord, help him." I had never experienced a Sunday service like this one. The enthusiasm and love coming from these fine people truly blessed me.

On a summer afternoon two years later, a car turned into the driveway of our Crystal Lake cottage. To our delight, here was Leonard, his wife, one of their daughters, her husband and their two children. The daughter, Doreen, was now a U.S. school teacher and music director. Her husband also taught. We had a great time together, and later that year Doreen brought her church choir to First Baptist for a Sunday of musical worship. Some years later, Katherine and I visited her church in Jamaica—Jamaica, New York. We keep in touch with Doreen to this day. Leonard, a truly good man, made the transition to eternal life several years ago.

As time permitted, I had begun to present occasional talks to local church and civic groups to publicize ORBIS. In late July, I flew to

Princeton, New Jersey, invited by Rotarians there to speak about the organization. This expanding PR work would shortly lead to a national event I had been mulling over since I acquired the Waco. I had put the idea on hold, but I felt the time was nearing to put it into action.

The next month I journeyed to Panama to fly the DC-8—with First Officer Bill Bradford and Flight Engineer Ken LaPointe—to Arequipa, "gateway to the land of the Incas" in southern Peru's Andes. The airport, in thin air 7,500 feet above sea level, required us to touch down at a racy ground speed, an attention-compelling end to our four-hour flight.

The Spanish Baroque architecture of this isolated but surprisingly large center had made it known as "The White City." Since Arequipa was in an active earthquake zone, most of its buildings were one-story, the twin-towered cathedral a notable exception.

The next day, I was homeward-bound but would return to Arequipa in a couple of weeks to fly the DC-8 600 miles up the coast to Lima, Peru's capital city. Dave Ormesher, an active United Airlines pilot, and I flew that 90-minute cruise over the majestic Andes to the "City of Kings," so-named by Pizarro, the Spanish conqueror of Peru.

Oliver, no desk-bound executive director, put in an appearance on nearly all ORBIS missions. He awaited us in Lima, and he and I returned to New York on Aero Peru, first class courtesy of the airline.

In mid-October, Oliver, his wife Nancy and their two children drove to Waverly on a Sunday to attend one of my church services at First Baptist. Memory tells me I preached an unremarkable sermon, on a 1 to 10 scale no better than a 4. Following the service, Oliver and family, several regular parisioners, Katherine and I lunched at the Elkview Country Club. Oliver, ever his charming British gentlemanly self, told of an experience I remember to this day. One of ORBIS's major contributors, a Texas oil man of advanced years, was a good friend of then-President George H.W. Bush. He arranged a meeting with the president to introduce him to Oliver. When they were ushered into the Oval Office, Oliver delighted in recounting, the oil man in a state of sudden fluster, blurted, "Mr. President, may I present Oliver Twist, son of Lord and Lady Godiva?"

I had been in the company of the oil man from Texas, and can vouch for the fact that in his very old age, he often had difficulty in bringing the right words to the surface.

On my next Cessna trip, October 24, I flew Clifford Fire Department Chief Jim Kenyon and an associate to Somerset in Southwestern Pennsylvania, where they took delivery on a new fire truck. One more flight, a brief November visit to John and Carolyn in Symsbury, ended my aerial adventures for the year.

Then came disaster. On a windy, rain-lashed night in early December, a phone call. Sandi Jenkins, the late Duane Johnson's daughter, now helping to manage Clifford Airport, was in tears.

"Oh, Jack, I have absolutely awful news. The airport hangar has just collapsed on both your airplanes."

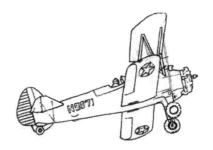

28
CHAPTER

"BARNSTORMER'S MUTUAL"

I scrambled into my Honda and rushed through the pounding rain to the airport. A patchwork structure of cinder block walls with a metal-sheathed wood frame roof, the hangar had stood for 40 years. I'd considered it indestructible. Now, in a state of shock, I found it in shambles.

The four aircraft inside were stored in a row, all facing east. The estimated 60-70 mph east wind had collapsed the entire roof. My Waco, second in line, was seriously damaged. Its center section supported the collapsed roof. That had prevented even more damage to the adjacent two planes, a Piper Tomahawk and a Bellanca Citabria.

I worked my way into what was left of the hangar and discovered my Cessna's fuselage was crushed, and the wing had been damaged, but the engine and propellor appeared to have survived.

The main spar of the Waco's upper wing had been broken. The tail assembly was crushed, but the fuselage, engine and propellor appeared to be still sound.

Sandi threw her arms around me and wept. I came close to weeping myself. The owners of the other two planes were saddened by their losses, but they seemed to feel even more deeply for me and the stricken Waco.

In the morning, a group of us met at the disaster site, including Tom Collins, who worked for a company that erected commercial signs. He had brought in a company crane.

With the crane, Tom gently lifted the roof off the Waco. Many willing hands then pulled the old ship out of the surrounding carnage. After a careful inspection of the damage, I believed she was repairable. The other three aircraft, though—including my Cessna—had been battered down to salvage value.

Following Duane's death nine years ago, the airport had been operated by his widow, Marion, with the help of her daughter, Sandi. In the aftermath of the hangar disaster, someone said to me, "You've been paying hangar rent, so Marion is liable."

I knew she had no insurance on the building and no assets other than the airport. Even if she had, suing her was unthinkable.

The only insurance I carried was liability. With hull insurance premiums sky high, I was a believer in author Richard Bach's view that "Barnstormer's Mutual" was the only practical policy for vintage aircraft. What did it cover? Only blind faith that the pilot would always have a suitable emergency landing field available. Barnstormer's Mutual did not include hangar collapse. In fewer words: I had no insurance to cover the crunching of my aircraft by a collapsing roof. But I was determined the Waco would fly again, and I would foot the bill.

This was not an uplifting finish for year 1986.

Through our son John, I knew of Hugo Bartel, an expert aircraft mechanic who had worked for Canadair and now operated an aircraft repair business at Cove Valley Airport near Altoona, Pennsylvania. I called Hugo. The next day, he arrived at Clifford Airport towing a trailer. Considering the extent of the damage, I decided a complete rejuvenation was in order. We detached the Waco's wings, secured the wreckage on the trailer and Hugo towed my battered flying machine to Cove Valley.

For a new set of wings, I called John Shue, a Waco specialist in York, Pennsylvania. He agreed to build new upper and lower wings, using the old undamaged fittings. John promptly drove his truck to Cove Valley and carted the damaged wings to York for their salvageable parts in the rebuild. Both John and Hugo were meticulous craftsmen. Their estimated time for restoring the Waco: one year. But it would take almost two. Arrangements for the crumpled Cessna turned out to be simpler. Hugo bought it.

In late January, 1987, Dave Ormesher and I flew the ORBIS jet from notorious Cali, Colombia, to nearby Medellin, a quick 200-mile hop along the northern Andes. I had then planned to leave promptly for home. Unexpectedly I found myself appointed arbitrator in a conflict between Pat Healy and "Roy," a black aircraft mechanic we had recently hired to deal with the plane's recurring mechanical glitches. While Pat and Roy had been working on one of the engines, a bolt had refused their efforts to remove it. "We may have to 'nigger' it out," Pat had said. Roy had claimed that to have been a racial slur. I had never before heard that term, but it is actually an old lumberman's reference to a long-toothed, power-driven lever used in logging operations.

Oliver was in Medellin when I arrived, and he asked me to mediate the dispute. I knew Pat was no racist. Yet his explanation and apology had not satisfied Roy. I believed the best way to go about resolving this confrontation was to bring all four of us together-including Oliver—to discuss the matter openly. We soon realized Roy's understandable sensitivity was the result of several unfortunate events in his past. It became clear that Pat's remark, though not well chosen, was not at all meant in any racial sense. The matter was resolved amicably.

I went on home, only to return to Medellin in late February to fly the DC-8 to Tegucigalpa, Honduras. ORBIS had accepted an invitation for a three-week mission there, but when the Honduran Air Authority was asked for clearance, the answer was *nada* chance! The runway was too short, a mountain rose at one end and no plane as large as ours had ever landed there. The Air Authority refused to take responsibility for approving our arrival.

Pat and I journeyed to Tegucigalpa from Miami via an Honduran airline. Armed with DC-8 performance data, we set up a meeting to prove ORBIS could safely bring off the mission. The Honduran airline's Boeing 727 jets, we reminded the Air Authority officials, regularly operated in and out of Tegucigalpa with no problems.

"*Si, Senors,* but they are smaller and have better performance than your DC-8."

We discussed the impasse over several days. In the end, the Air Authority reluctantly granted approval, with ORBIS signing an official waiver to absolve the Air Authority of any liability should we drive our machine into the mountain or otherwise come to grief.

With the area noted for drug running, other clandestine goings-on and general turmoil, I wasn't unhappy to get back to Medellin in time for our scheduled departure from there February 18.

Eric Friedrichsen flew with me on this one. Since the runway at Tegucigalpa tilted on a two-degree downslope from the mountain end, we decided to land upslope toward the mountain, whatever the wind direction. The airport's 3,600-foot elevation meant the air would be just a bit on the rarified side. Early morning would be the optimum time to land. Winds should be calm.

With the stage set for potential drama, we took off at dawn for the two-hour, 30-minute flight across the western Caribbean and Nicaragua. Crossing into Honduras in fine weather, we made a couple circuits of the airport.

Hundreds of people had gathered around the field's perimeter to watch the arrival of the largest airplane ever to attempt landing there. The event was sure to be well-photographed, and I had a sudden vision of German movie director Erich von Stroheim filming a World War I risky landing sequence.

"Keep der camera rolling on der ship. Dere may be a crrrash!"

I made the approach at absolutely minimum safe speed, put it down "on the numbers," and we rolled to taxi speed just two thirds of the way up the strip. Sorry, Erich.

Nor did the DC-8 have any trouble taking off downslope away from the mountain when the mission ended three weeks later.

Home again, now bereft of any aircraft of my own, I felt that void so keenly I couldn't resist buying a two-place Cessna 150. The "previously-owned" plane was in good shape for the short time I intended to keep it. It bore license N704UC—and we called it "Uncle Charlie."

About this time, ORBIS, never operating with much of a financial cushion, was in search of a line of credit. I spoke with a friend of mine, Larry Stetler, president of PNC Bank in Scranton and a member of First Baptist. A meeting was set up, and Oliver drove to Scranton. Larry was aware Oliver's father, Lord Cardamon, had served as British ambassador to the U.N. and that Pennsylvania's former governor, William Scranton, had also been a U.N. ambassador. He had known Oliver's father well. A resident of nearby Dalton, Governor Scranton, a close friend of Larry Stetler's, now maintained an office in the bank's executive suite, and all four of us met over lunch in the executive dining room.

Major corporations would sometimes sponsor an ORBIS mission. Governor Scranton, now a member of the board of Scott Paper, offered to try for a sponsorship from that company.

My foray into high—well, moderately high finance—was a success. The line of credit was established, and in August ORBIS conducted a mission in Santiago, Spain—sponsored by Scott Paper.

The day had ended well for ORBIS but not so well for Oliver. On his way home to Long Island, he managed to prang his Toyota. He was uninjured, but the car needed major surgery.

In late spring the DC-8 was flown to Dallas for a "heavy mainte-nance" check-up, including work on the balky radios. Bill Bradford and I reported to Dallas May 7 to fly the jet to Houston with Pat Healy as flight engineer.

While we were still parked on the Dallas airport ramp, we made the standard radio check with the tower. Loud and clear. All three of us were elated. We finally had radio equipment we could depend on. We began to taxi out and changed frequencies as required.

No response.

We tried another mike.

No response.

With Dallas a notably busy airport, we dared not taxi further without clearance. We could hear ground control calling us, but we were elec-tronically mute.

In desperation we eventually made contact on some obscure fre-quency and were cleared to taxi to a holding area. Pat went to work on the radio equipment that seemed to have stumped the experts. Thanks to his resourcefulness, we finally were able to launch for Houston, ORBIS's home medical center. There we set that airport's radio wizards to work on our ever-obstinate communications equip-ment.

Two days later, with the radios back in order—we hoped—we flew on to Santo Domingo in the Dominican Republic for the next mission. Milt Massey, my friend from the Waverly church and a generous sup-porter of ORBIS, flew jump seat. On that three-hour, 30-minute jaunt, the radios did what they were supposed to do.

In June, 1987 the search committee at Waverly's First Baptist called a full-time pastor, Jerry Hoch. He and his family would move into the adjacent parsonage. Jerry seemed just right for the church, and we all were pleased. I continued to provide pulpit supply here and there in the Abingtons until 1990 when I accepted another call to serve Clifford Baptist as interim pastor.

When the mission sponsored by Scott Paper was completed, Eric and I flew the DC-8 from Spain to its next destination: Moscow. Ophthalmology research in the Soviet Union had broken new ground with the development of an operation called keratotomy, a surgical adjustment of the cornea. The procedure was said to eliminate the need for eye glasses for many patients. The Soviets were eager to demonstrate the technique. With close contacts in the Kremlin, the head of the Soviets' Department of Opthalmology had invited ORBIS to visit Moscow for what the Russians and ORBIS termed "an exchange of skills." I couldn't resist the opportunity to take Katherine along on this unusual trip. Oliver, too, came with us.

At the time most of the air/ground communication was in Russian. All altitudes, air speeds, weather ceilings and wind velocities were transmitted in Russian using the metric system. We were required to add an English-speaking Russian navigator to our flight crew, and we were restricted to a narrow air corridor. Despite all the complications, the flight was a good one.

At Moscow's Sheremetievo airport and at Hotel Kozmos, we waded through a plethora of bureaucratic delays. But we were determined not to be pegged as "Ugly Americans." Through the two-hour wait in the hotel for room assignments, we all remained pleasantly calm, an accomplishment I felt was duly noted by observing eyes.

During our two-week stay in the capital city of the soon-to-collapse Soviet Union, political barriers dissolved and we had an enjoyable time. Especially memorable was a visit to one of the larger hospitals where we observed keratotomy operations. The patients were placed on a sort of merry-go-round operating "wheel," their feet toward its center. A surgeon stood at each patient's head and performed a step of the operation. Then the wheel would rotate one space. The surgeons stayed in place and each repeated his part of the procedure on the just-arrived patient. Though it struck me as coldly impersonal, the medical round-about assembly-line approach did appear to save a lot of time. The Russians were obviously proud of it.

All of us were given tours of the Moscow area and were kindly treated. On our last evening in the city we were entertained at a dinner and hugely enjoyed a spectacular show of Russian dancing. This was followed by hearty exchanges of appreciation—with the help of a Russian interpreter. Everyone from ORBIS, introduced by Oliver, spoke a few words. When Oliver called on me, he mentioned I was not only the flying hospital's captain, I was also a pastor. That stumped the interpreter. After much discussion, she settled uncertainly on the Russian word for priest.

Next morning we lifted off for Leningrad and a two-week "exchange of skills" there. Eric flew this leg in rain with low visibility and made an excellent approach and landing in absolutely minimal weather.

Again we were treated grandly, visited the city's great museums and palaces with a climactic tour of the exhibition centered on the German Army's 400-day blockade and siege of the city in World War II. Residents had been reduced to drinking hair oil and eating vaseline and had made soup from furniture glue and wallpaper. A million died before the Germans, having failed to conquer the city, were routed.

Eric returned home via Finnair and Pan Am. Katherine journeyed by train to Helsinki, Finland, then from there home on Pan Am. Dave Ormesher arrived in Leningrad, and on September 5 he and I flew the DC-8 to Sarajevo, the capital of Bosnia-Herzegovina. Viktor, our mandatory Russian navigator, accompanied us on the flight out of Soviet airspace. In the short time I had known him, I'd found Viktor a decent and friendly fellow airman.

In this early autumn of 1987, Sarajevo was a lovely city. The people were friendly and seemed to enjoy life. The three-way struggle among Bosnia's Serbs, Muslims and Croats was five years over the horizon. I stayed a few days in the city that still showed the architectural influence of its four and a half centuries under the Turks. In fact, its present name was derived from *serai,* the Turkish word for palace. The 1984 Winter Olympics site was still impressive, and all was peaceful in Sarajevo. Five years later, most of the city would be in ruins with thousands killed. Another instance of civilization still in its infancy.

I returned home due for an FAA physical, strictly routine, but I was soon to face staggering news. At age 66, I had developed prostate cancer.

THE YEAR TO LIVE A DREAM

I had heard that a macrobiotic diet had brought about cures for some cancer patients. I launched into that regimen. Katherine stocked supplies of Japanese *miso* soup, seaweed and other such "foods," and she faithfully saw to my staying on that uninspiring diet.

I began losing weight rapidly. Neither that nor the cancer affected my FAA physical legality. My next ORBIS mission was to fly the DC-8 from Athens to Larnaca, Cyprus. Mike Lyon and I made that one-hour, 30-minute flight October 17, 1987.

I hadn't seen the ORBIS people since Sarajevo but all had heard I had been diagnosed with prostate cancer. On the macrobiotic diet, I had already lost 30 pounds. I was sure the crew assumed the disease had taken hold with a vengeance. They were clearly touched by my gaunt appearance.

Returning to Crystal Lake, I still had no physical limitations. I continued my weekly commutes to the ORBIS New York office and was perfectly able to fly Uncle Charlie, the Cessna, when schedule and weather permitted. I also spent a good bit of time with my 93-year-old mother before her life on earth ended several months later.

In that fall of 1987, our daughter Jackie told me of an article she had read concerning a Canadian medical development said to have helped many cancer patients.

Might it be worth a try?

The medication turned out to be Flutamide, developed by Dr. Ferdinand La Bris at the University of Ottawa. Canadian Dr. Brian Leonard, one of our volunteer ophthalmologist friends with ORBIS, offered to check out Flutamide for me. Though at that time the drug had not yet been approved by the U.S. Food and Drug Administration, a number of American oncologists were using the protocol.

Dr. Leonard arranged a consultation with Dr. Roy Berger of North Shore Oncologists in Port Jefferson on Long Island. On his recommendation, I went ahead with the treatment. In November, 1987 I began taking a daily tablet of Flutamide plus a daily self-administered injection of Lupron. Eventually, the injections should decrease to one a month.

An important factor in healing, I was—and am—convinced, is prayer. Hundreds of people I had come to know over the years began to pray for me. At one point, a former ORBIS coordinator and dear friend, Saundra Tkacs, surprised me with a call to tell me she had arranged to gather together her church's entire congregation for prayer in my behalf. "Jack," she assured me, "I know you will be healed."

On March 12, 1988 John Harris and I flew the DC-8 from Bamako, Mali, to the Island of Djerba off Tunisia's Mediterranean coast. The mission just completed in Bamako had been largely concerned with "river blindness," lesions of the eyes caused by filarial parasites invading the blood stream. Without prompt treatment, vision could be destroyed.

The 2,000-mile trip to Tunisia was spiced with a back-of-my-mind apprehension concerning a leak in number 2 main fuel tank. Persisting for some months, the leak had been treated with sealants. It still dripped, but not enough to ground the aircraft. Despite that nagging concern, we landed in Djerba as scheduled.

I left the next day then returned two weeks later, this time with Eric Friedrichsen, to fly the DC-8 to Frankfurt, Germany for some essential maintenance and a PR effort.

Enthusiastic German media met our flight, and when I was interviewed, quite a bit of interest was shown in my having flown the Berlin corridors 35 years before.

In May, Katherine and I drove to Damariscotta, Maine, about 25 miles northeast of Brunswick. In all the flying I had done to and from some pretty rough-and-ready places, I had suffered no injury. Ironically

Katherine, visiting a lighthouse during our pleasure trip to Maine the year before, had broken her ankle. The local doctor had installed a temporary steel plate. Now we returned to Damariscotta, the scene of that trauma, to have the plate removed by the same doctor. We arrived as a couple and a week later—minus the ankle plate—departed as a trio with "Snoopy," a golden retriever we had been unable to resist "Down East."

That same month I again flew Uncle Charlie out to Cove Valley Airport to check progress. The Waco was looking better but still far from flyable.

I continued to put in my one day per week at ORBIS headquarters in New York City. In late May the DC-8 was about to complete a three-week mission in Zagreb, Yugoslavia. Next stop, Amsterdam. I had a hard time assembling a flight crew for that relatively short hop. I needed another qualified pilot. Not one of the roster's volunteer pilots was able to join me. In desperation I recalled that son John had a friend who was current on the DC-8. I called John, and what luck! His friend, Nick Venn, would be glad to arrive in Zagreb in time for the flight. On June 17, Nick and I flew the ORBIS plane to Amsterdam as scheduled, for a publicity and fund-raising visit in the Netherlands.

Through the summer I put in some hours as instructor in Uncle Charlie, the Cessna 150, and continued my airborne visits to Cove Valley where the Waco was beginning to look like a flyable airplane again. John Shue had completed the new wings and transported them to Cove Valley by trailer. Though the old fittings and drag and anti-drag wires had been usable, John had built new spars and ribs to original Waco specifications. He had also managed to find a replacement vertical fin and rudder from old Waco parts salvaged by some fortunately foresighted people.

Since the old classic would soon be airworthy, I decided to accept an unexpected offer to buy Uncle Charlie. On July 17, $12,000 changed hands and the Cessna 150 had a new owner.

The high point of the summer was an invitation to fly to the general aviation gathering at Oshkosh in rural Wisconsin. Organized by the Experimental Aircraft Association, the informal week-long get-together had originated in Rockford, Illinois, then moved to Oshkosh in 1970. It now attracted thousands of pilots for a week-long extravaganza of privately-owned aircraft on display, air shows and special events.

Back in June, ORBIS volunteer pilot Mike Lyon had called to ask if I would be interested in flying a classic Stearman to the Oshkosh event. The old biplane was owned by Mike's friend Bill Rose, who maintained and flew some 20 vintage aircraft at his private airstrip in Barrington, Illinois. Bill and several of his friends planned to fly nine or 10 of his planes to the Oshkosh meet, including two Ryan STs, two de Havilland Chipmunks, a Fairchild 22, a Grumman Goose and the Stearman. During the week-long event the Rose contingent would have a pair of trailers at a nearby campsite to provide food and drink.

This was an offer I absolutely could not refuse. Katherine and I flew to Chicago and were treated to a limo ride 15 miles northwest to Bill Rose's home in Barrington. We found Bill a kind, generous man beneath a no-nonsense exterior. We met his wife-to-be, Myrt, a lovely woman with an unusual aviation connection. She had been a wing-walker, standing on the top wing of a biplane while the pilot performed acrobatics. Also on hand were Eric Friedrichsen, his wife Verna, and several other pilots I knew. Bill had arranged accommodations for all of us in his home and guest house, a grand get-together before the main event up in Wisconsin.

During the couple of days we stayed in Barrington, Bill checked me out in the Stearman at his farm's airstrip a few miles west. I shot a series of take-offs and landings until I felt at home in the first Stearman I'd flown since my crop dusting days 40 years ago. With my Waco out of commission for more than a year, I was elated to be back in an open cockpit.

For our departure for Oshkosh, Katherine and I, properly helmeted and goggled, led a flight of five of Bill's aircraft. With the other four planes trailing behind us, we crossed the Wisconsin border in clear weather, made a fuel stop at Waukesha just west of Milwaukee then approached Oshkosh on the west shore of Lake Winnebago.

The landing site was an air traffic beehive, and the Stearman had the only radio in our flight. The tower operators, awash in incoming traffic, were outstanding. We flew inbound on a precise approach heading with minimal spacing between aircraft. All five of us landed safely. We parked among the hundreds of planes already there and headed for Bill's compound.

Our week at Oshkosh was an unforgettable delight. Each morning we flew out for breakfast, usually 15 miles north to Appleton. Katherine and I enjoyed a flight in Bill's amphibian Grumman Goose—another link with the past—landing on Lake Winnebago. Every day at Oshkosh we enjoyed an airshow. Each evening we had supper in the open. For our final dinner, Bill had lobsters flown in, the climax of a marvelous week.

In the years since, the Oshkosh AirVenture has become a massive annual event. In 2002, 11,000 airplanes assembled at the AirVenture.

With 10,000 attendees in 1970, the event had grown to 800,000 by 2002. The huge fly-in has been termed the "Woodstock of Aviation" but it dwarfs that namesake.

Home again and personally planeless, I flew one of Bob Seamans's Cessnas to Cove Valley. The prognosis of my Waco doctor: three or four more months before she could fly home.

Following the Oshkosh venture, Ken LaPointe, United instructor pilot Dan Lynch and I relocated the ORBIS jet from Hyderabad, India to New Delhi. Back home, I continued my trips to the New York office and faithfully kept to my schedule of monthly visits to my Long Island oncologist—plus a blood test and bone scan every three months.

In December, great news! The Waco was ready for a test flight. The day after Christmas, I drove to Cove Valley. The old girl was wheeled into the sunlight, her new fabric sparkling crimson, drum tight, eager to be aloft. What a great feeling of release to race her down the runway, lift off and soar into the crisp winter sky.

With a few minor details still needing attention, I had to leave her there. In two weeks, I could return and at long last fly her home.

Following his historic transatlantic solo flight in 1927, Charles Lindbergh felt he must use his worldwide celebrity status to promote aviation. Backed by the Guggenheim Fund for the Promotion of Aeronautics, Lindbergh took off from Mitchell Field, Long Island on July 17, 1927, to fly the *Spirit of St. Louis* on a widely publicized three-month tour of all then-48 states, visiting 82 cities. When he returned in October, he had covered 22,350 miles in 260 flying hours, and the Guggenheim Tour was a public relations sensation.

For decades, I had thought about duplicating Lindbergh's tour route, an ambition reinforced by my meeting Lindbergh and flying him as a jump seat passenger in 1970 on that Pan Am cargo trip. Now at age 68, and continuing treatment for prostate cancer, I determined the time had arrived to get serious about my nearly life-long dream.

When I bought my Waco in 1966, I felt the classic ship just might be the perfect plane to recreate the 1927 tour. What had held me back all these years was the conviction I shouldn't make the flight just for its own sake. I needed a higher purpose. And now publicizing the work of ORBIS struck me as an eminently worthy justification to live the dream.

In New York, I laid out my proposal for ORBIS officialdom's consideration. With the entire ORBIS staff enthusiastic about the idea and the potential for national publicity, it was a sale. Oliver contacted one of the PR firms doing pro-bono work for ORBIS gratis—and was told flatly they wouldn't touch the project. An ancient airplane with no state-of-the-art navigational equipment? And a somewhat elderly pilot? As they put it, expectations of success were not positive. In simpler words: No, thanks.

Totally undeterred by such lack of faith, Oliver determined, "We'll handle the PR work ourselves."

He turned to ORBIS's own internal affairs coordinator, a brilliant young woman named Holly Peppe. With a Ph.D from Brown University, Holly had written the only definitive biography of the celebrated American poet, Edna Saint Vincent Millay and had taught at Brown. But her real passion was humanitarian work. Oliver handed her the responsibility for all the Lindbergh tour PR advance work and media coverage.

ORBIS would not only conduct the publicity campaign. The organization would also wangle free fuel, hangar space and lodging wherever possible and provide monetary assistance for my road crew, including rental of their vehicle. Such was the faith of Oliver and ORBIS. I readily signed an agreement to absolve the organization of any liability should anything untoward occur, and the project—with many people contributing—was a go.

But first:

On January 7, 1989, Dan Lynch, Pat Healy and I flew the DC-8 from Bangkok, Thailand to Dhaka in central Bangladesh, an abjectly poor country where anything at all that ORBIS could do would be a major plus.

On my return, son John flew me on a frosty mid-January day to Cove Valley. At long last, the Waco was coming home. Not at all minding the icebox-frigid cockpit temperature, I flew the old girl back to Clifford.

The demolished hangar had not been rebuilt—and never would be. But during the lengthy period while the Waco was laid low, Bob Wallis, a friend of mine and a Stearman owner, and I had bought two acres fronting the airport's east-west runway. We each had built small hangars there, side-by-side. As I rolled the Waco into its new hangar, I was elated that the key part of the 48-state tour preparation had fallen into place: I had the plane.

The next month, Pat Healy and I scrounged a ride on a Flying Tiger 747 cargo flight to the Philippines. There we were joined by Oliver for the DC-8's transfer to Port Moresby, New Guinea. During our four days in Manila, Oliver was stunned by his visit to "Smokey Mountain," a massive garbage dump in the city's outskirts.

"Incredibly sad," he told me. "I saw people living on top of the dump, spending their days picking through the garbage hoping to find something to use or to eat."

February 18 we took off for New Guinea, my turn to fly—and to be at the controls when number three engine decided to quit. We went through the restarting procedure. The engine would run for a few moments then stop dead again. Fortunately, we were about to descend into Port Moresby and didn't need all four engines to make a safe approach. We landed with number three shut down. Its malfunctioning fuel control was soon repaired.

The tropical afternoon was beautiful; the Coral Sea, scene of desperate World War II naval battles, sparkling and serene. I couldn't help but think of all the casualties inflicted here in the Japanese attempts by land and by sea to capture the town for its port and the control of southeastern New Guinea.

Eager to get home to continue preparations for the Lindbergh tour attempt, I flew to Sydney, Australia via Qantas, the Australian airline, overnighted there then caught a Qantas flight eastbound.

I had hoped to begin the tour where Lindbergh had begun his, the same month and the same day 62 years ago. But Mitchell Field on Long Island was now the site of urban development. As a suitably near replacement, I chose Bayport Aerodrome, a small grass airfield on the shore of Great South Bay.

In May, 1989 Katherine and I flew the Waco to York, Pennsylvania for Waco expert John Shue—the rebuilder of its wings—to make a complete inspection of the reconstructed old ship. He went about it like a suspicious internist, pronounced the machine entirely shipshape for the projected tour, then made a remarkable offer.

"Jack, if you have any trouble with the plane along the way, call me and I'll come to wherever you are to work on the problem."

When I prepped the Waco in July for the tour, I noticed a loose tail wheel bearing. I called John in York, and true to his word, he drove to Clifford the next day to replace the bearing.

In late May, Eric Friederichsen and I arrived in Beijing, China to fly the ORBIS jet 700 miles northwest to Ulan Bator, the capital of Mongolia. I had hoped Katherine could be with us on this one, but her mother's health was not good, and Katherine's caring for her was of higher priority.

All but four of the doctors and nurses had already left by train for Ulan Bator to prepare for the plane's arrival. Eric, I and the remainder of the group spent a few days touring Beijing and the surrounding area.

About 70 miles north of the city, we visited a portion of the Great Wall and walked it a mile or so. I found the whole idea of that massive 1,500-mile-long, 2,200-year-old construction absolutely overwhelming, with several hundred miles of it still intact today.

Equally exciting for me was our visit to the Beijing's Forbidden City, the immense, walled-in palace enclosure of the Chinese Emperors. Our tour of the palace museum was narrated, to my surprise, by Peter Ustinov on tape.

Then we witnessed a remarkable event in Chinese history. Our brief stay in Beijing coincided with the protest gathering of 100,000 students and workers in Tiananmen Square, an incredible happening in this Communist Party-ruled nation. Protesters in 20 other Chinese cities joined in, and for weeks, the crowd in Tiananmen Square camped in the open, refusing to leave. The vast square was alive with the excitement of change, and at the time we were there, it seemed possible. The government appeared to be dithering.

Down in the square, I met a young English-speaking Chinese man, a lawyer.

"Your group is behaving so well," I told him. "I'm sure the government will have to listen."

"That will not happen," he said sadly. "The government will use force."

Shortly after we left for Mongolia, in rolled the tanks and troops. Who can forget the TV footage of a lone man's blocking the path of a Chinese Army tank by standing his ground as it rolled up to him—and stopped? A superb act of defiance, but the reports of the ensuing death toll vary from 500 to 7,000, with 10,000 injured, 10,000 arrested and 31 executed.

During the preparation for our departure from Beijing's airport, we ran into notable information gaps.

"What's the weather enroute?" we asked.

"It should be . . . okay," was the forecaster's response.

"Might you have a spot weather-on-terminal forecast?"

"No, but it should be okay."

"How about winds aloft?"

"Should be westerly."

"Any contact here at all with Ulan Bator?"

"No, but that's not unusual."

"What's a good alternate airport?"

"Back here."

Considering such a non-committal "weather report," we took off carrying a lot of fuel. We had managed to get our hands on a diagram of the Ulan Bator Airport. With high ground at one end, it was a one-way landing strip for large aircraft. During the two-hour, 15-minute flight, the weather was "okay," as predicted. Navigational aids were unavailable in this remote part of the world, but we arrived . . . okay.

The Mongolians, a proud people under a Communist regime since the early 1920s, greeted us with great enthusiasm. We were put up in their best hotel, not luxurious but adequate. On a tour of the city's museum, we were impressed by the emphasis on the nation's ancient hero Kubla Kahn, founder of China's Mongol Dynasty. Kubla Kahn's better known grandfather, Genghis Kahn, the unifier of the 13th century Mongol tribes, was given notably less attention.

Eric and I returned to Beijing on a Chinese Airline jet. From there we journeyed on to the U.S. via United Airlines to Tokyo then caught a non-stop Pan Am flight to New York.

With the target date for the Lindbergh tour coming ever closer, preparations were now fully underway. I collected all 37 aviation sectional charts of the U.S. and chose airports used by Lindbergh—or substitutes as close as possible to those 1927 airports no longer in operation. ORBIS was busy with the public relations schedule for maximum TV, radio and press coverage.

As a part of the growing publicity campaign, son John and I had flown the Waco to Mt. Vernon, Ohio, in June as a feature of the Waco Club's annual meet. We found the participants already excited by the prospect of a Waco's flying the 48-state tour.

With the replacement of a not-so-reliable turn-and-bank indicator to keep me rightside up in IFR weather, the Waco was ready. After I arranged the ORBIS pilots' schedule for flights while I would be flying the tour, I was ready too.

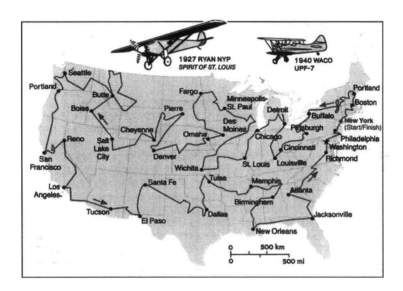

Route of Charles Lindbergh's 1927 tour during which he flew his legendary *Spirit of St. Louis* Ryan NYP airplane 22,350 miles stopping in each of the 48 states. During 89 days in the summer of 1989 Jack Race recreated his hero's trip, flying his own 1940 Waco open-cockpit biplane, *Spirit of Orbis*.

"HE'S NOT QUITE AS TALL, BUT HE LOOKS LIKE CHARLES A. LINDBERGH!"

"One hundred fifty well-wishers, including fellow flyers, Baptist clergymen and church members, gathered at Clifford Airport Wednesday to bid farewell to pilot John T. (Jack) Race as he began retracing Charles A. Lindbergh's historic 1927 transcontinental flight . . . . The Crystal Lake resident, a retired Pan American Airways captain and chief pilot for Project ORBIS, expects to make 82 stops in 48 states, covering more than 20,000 miles, between now and mid-October."
—*The Scrantonian-Tribune,*
Scranton, Pennsylvania,
July 20, 1989

This could have been a scene from aviation's 1930s "golden era." A tiny sod airfield bordered by trees and rolling farmland. A bright red biplane, its radial engine ticking over in the humid July morning. In its rear cockpit, the helmeted pilot adjusting his goggles, his white silk scarf adding a bit of dash.

But the year was 1989. The airfield was northeastern Pennsylvania's last commercial airport with a sod runway. The airplane was a restored Waco UPF-7. The pilot was myself, about to take off on the flight I had dreamed of for decades, flying the same route of Lindbergh's celebrated 1927 Guggenheim Tour to all 48 continental states.

Now as I made my final check of the few instruments in the Waco's cockpit, I thought of the differences—and startling similarities—between Lindbergh's tour of the U.S. and my coming attempt to refly it.

First, there was the contrast of our airplanes. The *Spirit of St. Louis* was a single-engined monoplane with an enclosed cabin. My Waco was an open cockpit biplane. Placed side-by-side, the two planes might have fooled the casual bystander into deciding that the *Spirit of St. Louis* was the more advanced design. Interestingly, both planes had the same horsepower. Lindbergh's engine was a 220-hp Wright Whirlwind. Mine was a 220-hp Continental. And we shared the same cruising speed: 105 mph.

The *Spirit of St. Louis* and my Waco carried the same rudimentary navigation instrumentation: a "wet" compass. Lindbergh had an additional item, a drift meter. I had a radio for air-to-ground communication, but there was no modern electronic navigation gear aboard the Waco. This flight, like Lindbergh's, was to be navigated by "dead-reckoning"—the use of compass headings, elapsed times and visual checkpoints.

The two planes differed in age by only 13 years. The *Spirit of St. Louis* was built in 1927. My Waco was of 1940 vintage, coincidentally the year I first soloed. A much greater difference was in the age of the two planes at the times of their flights. Lindbergh's specially-designed Ryan NYP (Lindbergh's designation for New York to Paris) was only a few months old. The plane I was readying for take-off was just one year shy of a half-century in age.

There was almost as big a difference in our ages. Lindbergh had flown his Guggenheim Tour at age 25. I was about to shove off on my 82-city tour at the age of 68.

Lindbergh had begun his tour on Long Island July 20, 1927. Now, 62 years later, I was determined to set out on July 20, 1989. Today, though, was July 19. And I was about to leave Clifford Airport 10 miles northwest of Carbondale in the foothills of Pennsylvania's Endless Mountains. Destination, southern Long Island. The official take-off on my re-created 48-state tour was scheduled to take place there tomorrow morning.

Here in rural Clifford, though, more than a hundred people stood along the sod runway to watch this departure from the Waco's home field. Members of the local press were here to see the take-off for Long

Island. One, Nan Waters, a feature writer for the *Sunday Scrantonian,* was delightfully carried away with it all. "For several years," she wrote in the following Sunday's edition, "we've thought that Jack Race reminded us of someone. As we shook hands with him Wednesday morning and wished him, 'Godspeed,' we suddenly realized who it was. He's not quite as tall. But he looks like Charles A. Lindbergh!"

On this flight, and for the first official leg of the tour, I had a passenger. Katherine, my indulgent, patient—and adventuresome—wife for nearly 50 years, was properly outfitted with helmet and goggles in the front cockpit. She had stood by me through five decades of an aviation career from the Aeronca "Flying Bathtub" to the Boeing 747. Now eight years after mandatory retirement from Pan American, I was about to take off on a journey whose length would almost equal that of a trip around the world.

In the Waco I carried a sleeping bag, tie-down equipment and a tool kit. After flying the first leg with me, Katherine would serve as chief of the ground support crew. She, her sister and brother-in-law—Betty and Walter "Rip" Russell—were to follow the tour by road in a rented 1988 Oldsmobile station wagon. In addition to their luggage—and mine—the car was loaded with a spare magneto and a set of plugs for the Waco, plus selected spare parts—and medications for my cancer treatment. One wag asked if we were taking along any bailing wire. We told him there should be plenty available along this wide-ranging route.

My ground crew and I planned to meet at three- or four-day intervals along the planned route. Lindbergh, too, had back-up on his tour. His support vehicle was another aircraft, flown by Philip Love with a mechanic and a writer as working passengers.

Just before take-off, everyone joins in a circle of prayer. At 11:10 a.m., I salute the crowd with a farewell wave and nudge the snorting Continental. We bounce to the downwind end of the field. I run through the take-off check, turn into the wind and lock the tail wheel. I ease the throttle forward. The engine's mutter builds to a roar. Tail up. The main gear bounds along the uneven grass. Then we are airborne in the cool morning haze.

If you have never flown in an open cockpit, you have missed one of aviation's most exhilerating experiences. The engine beats your ears with a blare of power. Lean to the side of the windscreen and the solid slipstream buffets your face. You feel the air's fluid strength to keep the wings aloft. There is no intervening window between you and God's earth below. This is truly flying, a sensation never experienced by the earthbound—or the jaded jet passenger.

At 2,000 feet, we levelled off on a 123-degree heading just below the base of a broken cloud layer. The weather: hazy beneath the ragged edge of a stationary warm front. The rolling hills of the eastern Poconos drifted below.

We crossed the southern tip of New York State. The murky Hudson River fell behind. Last checkpoint before crossing Long Island Sound: Norwalk, Connecticut. Then for 17 miles, water and sky blended. No horizon for reference, the same deceptive visual condition that would lead to young John Kennedy's crash and death a decade later.

Safely over Long Island I spotted the small, whimsically-named airport just east of Sayville on Long Island's south shore. I throttled back and we began the long descent into Bayport Aerodrome.

Our landing on the 2700-foot grass strip was less than picture perfect. Katherine held a train case on her lap, and when I began the flare-out, the case impeded the rearward travel of the dual control sticks. The level-out was about to become something destructively different when she suddenly realized the case was better placed at her side. With that, landing became possible—but ungracefully porpoiseful.

Safely down with damage only to ego, we were greeted by several local pilots and friends who had prepared a cook-out at Bill Ahern's hanger. After an evening of hangar stories, a car was made available, and Katherine and I drove to the Eden Roc motel about three miles from the aerodrome.

Sleep at the motel didn't come easily. Tomorrow was the day I had dreamed of for so many years. I was gripped by the excitement Lindbergh had surely felt 62 years ago here on Long Island.

Now, on July 19, 1989, in the darkness of the motel room, I stared sleepless at the ceiling. I recalled my two meetings with that friendly, concerned, pre-eminent airman of aviation's golden age. I worried about the muggy weather. Would it clear enough for me to begin the long journey to commemorate his 1927 cross-country trail blazing? Would I be able to keep to the tight scheduling of media coverage to support the ORBIS humanitarian effort that had become close to my heart?

At daybreak, rain streaked the windows of our motel room. This had to be some gross climatic error. Last night the weather had cleared so nicely. Now this?

The Waco had been housed under cover in Bob Fritt's spotless hangar, fine-tuned and refueled for the flight to Hartford. The night sky had looked clear, promising good weather today. Now nature was playing a joke. Not only was rain pouring down. Peering through the motel window, I estimated the clouds to be no higher than 100 feet.

Take-off had been planned—and widely publicized—for 11:00 a.m. I knew Oliver Foot and many of the ORBIS staff must already be pulling into Bayport Aerodrome for a heavily promoted press conference scheduled to begin at 10:00 a.m.

I called Flight Service for a weather update. Response: Instrument flight rules all day. I knew weather could be whimsical, so I tried to stay optimistic. Katherine and I checked out of the Eden Roc and in our borrowed car, drove back to the airport.

The murk out there was no less dismal. Several pilot friends had planned to fly in from nearby airports then fly across Long Island Sound with me, a proper send-off on the first official leg of the tour. Now they called, forced by the weather to bow out.

Delaying the flight was easier than delaying the press conference. At 10:00 a.m., right on schedule, the Great Send-Off began in Bob's hangar. Oliver greeted the crowd then came interviews. A reporter from *Newsday* loudly asked if the Waco, now named *The Spirit of ORBIS,* had been painted red so she could be easily spotted if we went down. He also wondered if I had in the back of my mind a bit of worry over my age—and the age of my airplane. I did not, I told him. I had faith in both, or I never would have attempted this sure-to-be-demanding journey.

In Lindbergh's day, I could have taken a shot at "needle-ball-and-air-speeding" out of there on the Waco's meager instruments. Back then there would have been no other IFR traffic to contend with, and no tale-telling ground radar. But in 1989, Bayport was in the thick of a crowded FAA air traffic control zone. Any attempt to pick my way through it in a plane not fully equipped for IFR conditions would have been a license-revoking offense.

Concerning the rotten weather, everyone—well, almost everyone—assembled at Bayport Aerodrome was sympathetic. Some had driven from Clifford to see me off, including our daughter Jackie, her husband Bill DeNike and their children. There were some skeptics in the crowd, though, who were convinced I couldn't pull off this projected aerial odyssey.

I hated to do it, but in the early afternoon, I made the decision to stand down. There went my intention to start the tour the same date as Lindbergh had set out 62 years before. I rescheduled take-off for 11:00 a.m. tomorrow.

The rain refused to let up. We spent Friday, July 21, sitting around Bob Fritt's hangar, chatting with the scattering of veteran pilots who had dropped by for a few hours of "hangar flying." One of them, George Mitchell, a man of impressive faith, owned an Aeronca Champ.

He was determined to escort the Waco out of Long Island—if the weather ever broke.

In the late afternoon I noticed the thick overcast seemed to be thinning just a bit. Or was that wishful thinking? If conditions would improve to bare visual flight minimums, I was determined to set out tomorrow.

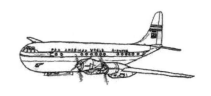

31
CHAPTER

WEATHER FORECAST: RAIN

At long last, on the morning of July 22 the weather began to break. I determined to take off for Hartford's Johnnycake Airport at 11:00 a.m.

My preoccupation with meeting the schedule went beyond personal satisfaction. Holly Peppe had conducted a superb advance publicity campaign with stories in newspapers coast-to-coast, magazine coverage including *National Geographic* and *Flying,* and publicity in newsletters of many national organizations. She had planned events at most airports on the tour, all of them tied into my staying precisely on the widely publicized schedule.

After prayers with George Mitchell and his wife, Katherine and I climbed aboard *Spirit of ORBIS.* By now the only media coverage at Bayport was a pair of die-hard newspaper reporters, bless their persistent souls.

We waved to the gaggle of Aerodrome regulars who had stood by us through the long wait for this moment. I gunned the engine. Rolling. Tail up. And we were finally off on the long planned, eagerly awaited 82-city tour.

Visibility had cleared nicely with an overcast at 1,000 feet. Behind us, George lifted off in his Aeronca and climbed to fly alongside to Long Island's north shore.

As we neared Long Island Sound, the ceiling began to drop. George dipped the Aeronca's wings in a farewell salute and peeled away toward Bayport. Beneath the lowering clouds, Katherine and I skimmed across the sound no higher over the dark water than 100 to 200 feet.

Then the ceiling began to lift again. We passed west of Bridgeport, then to avoid a 1749-foot radio tower in Waterbury, swung wide around that city.

We approached Johnnycake Airport—another grass field—from the west. This time Katherine had her traveling case well secured, and I made what I considered an elegant touchdown.

Holly had rallied a fair-sized Saturday crowd to witness our completion of the first official leg of the tour. Eric Friedrichsen was among those welcoming us to Hartford, along with ORBIS audio-visual producer Ozzie Font. Airport Manager Frank Gallagher offered free overnight hangar space, but already two days behind schedule I decided to press on to Providence, Boston and Portland, Maine before day's end, thus catch up a day. So my stay in Hartford was a mere 60 minutes, but coverage in the area's papers the next day was excellent, a solid boost for ORBIS.

As planned, Katherine joined Betty and Rip in the station wagon, which we had begun to call the "van." Though we would have no direct contact between plane and van throughout the tour, we had carefully planned more than two dozen locations where we would rendezvous along the flight path. Off they drove toward our next planned get-together at Albany. Then with Ozzie in the front cockpit, he and I took off at 1:34 p.m. in weather improving from pretty good to good. Fifty minutes later, we landed at Providence North Central Airport in Rhode Island.

Unfortunately my being behind the tour's published schedule cost us media coverage here. Providence turned out to be one of the few ports of call with no resulting publicity, though one reporter did call the airport to confirm my arrival. After taping footage at the airport to add to that he had recorded during the flight, Ozzie departed for New York aboard a commuter flight.

At 3:00 p.m. I rushed back in the air headed for Tew-Mac Airport, Boston, the first section of the tour I flew alone. Now responsible only for *Spirit of ORBIS* and myself, I felt a renewed sense of elation.

This 48-mile hop did land to an encouraging welcome. In the modest crowd, Mindy Pollack represented the Massachusetts Society of Eye Physicians and Surgeons. Former ORBIS Dr. Joe Burke presented a congratulatory certificate, and the next day's newspapers carried excellent coverage. But with the airport personnel a bit laid back, no help appeared on the flight line. "Help yourself," I was told in the Tew-Mac Aviation office. I found the pump locked and returned to the office. Someone stirred himself enough to unlock it then walked away. I handled the pump myself.

At 4:45 p.m. I rushed off again to follow the coastline in pleasant weather to a much busier airport, Portland International. But again, arriving a day late had cost us major press coverage. A couple of reporters did show up for my 5:30 p.m. appearance, though the public did not. The gathering of folks at Portland, including fellow Pan Am check pilot Ralph Hunt, had taken place in vain the previous day. Timing is everything.

Tom Carr with Northeast Flying Service had arranged for hangar space and lodging. With the hope of getting back on schedule tomorrow, I repaired to the nearby Comfort Inn finding a modicum of comfort in the fact that Lindbergh himself hadn't experienced smooth sailing on this leg of his tour. On his Boston-Portland leg, he had circled the Portland Airport for three hours hoping a heavy fog would clear. Finally he diverted to Concord then flew back to Portland the next morning, a day late in his schedule.

Now similarly one day late, I too was headed for Concord, New Hampshire. Before breakfast I took a half-hour walk and found myself playing that frustrating mind game: What if?

What if I had left Bayport a day earlier, flown *east* along Long Island's south shore then turned north toward Groton? I'd been so mentally locked into my announced plan I hadn't checked conditions eastward. I could have rented a car for Katherine to drive to Hartford. Flying alone, I would have felt freer to explore iffy options.

What if I had found a way to reach Concord on schedule? The publicity was to include a welcome from Boy Scouts, Girl Scouts, Daniel Webster Junior College, a high school band, a commendation personally presented by Governor Judd Grey, an interview with the Nashua Historical Society, an invitation to speak at the American Baptist Church, a special dinner that night . . .

All that was to have happened yesterday, but flying through the MacArthur Control Zone in below-VFR minimums with IFR traffic all around would have been risky, in addition to violating regulations

After breakfast, I returned to the airport. At 10:00 a.m., I took off for Concord, a day late—but not entirely out of the publicity loop. The New Hampshire Historical Society's representative Laura Eames, who had worked so hard on yesterday's event, had salvaged part of her program. A small contingent of Boy and Girl Scouts, several members of the Historical Society and a reporter greeted me at the airport.

I hangared the Waco overnight in the same hangar that had housed his *Spirit of St. Louis* on Lindbergh's tour. After lunch with Laura and several of her friends, she took me to the hotel where I would overnight—the same hotel where the gala dinner was to have been held the previous evening. Some of the decorations were still in place, and I was overwhelmed with the disappointment of having let down the Historical Society. In my room I found a huge basket of fruit, courtesy of the church where I had been invited to speak this morning. Compelled to walk to the church to offer my apologies in person, I found it closed. Later I wrote to the pastor to thank him for the basket and explain in detail the reason for my non-appearance.

Concord offered one last downer. As I unpacked my kit for the night, I discovered my Bible was missing. I'd left it in Portland. My good friend and colleague Manny Manioudakis had given me the Bible on my retirement from Pan Am. It had special meaning for me. I called the Comfort Inn. From there the Bible was mailed to Clifford then relayed to Katherine on the road. Ten days later, I had it back in hand.

All in Concord was not gloom, though. Old fellow Pan Am pilot Bill Malcolm surprised me with a call from the lobby. Having read my itinerary in his local paper, Bill, a Canadian American, had driven down from St. Stephens, New Brunswick to greet me. We had a grand evening together. Bill stayed at the hotel and in the morning drove me back to the airport in his VW.

As I pushed the Waco out of the hangar, a Piper Twin Comanche touched down. To my surprise and delight, here were son John and grandson Josh to see me off into the morning haze on schedule at last—thanks to Lindbergh's delay here. I took off with plane and spirits lifting.

Next stop, Springfield, Vermont, and a welcome by a goodly crowd including an elderly gentleman named Andy Johnson. He had been among those awaiting Lindbergh's arrival at this same airport on the same day in July in 1927. His most vivid memory, he told me, involved a fellow who had stood close behind him and as Lindbergh approached, pointed skyward and shouted, "Here he comes!" Then the loud-voiced fellow deftly relieved the diverted Johnson "and quite a few others of our wallets." This time, Andy Johnson had a less expensive experience, gamely making his way to the Waco with the aid of his walker to pose for a photo with me. The picture appeared in Ludlow's *Black River Tribune* July 26.

Old friend Woodie arrived from his home in Hanover, New Hampshire bearing a supply of most welcome sandwiches. He and I enjoyed a fine get-together before my afternoon take-off for Albany, New York.

Rensselaer, the appropriate Albany area airport for the tour, lay just across the Hudson from South Albany. A single runway field, it hadn't seen much use in recent years. In persistent haze, I timed my progress from my last checkpoint—Bennington, Vermont—but when I should have been right over Rensselaer Airport, I couldn't spot it. I made a slow 360° turn. There it was, a mile to the right. I spiralled down and was surprised to see a welcoming committee smack in the middle of the runway. Not people. A herd of deer. I dropped down in a low pass and they scattered.

Airport Manager Barbara Fioravanti and a small gathering greeted me, including a reporter—and my van crew who had arrived right on schedule. "Spent a miserable night here," they told me, "in a motel we will not go back to."

"I have my sleeping bag in the front cockpit. We could all sleep under the wing." I was kidding, but when the crew left to search the area for more amenable lodgings tonight, sleeping under the wing struck me as a good idea. I unfurled the sleeping bag and enjoyed a mid-afternoon nap.

Suitable quarters having been found, the crew returned, we hangared the Waco and drove off to that motel.

Early the next morning, the van and crew departed for Buffalo where we would next rendezvous. At 10:30 a.m. I left snoozy Rensselaer for Schenectady.

In 22 minutes, I glided into Schenectady County Airport to be met by Liz Tiffany representing the airport's Aerospace Museum, several media folk and an enthusiastic crowd. After a tour of the museum and a pleasant luncheon hosted by Liz, I dashed off again at 1:30 p.m on the flight to Syracuse.

Near the mid-point of this 164-mile upper New York State jaunt lay the town of Little Falls. A woman living there had called the ORBIS office and mentioned that during Lindbergh's tour, he had circled Little Falls, New York as a greeting from his hometown of Little Falls, Minnesota.

I couldn't resist circling Little Falls at 1,000 feet, but I never did learn whether the good woman saw my nostalgic double orbit.

At Syracuse's Hancock International Airport, an impressively busy airdrome, I was struck with the distinct impression the tower folk did not suffer airplanes of my ilk gladly. But at the General Aviation Terminal, TV and newspaper coverage was plentiful. I was officially welcomed by Dr. Bob Hampton, an ophthalmologist who had served on several ORBIS missions. His wife Jan, a nurse, had also flown with ORBIS. Bob's interest in my arrival was not solely ORBIS-inspired. An experienced pilot, he owned a Mooney based in Syracuse.

Dr. Bob had mustered extensive media coverage. The Central New York Pilots Association and the Aviation Historical Society had arranged a dinner that was attended by some 100 that evening at the airport. Then Bob put me up at his home for the night. In appreciation, I invited him to ride in the Waco's front cockpit to Buffalo tomorrow.

Flier's Lindy vision means hope for poor who are blind
—The Buffalo News

We took off at 10:00 a.m. July 26. Again I had the feeling I was a burden to the personnel in the tower, but I couldn't really blame them. They had enough of a challenge managing frequent arrivals and departures of scheduled airliners and didn't really need an antique biplane in the middle of all that jet traffic.

With Bob Hampton mightily enjoying the ride, we arrived in Buffalo right on schedule. I was to stay here several days to tie into a highly promoted open house scheduled at the airport July 29. The event would celebrate a $500,000 FAA grant to finance a new runway and ramp. ORBIS had been offered a booth to promote the tour.

So we enjoyed double coverage. TV and press were on hand when Bob and I landed. During the Saturday open house on a windy day with occasional rain showers, the van crew handed out a lot of PR material to a sizable crowd.

As the afternoon wore on, I realized many at the open house hoped to see *Spirit* fly. I felt the time was appropriate to head for my next stop, Erie, Pennsylvania.

After a 55-minute flight, I landed at Erie's Wattsburg Airport. Though no media coverage had been planned here, several people appeared to welcome my arrival. I visited for about an hour then pressed on for Cleveland—an easy one-hour flight by "water compass": following the Lake Erie shoreline.

As I neared Cuyahoga County Airport in the outskirts of East Cleveland, I noticed the sky to the west darkening and becoming overcast. At the airport, a small crowd greeted me, including several reporters and two ladies who recalled for me their memories of Lindbergh's landing here during his tour. One of the reporters interviewed me at length. Her impressively accurate article appeared in the *Cleveland News Herald* the next day.

Most touching was the 16-year-old working at the airport as a line boy. After my interview and conversations with people in the crowd, he walked up to me and said quietly, "I'd like you to have this. I want to help ORBIS." He held out a five-dollar bill.

As he helped me refuel the plane and move it to a nearby hangar, he told me about his ambition to become a pilot. I was impressed with his sincerity and I hope that today he may be an airline captain.

Beckett Aviation generously provided fuel, hangar and a car, all at no charge. I drove to the Willoughby Travel Lodge for the night. Sometime during the wee hours I woke to discover light rain falling.

Back at the airport after breakfast, I was becoming concerned about what I could expect on my way to Pittsburgh, the next scheduled stop. Weather forecast: rain.

At 9:00 a.m. I took off in a light drizzle. Visibility was good enough; about seven miles. At 2,000 feet I leveled off just below the overcast. Thirty minutes later the clouds lowered and misty rain began to cut the visibility. I eased down to 1,000 feet.

Thirty miles northwest of Pittsburgh, now in heavy rain with a persistently sinking ceiling and visibility closing in, I realized landing at Pittsburgh Metro in the busy Pittsburgh Traffic Control area was no longer a wise intention.

About 20 miles northwest of the city, I put down at Columbiana County Airport, landing on the single runway in pelting rain. Spotting no one at all outside, I taxied to the tie-down line, snapped the cockpit cover in place and trotted through the downpour to the fixed base office. I found just two dejected people in there sitting out the discouraging weather.

I called Holly in New York to tell her I hadn't entirely given up on reaching Pittsburgh Metro, should conditions improve. Since rain was also drenching that airport and publicity opportunities would be scant to none, she doubted my landing at Metro would accomplish much in the way of PR.

"I'll try to press on to Wheeling," I decided. An official welcome was already being assembled there.

I checked Wheeling's weather. A 1,000-foot ceiling with three-mile visibility in light rain.

When the rain eased at Columbiana, I took off in what had subsided to a drizzle, flew west across the Pennsylvania-West Virginia line then followed the Monongahela River south for 30-some miles. The only problem was the multitude of stacks and utility towers along both shores. Some reached as high as 800 feet. I stayed close to the river's center.

As Wheeling drew near, the rain increased and the cloud layer began to press lower. I called the tower. Visibility, I was told, had closed to two miles—just under the minimum for visual flight.

In spite of the deteriorating conditions, I determined to land at Wheeling. I knew I would have some explaining to do if a violation was filed against me, and that definitely would not be publicity ORBIS was hoping for.

The control tower operator seemed to sense my situation. As I approached the field, he came back on the air.

"Waco 130, the visibility is now three miles. You are cleared to land on any runway. There is no reported traffic."

Visibility of three miles made a visual flight regulation landing permissible. In relief, I thanked the tower, throttled back and glided in. As I parked in front of the terminal, rain again poured down. Getting soaked in the process, I wrestled the cockpit cover into place. Then I rushed to the terminal.

Two women from the local Historical Society, all that was left of the welcoming committee, met me at the entrance. The reporters, certain I would never appear in this miserable weather, had all scurried back to town.

Inside the terminal I was greeted by the airport's manager, Tom Tominack, a devoted Lindbergh enthusiast. Two years earlier the airport had hosted a gala celebration of the 60th anniversary of the Lone Eagle's landing there.

To my delight, the terminal's interior decor was that of the 1930s, including a replica ticket counter of that era. Aviation memorabilia was everywhere, with one wall devoted to Lindbergh with pictures, news accounts and replicas of aviation items past. Then a big surprise. On that same wall commemorating notable historic events, Tom had posted news of my flight and a photo of the Waco.

Someone had called one of the departed reporters, and he hustled back to the airport to interview me at great length. I spent some time in Wheeling's impressive terminal, and a kind soul wheeled his Cessna out of his T-hangar so I could roll *Spirit* in for the night. Then I drove to a motel in a car provided by the airport.

A room had already been reserved for me, and despite Mother Nature's efforts to rain me out, I relaxed with a feeling of accomplishment after all.

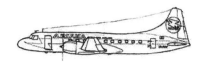

ACROSS THE U.S. BY MAP AND COMPASS

July 31 dawned—barely—with dense fog blanketing Wheeling. I drove to the airport early and called Flight Service. Fog and 100- to 200-foot ceilings with less than a mile visibility for most of my planned route to Dayton, Ohio. No improvement expected today. More of the same tomorrow. To follow my brief Dayton stop, a major PR event had been planned today at Cincinnati. Now it had to be cancelled.

The next morning was no better, but Flight Service did forecast improvement in the afternoon. At 3:00 p.m. Wheeling's visibility increased to a scant three miles, VFR minimum, with a 1,000-foot ceiling.

I took off and flew low level toward Dayton. At this ground-hugging altitude, I kept a sharp eye out for radio towers, some of them higher than I was. Radio transmitting towers were to be a nagging worry when I had to fly low in poor visibility, something Lindbergh didn't have to look out for back in 1927. Nor did traffic controls exist then. On the other hand, he'd had no detailed aviation sectional charts. Lindbergh had navigated with road maps.

With my eyes flicking to chart and compass, the flight to Dayton proceeded smoothly, though my forward vision between the top of the engine and the bottom of the upper wing was never superb.

With improving visibility at the Dayton end, I landed at the Wright Brothers' hometown at 5:00 p.m. A small but enthusiastic crowd of about 10 greeted me: a newspaper reporter, several airport employees and a woman with her two sons. The young boys asked for autographs, and I was happy to comply.

Pie-in-the sky dream? Not for vintage biplane fans
—Dayton Daily News

With *Spirit's* fuel tanks topped off, I soared away again, now headed for Cincinnatti's Lunken Airport, 45 minutes south. At one time the city's major airport, Lunken had been built on low ground in something of a bowl not conducive to jet age expansion. While the city's newer international jet port boomed some 10 miles to the west, "Sunken Lunken" still served smaller aircraft.

As I rolled up to the terminal, I was happy to see Katherine and the others in the van crew right on schedule. Among folks greeting me was talented writer Ann Pester. Ann had arranged a great welcoming extravaganza here at Lunken, but I was so far off schedule it had all collapsed.

The van crew assured me they were having a grand adventure with sight-seeing along the way—and without any difficulties with the rented Olds station wagon.

Daybreak again brought fog that cut visibility below one mile. However, controlled airports have available a special VFR clearance in such minimal conditions. I called the tower and was granted take-off clearance with restricted heading and altitude. I climbed out of Lunken at 11:12 a.m. An hour later, with far less than the best visibility enroute, I landed at Bowman Field, Louisville, Kentucky.

I was welcomed by aviation enthusiast Ed Peck, a former Central American Airways executive who had read National Geographic Magazine's mention of my proposed tour. Ed had arranged for Louisville newspaper, TV and radio coverage. After he and I had lunch, we drove to the home of Lynn and Jim Thomason where I was invited to have dinner and spend the night. Lynn was the daughter of Dorothy and Larry Stetler.

In the morning, thanks to Lynn's PR work I appeared as a guest on a WAVC-TV talk show. Despite a touch of pre-show jitters, I found I enjoyed that brief "show biz" appearance.

Ed returned me to Bowman Field—and guess what? Visibility had deteriorated below the three-mile VFR limit. But shortly conditions improved. A green light from the tower cleared me for take-off on the one-hour, 15-minute flight to Indianapolis Metro Airport.

As I neared Indianapolis, the skies brightened. I landed in pleasant afternoon warmth to a spirited greeting from my van crew, a goodly number of interview-eager media reps, ORBIS ophthamologist Dr. Keith Engel and my old high school classmate, Jack Patton.

Next morning I enjoyed fine visibility through the two-hour flight to Detroit's Mettetal Airport. This time the weather challenge enroute turned out to be a dodge 'em scatter of thunder showers. Just north of the city, tiny Mettetal offered a single north-south paved runway. I could have done without the 20- to 30-knot wind gusting in from the west. My final approach and touchdown in that strong 90-degree cross-wind were just about all the Waco and I could handle. But we managed not to embarrass ourselves.

By prearrangement, the van had been driven on to Chicago. Scott Lorenz, whose family owned the Mayflower Hotel, and flying enthusiast Judy Van Hook met me at Mettetal's modest terminal. We hangared the plane then I enjoyed dinner at the hotel with Scott and his parents. When I appeared for breakfast, I was delightfully surprised by Jim Fisher, one of my closest friends from our World War II ferry pilot days in England.

Before noon, I took off for Grand Rapids. The weather front with its thunderstorms and strong winds had moved east. My hour-long flight west was serene.

I landed at Hastings Airport, a small operation with no paved runways. Having made that appearance to conform with Lindbergh's route, about an hour later I took off again. Now I headed for Bill Rose's private strip northwest of Chicago, not where Lindbergh had landed for his Chicago stop, but close enough. A direct route from Grand Rapids would have taken me across the southern end of Lake Michigan and into O'Hare International Airport's bustling traffic control zone. Instead, I headed for the lake's south shoreline then gave O'Hare a generously wide pass to the west.

As I neared Bill's private field, a Stearman biplane eased into formation just off my left wings. In the rear cockpit, I recognized Mike Lyon. And up front, with a delighted grin: Katherine. Her enthusiasm for this three-month adventure was a major part of my determination to see it through. Mike, Katherine and I flew in formation until I peeled off for the landing.

Spirit was due for an oil change and a general going over, all of this handled in Bill's hangar by one of his capable mechanics. Despite impending surgery, Bill, ever the gracious host, arranged for Katherine and me to stay in his guest house.

The following day, August 6, was Katherine's birthday. We spent it with Bill and Myrt Rose, including a special birthday dinner. At 9:00 in the cool breezy morning, *Spirit* and I took off for Springfield, Illinois. There I was greeted by a small but enthusiastic group, chatted with them briefly, then forged on to St. Louis Regional Airport near Alton in western Illinois.

St. Louis Regional was our staging area for a complex, precisely timed and heavily publicized event at Spirit of St. Louis Airport west of the big city. Arriving at St. Louis Regional in the late morning, I was met by ORBIS's video producer Ozzie Font and the pilots of seven biplanes. After lunch, we all took off to fly in formation to Spirit of St. Louis Airport 35 miles southwest across the Missouri River.

Our dramatic arrival had been engineered by hard working Walter Hubert, who himself piloted a Waco in our eight-plane formation. The only pilot on this nostalgic flight I had previously known was Tom Flock, whom I had met at a Waco fly-in in Ohio. From the front cockpit of Tom's plane, Ozzie Font shot spectacular footage during the flight, a short hop lengthened to 50 minutes by our wide swing around the St. Louis traffic control area.

We landed precisely at 2:30 p.m. as scheduled and taxied en masse to the designated reception area. There we were met by a contingent of ORBIS doctors and nurses and plenty of media folk—print, radio and TV. I received a series of undeserved accolades and proclamations. Many young people pressed for autographs. I accepted all this as graciously as I could manage, but I couldn't help but feel unworthy of all the personal attention. The purpose, after all, was to promote ORBIS, not me. A gala evening affair at the jet center topped off a day in which everything had gone precisely right.

Next morning, August 8, I made my 26th take-off of the tour, this day heading for Kansas City. Two and a half hours later, in fine weather, I brought the Waco into Downtown Airport, the same airport where Lindbergh had landed, along the Missouri River on the Missouri side. The van crew appeared on schedule. Our host, Art Parchen, was a bubblingly retired entrepreneur, fellow pilot and now a researcher/lecturer on Amelia Earhart. Art and his wife Marilyn graciously invited the crew and me to overnight in their home. Art had arranged for TV interviews including my appearance on a Kansas City TV talk show. All of this garnered a batch of first-rate publicity for ORBIS.

The next stop would be Wichita, Kansas, but I would not see the van crew until Minnesota where they would renew my supply of Lupron for my daily self-adminstered injections. Since I was scheduled to stay in Kansas City until the 10th, the crew and I visited the Amelia Earhart Museum in nearby Atchison, with Art as our guide. Visiting the museum's exhibits of memorabilia celebrating Amelia Earhart's life and times was an unforgettable experience.

The next day, August 10, I left for Wichita. As I neared that city, I flew through a couple of light showers then just after 11:00 a.m., landed at Maize Airport northwest of town. Maize lacked a paved runway but it did have an old Stearman duster and a Tiger Moth. Sid Tucker, who had arranged for my use of the airport, owned the venerable British biplane. I was treated to a tour of the Flight Safety Training Center at Wichita Mid-Continent Airport and a complimentary night at the Airport Hilton.

On the morning of the 11th, I departed northeastward for Rosencrans Field back in Missouri at St. Joseph. In 1943, I had received my Army Air Force multi-engine and instrument training at Rosencrans, flying Cessna AT-17 Bobcats and Curtiss AT-9s. I was eager to see how nearly half a century had affected that old USAAF base.

Pilot retraces Lindbergh's tour of 1927
—St. Joseph Press Gazette

Before landing, I circled the field, trying to spot anything from my time there as a new 2nd lieutenant. I looked in vain. All had changed. I landed, taxied to the FBO area and walked into the Express Flight, Inc., office. ORBIS had told manager Pat Macreary I would be arriving, and he had a reporter and photographer on hand. After I was interviewed, I asked several of the local folk if they knew of the Army Air Forces Training Center here back in the 1940s. Not a one of them did, though a couple recalled having heard vaguely from someone else there had been something of that sort way back in the dim mists of time.

I tried to locate the site of the old flight ops building and its ramp. Not a clue. After a few hours at Rosencrans, I remounted *Spirit* and we winged away for the Tri-Cities: Moline, Rock Island and Davenport, straddling the Mississippi River—the Illinois-Iowa line.

Navigating with the use of only the compass and a map, especially in an open cockpit, demanded total concentration. I could easily miss check points clearly shown on the sectional chart but not so easily recognized below. Some map features were not obvious surface features, and the Waco could wander while I was preoccupied with the map and my meager instruments. I'll admit at times I was less than certain of exactly where I was, most often in areas where few checkpoints existed, though I always had a bracketed position.

Yet I found the most stress not in the flying, but in the constant pressure to keep to the schedule for PR purposes. Without that overriding concern, the three-month trip would have been totally enjoyable. But the purpose, after all, was the PR benefit for ORBIS.

During the three hours in the air enroute the Tri-Cities, I spotted just one other aircraft. Remarkably, it turned out to be another Waco. Barrel-rolling above distant broken clouds, its pilot clearly was having a grand time.

At Davenport, Iowa, I was greeted by what had become the more-usual-than-not small but avid group of people with a reporter and photographer. When they dispersed, George Brown from Morris, Illinois, stepped forward, gave me a lift to a nearby motel—and became a friend.

Sunday, August 12, I took off for Milwaukee. The forecast promised spotty light fog and haze with three- to five-mile visibility. I decided to deviate a bit from a straight course and fly over my old crop dusting lands.

I easily picked out Rochelle, Illinois, though the area had changed. The airport west of town was no more, but a large paved runway now lay south of Rochelle. Some of the fields I had dusted in 1948 and '49 were still recognizable. As I settled back on the heading for Milwaukee, I found myself thinking this calm, hazy Sunday morning would be just right for dusting.

At Milwaukee's Timmerman Field, a larger than usual crowd surrounded me—reporters, cameramen and quite a few people from the Experimental Aircraft Association. Barbara Scheibe, manager of Gran-Aire, Inc., was most hospitable. Fuel and hangar space were made available, and I stayed gratis at the Milwaukee River Hilton. The next day, son John arrived in his Piper Twin Comanchee, taking time out from visiting his daughter in Traverse City. The morning of the 14th, I left for Madison, a 35-minute flight westward beneath a low overcast with occasional rain.

Rows of corn flanked Blackhawk Airport's narrow 2,600-foot runway. Traditionally "knee high by the Fourth of July," the corn now stood considerably higher than that. I circled and lined up to land into the gusty west wind. On short final, a sudden and strong current rammed us downward. The old reflexes kicked in and I managed to put the Waco on the runway without bending anything. When I taxied to the small parking ramp and dismounted, airport manager Mary Taylor greeted me.

"Glad to see you got out of that downdraft without real trouble," she told me. "It happens on windy days here, and I've seen more than one pilot land short of the runway."

She and her husband were most accomodating. They helped hangar *Spirit,* drove me to the Fairfield Inn for the night, then picked me up in the morning.

Captain Jack stops in South St. Paul during flight to combat blindness

—South St. Paul Review

Another low overcast day with spotty rain. Flight Service forecast a 500- to 1000-foot cloud base with intermittent rain for most of my 230-mile route to Minneapolis/St. Paul. I had planned to shove off at 9:00 a.m. I stayed put. But the weather didn't get any better. At 10:15, I took off anyway, realizing I might have to turn back. Flying at 500 feet, I dodged dark rain areas until conditions did improve as I reached the Mississippi River. The sun poked through breaks in the overcast and I flew 1000 feet above the river toward South St. Paul's Fleming Field.

A few miles south of the airport, I veered west to circle the town of Savage as Lindbergh had. A wealthy admirer of the Lone Eagle had asked me to offer such a reprise, promising good publicity would result for ORBIS. Which, in fact, did. I landed to an enthusiastic greeting, especially from Ann Woodbeck, a freelance writer who turned out several excellent articles about the tour. That evening she hosted a dinner at her home, including the van crew. They had enjoyed a leisurely drive here, with a stop at the Mayo Clinic to visit Rill Rose who had signed in for knee surgery.

After a scheduled stand down day, I took off on the 17th for Lindbergh's hometown, Little Falls, Minnesota, an easy one-hour, ten-minute flight northwest. With pleasant weather all the way, I landed at Little Falls Airport well before noon. Some 25 people were on hand as I was welcomed by airport manager Rolf Turner and Chuck Stone, director of the Charles Lindbergh Historic Site. There I was given access to areas not available to most visitors, a privilege I most appreciated. Next came an appearance at the Little Falls radio station where I spoke for some 15 minutes. Returning to the airport, I took off around 2:00 p.m. for Fargo, North Dakota.

An hour and half later, under sunny skies, I landed at Jakes Field, a crop dusting enterprise operated by Dick Pratt and David Gust. The old chemical aromas took me back to my dusting days and the three of us had a grand conversation about agricultural flying. Then a kind soul drove me into the city where a newspaper interview had been set up.

After a night at a Days Inn, I was driven back to the airfield for my departure for Sioux Falls, South Dakota, 240 miles directly south. Navigation was simplicity itself: follow Interstate 29, my concrete compass. So navigation was no problem, but wind certainly was. A powerful and unremitting headwind cut my ground speed to about 55 mph. I noticed most cars on the interstate below rolled along faster than I. After only 50 miles, I found myself 17 minutes behind flight plan time. I faced a situation Lindbergh did not have to worry about. While his plane had been modified to cross the Atlantic Ocean with one fuel load, my Waco carried only enough fuel for three and a half flying hours plus a 30-minute reserve. With this strong headwind cutting my ground speed almost in half, I would have to make an unplanned stop enroute to refuel.

Plowing along at what felt like walking speed, I took a close look at my sectional chart for this sparsely populated area. And a few miles west of my route, I spotted an airport at the tiny town of Sisseton. I decided to pull in there for a fill-up. Despite the 30 mph wind, landing was not so difficult. The wind was straight down the 3,400-foot runway. Taxiing to the fuel pump in the persistent wind was more of a challenge.

Two and a half hours after take-off from Sisseton, fortunately with the headwind backing off a bit, I finally landed at Sioux Falls Great Plains Airport. In calm air that flight would have been a non-stop, two-hour 30-minute breeze; my trek from Fargo had taken four hours.

The van crew had already arrived, plus local resident Lauritz "Laury" Larsen, who regularly summered at Crystal Lake. A native American reporter—appropriately a Sioux—interviewed me at length, then after a quick lunch, I was airborne again. Destination, Sioux City, Iowa, 70 miles south and helpfully on my concrete compass route, Interstate 29.

The wind had lessened considerably. I landed at Sioux City's Martin Airport in mid-afternoon, hangared *Spirit* and repaired to a nearby motel. In the early morning, August 19, I lifted off for Perry Airport near Des Moines. The main runway had been pretty well torn up for reconstruction. Under lowering clouds and in a rain shower, I put the Waco down on an adjacent sod strip.

Armed only with compass, maps, and confidence
—Destination Discovery Magazine

Not all my stops were publicity productive, but to validate my Lindbergh tour recreation, I insisted on landing at or near every airport he had—and in the same sequence. After an hour or so at Perry's sleepy field, I took off for Omaha, Nebraska.

Climbing to 700 feet, I found that to be as high as I could go without flying into a solid overcast. Five minutes later, that descending cloud layer had pushed me down to 500 feet. Ten minutes after that, I found myself—as the Brits say—"scraping the chimney pots." Pressed ever downward by the still-lowering overcast, I had no sensible choice but to make a 180 and mush back down on Perry's soggy sod.

Not until the next morning did I depart Perry Airport a second time for Millard Field, Omaha, this time in clearer skies. The van crew had already arrived there, along with the press and TV. Following the media attention, the van crew and I gave *Spirit* a bath to wash away the mud splatters from Perry's sod strip. I changed the oil and gave the old girl a good going over, tightening a nut here and there. This with the help of our host, Ted Lange, owner of Werner Aviation.

Next, a morning take-off for Denver with a planned refueling and overnight stop at McCook, Nebraska. That had not been one of Lindbergh's destinations. His Ryan, with its much longer range, made the long pull from Omaha to Denver non-stop.

West of Omaha, low broken clouds hovered. I climbed to 3,000, putting the clouds below me. Then, to my surprise, the clouds became a solid undercast. According to the weather forecast, that was not supposed to be. I continued to 4,500, the approved VFR altitude for west-bound flight.

After an hour or so, I spotted a small break in the cloud layer below. I spiralled down to what I estimated should be about 500 feet above the ground. But I still had not reached the bottom of the clouds. I climbed back up. Then I saw breaks to the north. Thinking I must be just south of Grand Island, I turned toward those cloud breaks. Spotting a large open space in the cloud layer, I spiralled down again. At about 700 feet, I finally emerged beneath the overcast.

I no longer had faith in the forecast I'd been given at Omaha. With decent visibility, I located Grand Island and landed at Central Nebraska Regional Airport north of town for a serious recheck on the weather ahead. The forecast: better than what I'd just been through. I refueled and promptly took off for McCook, 120 miles west southwest. An hour and 45 minutes later, I set down at McCook, spent the night there, then took off in the morning for Denver. During that two-hour, 30-minute flight, several huge thunderstorms bloomed dead ahead. I gladly yielded the right-of-way and flew around them.

Back on schedule, I stood down in Denver, as Lindbergh had, until August 25. Before my take-off for Cheyenne, I was given a certificate of tribute by Colorado's state government, plus several other commendations. Thanks to local pilot and biplane enthusiast Christine Wolff, Denver TV and press coverage was notable. Thanks also to Christine, I was introduced to a friend of hers who had been flying over the Rockies for years. Soon to attempt my first flying over the Rocky Mountain range, I was eager for any information this veteran mountain pilot might offer.

"If at all possible," he urged, "do your mountain flying early in the morning. In the afternoon, you're likely to run into extremely rough air."

With a weekend airshow planned at Denver, aerobatic practice was underway Friday, the 25th, as I prepared to leave. Spectators were gathering to watch the practice. I was asked to make a low pass after take-off, a parting gesture I was glad to offer.

The temperature at the mile-high airport hovered around 80°. With the already thin air further degraded by the high temperature, with no discernable wind and with the fuel/air mixture necessarily leaned way back, my take-off was lengthy indeed. And it was followed by a sluggish, less than 100-foot-per-minute climb. After I swung around and gingerly made the requested low pass along the runway, I headed for Cheyenne, Wyoming, 100 miles north, just over the state line.

Cheyenne-based Plains Aviation had been the original purchaser of my Waco fresh out of its Troy, Ohio, factory in 1940. Now, 49 years later, the old plane would be returning to its first home. But Plains Aviation, I discovered after landing, was extinct. A couple of airport old timers did remember it, but even the hangar was no more.

A kindly woman who worked at the airfield drove me to the Capital Inn and picked me up the next day at bleary 6:00 a.m. I took off at 7:00, climbed to 10,500 and headed over the Rockies for Salt Lake City, Utah, nearly 400 miles west.

The weather: clear with unlimited visibility. As I had been told, the morning air over the deep valleys and towering peaks was pleasantly smooth. I found the craggy emptiness compelling, a huge expanse of raw nature defying civilization's intrusion.

Again unlike Lindbergh, on this long leg of the tour I had to put down enroute for refueling. I chose Rock Springs, Wyoming, some miles north of a straight-line course but a convenient stops in this part of the Northwest were few and really far between. The tiny airport nestled in a valley along Bitter Creek north of Flaming Gorge Reservoir. Tanks filled, I lifted off again at noon, climbed back to 10,500, still in remarkably clear skies

As I approached the Wasatch Mountain Range on the west edge of the Rockies just east of Salt Lake City, I ran through a patch of afternoon clear air turbulence. That mountain pilot back in Denver had been absolutely right. I throttled back, began my descent and landed at Salt Lake City Municipal Airport No. 2.

At the small terminal building, I spotted a large banner welcoming me to the city. A fine gentleman named Robert T. Race—no known relative of mine, though—headed the group that greeted me on the ramp. Following my appearance in an on-the-spot TV interview, he and his family hosted the van crew and me at their home. Then we overnighted at a motel. Just before I climbed aboard *Spirit* in the morning, Robert handed me an envelope.

"I'd appreciate your 'air mailing' this to my aunt in Santa Monica."

I taped it to the back of the Waco's front cockpit just before take-off.

Next destination: Boise, Idaho. That 300-mile pull northwest also required an intermediate fueling stop. Navigation was simple. I followed the prominent Interstate highway, with the fuel stop at Burley along the Snake River.

Two hours after refueling, I landed at a small airport south of Boise, accommodated the several media reps on hand then housed *Spirit* overnight in a crop dusting outfit's generously donated hangar space.

Now came the challenge of a stop at Butte, Montana. A direct route would involve a 350-mile pull northeast back across the Rockies—mountains all the way with no intermediate refueling stop available. I would be landing without my thin 20- to 30-minute fuel reserve. For an emergency, there would be only a few private strips well off the direct route.

I decided to fly first to Idaho Falls, a 200-mile pull east across less threatening terrain. I would overnight there, then head directly north 175 miles to Butte.

Ex-airline pilot flies around country to battle blindness
—Coeur d'Alene Press

I left Boise in good weather at 7:00 a.m. August 28. Two hours and 45 minutes later I landed at Idaho Falls, greeted there by a reporter and a TV news crew. At dawn the next day, I lifted off for Butte. In the brilliant morning sunlight, the mountains ahead were a magnificent panorama of light, shadow and earthtones. Over Interstate 15—much of that highway around 6,000 feet in elevation—I climbed to 10,500 feet. Most of the flight took me through a long pass. Mountain peaks pressed in on either side.

Two hours and 15 minutes after departing Idaho Falls, I touched down at Butte's Bert Mooney Airport, elated by a flight where truly the "Heavens and Earth declaimed the Glory of God."

I turned to clear the runway and was surprised and delighted to spot an ancient Ford Trimotor—the famed "Tin Goose"—landing behind me.

A reporter met me at the ramp, and while I told her about ORBIS and the tour, we ambled around the Waco. We both were startled to discover the right side of the fuselage drenched with oil, a serious leak. After the interview, I found the oil had spread from one, possibly two push rod housings. Tightening the retaining nuts called for a special tool I did not have, but a friendly mechanic promptly handed me one.

I climbed atop the engine and found one of the push rod housing nuts definitely loose. Hoping my work on the rebel nut had solved the problem, I phoned Waco specialist John Shue back in Pennsylvania and was reassured.

At dawn August 30, I left for Spokane, Washington, a three-hour, 20-minute flight that would "crowd" the Waco's maximum range. Back at 10,500 in good enough weather, I sighted an ominous dark area just south of my proposed track. I swung well around the storm but still bounced through its fringe turbulence.

Beyond Missoula, the sky began to clear nicely. I relaxed to enjoy the rest of the flight over heavily forested mountains, though I was saddened to notice several large areas of clear cutting. Spokane's river-edged Felts Field came into view on schedule, and I glided in. I was greeted by newspaper folk and, among others, friend Hal Swinburne from my Pan Am days.

Aviator retracing Lindbergh's route
—Spokane Chronicle

During a two-day stand down in Spokane, this time to let Lindbergh's schedule catch up with me, I spent considerable time attending to my flying machine. With the volunteer assistance of a local mechanic familiar with Wacos, we changed the oil, adjusted the brakes and conducted a general "tune up."

Friday, September 1, I was off on the three-hour flight to Seattle's Boeing Field. Soon after take-off, broken clouds thickened into a solid overcast. During the first part of the flight my map reading and compass attention was intense. When I reached the foothills of the Cascades, I planned to follow the highway through Snoqualamie Pass right into Seattle. But when I approached the east end of the pass, poor visibility told me I would have to fly very low with mountains all around me. Bad idea.

I spiralled upward to emerge above the clouds at 10,000. I knew once I crossed the Cascade Range I could let down over flat terrain. I flew west for 15 or 20 minutes. Timewise, I estimated I should now be clear of the mountains. Through a break in the cloud cover I caught a glimpse of the Interstate highway directly below. I began my descent.

Then something didn't seem quite right. If I were west of the mountains, the highway should be straight. But my concrete compass was winding through rough country. I was still over the pass—with shrouded mmountain peaks all around me. I hit the throttle, clawed for altitude and stayed on course another 20 minutes. When I let down through another break, this time I was over flat land at last. Soon I spotted the considerable air traffic over Boeing Field.

The tower cleared me in. Press coverage had been arranged by John Ferguson of the airport's Museum of Flight. He gave me a hearty welcome, as did Charlie and Margaret Bennett, old friends from my days in Afghanistan.

I had reached the West Coast—82 hours and 50 minutes flying time with 52 take-offs and landings in a mere 42 days.

"YOU CAN'T PARK HERE!"

The flight from Seattle to Portland, Oregon presented just one problem—a lot of swinging around restricted areas. As I taxied to the ramp at Portland's Hillsboro Airport, I was met by five exceptional people, the Hall Family; George, Jan and their three polite, interested children. Jan had been in contact with ORBIS since she had seen the tour story in *National Geographic* and had invited me to stay with them during my stop at Portland. In their vintage touring sedan, they drove me to their home in a pleasantly wooded area, a home with music and plenty of books, but no TV. This retreat into a less stressful past was a welcome break in my schedule.

Lindbergh had reached his next port-of-call—San Francisco—non-stop. The Waco's limited range required two stops enroute. Though Sunday, September 3, was to be a stand down day, I decided to fly as far as Red Bluff in Northern California's Sacramento Valley, with an intermediate fuel stop in Medford, Oregon. The scenery on the two-hour, 30-minute flight to Medford was spectacular; the Cascade Range to my left, the Pacific's expanse distantly visible to my right.

After a time I felt an undeniable call of nature. There is no relief tube in a Waco UPF-7. The Halls had given me a Ziploc bag of cookies for the trip and I had eaten a few. I stuffed the rest in my jacket pocket and went on from there. High over unpopulated terrain, I banked steeply left and dropped the bag 8,000 feet earthward, hoping for the best.

At Medford, Pat Richardson of the Southern Oregon Historical Society greeted me at the airport. After refueling the Waco and a visit with Pat, I took off south for Red Bluff, California. After an hour and 40 minutes over spectacular mountainous wilderness with Mount Shasta looming off my left wingtips, I glided into Red Bluff Municipal Airport.

At 9:00 a.m. Monday, the 4th, I shoved off for Oakland Metro International Airport across the bay. Designated number six in the landing sequence, I was bracketed by several large aircraft just ahead and another close behind. I kept my airspeed on final at 100 mph and quickly turned clear after touching down.

At the terminal, a red carpet rolled forth and a welcoming committee appeared, including the van crew and John Dobson, a volunteer ORBIS pilot. I was due for replenishment of my medical kit, and the van carried a three-month supply in a cooler to be drawn on as needed. Also meeting me at Oakland was Commander Jeff Fischbeck and family. Jeff was commander of the first submarine to navigate to the North Pole. He was the son of friends, Bob and Lynn Fischbeck, who were summer residents near Crystal Lake.

I planned to leave for Sacramento at 10:00 a.m. the next day, landing at nearby Placerville. An elaborate cook-out was planned there with a special appearance by the mayor and other local dignitaries. Alas, at take-off time a widespread overcast covered the intervening San Joaquin Range. Visual flight over those mountains was out of the question. I called Holly Peppe's assistant in New York, asking her to notify the Placerville folks I would be at least two hours late.

In some desperation around noon, I decided to take off in spite of the cloud cover still shrouding the mountaintops. The airport hummed with incoming and departing IFR-cleared aircraft. I notified the tower I planned to proceed eastward VFR and might I have clearance to climb VFR on top?

"Clearance denied." Much too heavy IFR traffic at all available altitudes. Hoping for a break in the overcast, I shoved off and headed for the mountains with two figures in mind. One, the highest elevation of the ridge line, and, two, the minimum IFR altitude crossing the ridge. I was sure I could climb above the cloud layer before reaching that minimum IFR altitude, thus avoid conflict with IFR traffic. As I neared the mountain range I asked Departure Control for clearance to climb IFR to VFR "on top."

The answer: "Maintain VFR."

I knew I was well below the minimum altitude for IFR traffic, and still would be even when I broke out on top. With a careful eye on my meager "blind flying" instruments—needle, ball and airspeed—I nosed up into the overcast. The key was the needle on the turn-and-bank dial. If I kept that needle absolutely centered at all times, I knew I would be flying dead straight—and with the airspeed well above stalling, no problem.

Within five minutes I broke into the clear above the overcast, congratulating myself on never once seeing the needle even nudge off-center. A few minutes later, I noticed nothing I did made it move off-center. The needle on the old instrument was firmly stuck in place.

Just after 1:00 p.m., I landed at Placerville—more than two hours late. But I was met by a still-friendly crowd.

"We had almost given up on you."

"Didn't ORBIS call you about the delay?"

Blank looks. Usually impeccably responsive ORBIS had fallen down on this one. Though the dignitaries had long since departed, the grill was still hot. I enjoyed a hamburger while explaining the weather problem. Those who had waited for me on faith alone were so gracious about it, I felt the event had been half salvaged and the local papers did carry some coverage the next day. I spent a couple of hours with these fine people while admiring the many vintage aircraft at the airport.

With a forecast of probable heavy turbulence below 15,000 feet over the Sierras, I left Placerville at 3:00 p.m. headed for a 90° crossing of that range in the area of infamous Donner Pass. With that unsettling turbulence prediction in mind, I began a full-throttle climb. As I neared 13,000 feet, the thin air had cut the Waco's normal 580-feet-per-minute ascent to a mere 100 feet per minute. I kept on at full throttle, expecting turbulence at any moment. At 13,800 feet, my climb rate had decreased to less than 50 feet per minute. I leveled off, still waiting for the first ominous bump—but I crossed the range in air as smooth as pond ice. And it stayed that way.

In the rarified air, I discovered if I moved my head rapidly, my eyes unfocussed for several seconds. Slower head movements solved that small problem.

On the east side of the mountains, I glided into Reno-Stead Airport, so-named in honor of Bill Stead, founder of the Reno Air Races there in 1964. With the 1989 races not yet underway, I was given an informal tour of the area while I waited for Bruce Gruenwald to pick me up for an overnight stay at the Gruenwalds' home. Bruce and his wife Mindy had read about my flight in *National Geographic,* hence the invitation. Following a barbeque that evening, I was guest speaker at Reno's First

Baptist Church, courtesy of Pastor Dr. Edmund Irwin. Early in the morning, I raced off for Santa Monica, another long haul with two intermediate stops.

After a two-hour, 15-minute grind through heavy haze with close attention to my navigation, I landed at Los Banos in the San Joaquin Valley between San Jose and Fresno. After refueling, I took-off for the hour-and-a-half leg to Santa Paula, about 50 miles up the coast from Los Angeles. The opportunity to visit Dan Sjoberg, one my my closest WWII friends, had made Santa Paula my choice for the overnight stop. And there I rendezvoused with Katherine, the crew, Dan—and Lisa Stetler of Wavery who had driven up from Los Angeles as a special greeter.

Culmination of a lifelong dream
—Santa Paula Chronicle

Noted as a base for many vintage aircraft, the nearly 60-year-old airport also served many Hollywood notables who were flying enthusiasts, among them Steve McQueen, Gene Hackman and Leonard Nimoy. Santa Paula was—and still is—serviced by Screaming Eagles Aviation.

Owner Doug Dullenkopf told me Dan Sjoberg had been taken to the hospital quite ill with cancer. I rushed there and found Dan better than I had feared, and we had a good half hour visit. That evening a champagne reception in the hangar centered around the Waco itself. While these festivities were in progress, a car drove onto the ramp. In the back sat a grinning Dan Sjoberg, on a pass from the hospital. That was a great moment for both of us, but alas, it was our last get-together. After I returned to Clifford, he wrote me that he was feeling better but when he'd endured a recent "bad patch," he'd had "a glimpse of the other side." Sadly, a few months later, Dan died.

On the morning of September 8, I departed for Santa Monica, a mere 40 miles southeast. Ten minutes after take-off, I noticed a Piper Cherokee 6 keeping pace on my right and closing in. Through an opening in the Cherokee's side, someone aimed a camera. I learned later he was Doug Dullenkopf, taking what turned out to be the absolutely best photos ever shot of the Waco in flight.

As I neared Santa Monica Municipal Airport, the tower informed me I would be number eight to land. I could see only two planes on their final approaches. When I reported I was turning to the base leg prior to final, the tower ordered me to continue on the downwind leg. I spotted another aircraft ahead. Then another behind me. Finally I was cleared to land, "but keep up your speed." A busy place. I was relieved when I cleared the runway.

I parked in front of the Santa Monica Museum of Flying and was greeted by Bill Worden and a respectable crowd. Bill represented the museum and Angel Flight, a group of volunteer aircraft owners and pilots who flew seriously ill people and their familes to distant destinations. Bill was accompanied by a sizeable crowd and the van crew handed out a small blizzard of ORBIS brochures. When the excitement died down, I managed to personally deliver Robert Race's "airmail" letter from Salt Lake City to his aunt in Santa Monica.

Santa Monica was as close as I wanted to get to the heavy air traffic around LAX—Los Angeles International—and that huge airport lay directly on the route to San Diego. Before take-off on the 10th, I had planned to fly a wide detour around LAX. Then Bill Worden told me VFR flights could be cleared right over the airport: 4,500 feet northwestbound, and 3,500 feet southeastbound, with strict radio silence both ways.

That worked out nicely. Clear of the LAX area I dropped down to 1,000 feet just off-shore and followed the coastline for an easy flight to San Diego-Montgomery Field. There I was joined again by the van crew—and by Milt Massey from Waverly, Pennsylvania, where we had become good friends through the First Baptist Church. Retired from RCA, he was a strong supporter of ORBIS—and loved to ride in the Waco. I had agreed to fly him from San Diego to Tucson where he would join his wife.

At this point, with two thirds of the tour behind me, I was becoming a bit testy. The physical strain? The pressure of meeting the schedule? The inescapable awareness of cancer? Come on, Jack, I told myself. Think of all those warm welcomes at almost every airport where you've appeared. And you're about to head east, toward home.

September 11 my support crew—Katherine, Betty and Rip—set out for their 500-mile drive to Tucson. Shortly after they left, Milt and I took off for our intermediate refueling stop at Yuma, Arizona. Beneath an overcast with lower clouds, we crossed the mountain ridges 50 miles east. Then we enjoyed smooth sailing in clearer weather across flat Imperial Valley close to the Mexican border.

When we pulled up to the refueling area at Yuma International Airport, we baked in stifling 110° heat. The temperature-thinned air made our take-off run unusually long. As we climbed out of Yuma, I was told later, the van crew barreling along Interstate 8 happened to spot us, the only time they had sighted the Waco enroute during the entire tour.

Three hours later, we touched down at Tucson's Ryan Field, greeted there by a small group of interested folks, a reporter and, shortly, by the ever-dependable van crew. Milt's wife, Billie, also met us at the airport, and she and Milt drove off for a vacation in Sedona.

In the early morning of September 12, the van departed for El Paso, Texas. At 8:00 a.m. I lifted off for the hour-and-a-half flight to Lordsburg, New Mexico, where Lindbergh had landed this same date in 1927. I was to be honored there by the mayor, and landed precisely at 9:30 a.m., as requested. As I cut the switch and climbed down, only a woman clutching a bouquet and a sparse handful of people stood near the ramp.

Where was the mayor? The expected crowd?

"You're an hour late," I was told. "You were scheduled to be here at nine-thirty."

I checked my watch. "It is nine-thirty."

"No, it's ten-thirty."

What? Then the mystery was solved. Arizona stayed on standard time while the rest of the country, including New Mexico, leaped an hour ahead to daylight time. Arizona's 9:30 was Lordsburg's 10:30. Taking off on Arizona's standard time, and now on New Mexico's daylight time . . .

Embarrassing indeed. But the durable flower lady who had waited presented me with two dozen of the most beautiful red roses I had ever seen. Lordsburg, I was told, was widely noted for its exquisite roses. Though the mayor had departed, he had left his proclamation for me. I spent an hour and a half with the patient and gracious few who'd had faith in my eventually showing up, then I headed for Texas.

Winging through rain showers enroute, I landed in mid-afternoon at El Paso International where small aircraft were not warmly welcomed. Thanks to Lawrence Smith of the El Paso Aviation Hall of Fame, I had been given special clearance. I turned off the runway as quickly as I could and headed for the hangar space kindly offered by Hughes Aircraft. An oil change was due, and I would give my old flying machine a complete inspection tomorrow.

The van crew and I were honored at a luncheon in the museum, replete with a proclamation, awards and a bunch of good publicity for ORBIS.

At El Paso I had hoped to find a replacement for my defective turn-and-bank indicator with its frozen needle. But such an antiquated instrument was not to be had—until the evening of my departure September 14. An accomodating fellow showed up with one he believed was operational. I paid him a modest sum and planned to install it in the near future.

In the morning, I set forth on another long pull, this one due north to Santa Fe, New Mexico, a four-hour flight not do-able non-stop in the Waco. For refueling, I made an intermediate landing in gusty wind at remote Socorro, New Mexico.

Holly Peppe, now back in action at ORBIS after a two-week hiatus, had arranged the Santa Fe event, coordinated locally by super-efficient Alice Dobson. The large crowd on hand was attracted by the ORBIS tour—and the inauguration of the airport's new terminal building. Orville Johnson, owner/manager of Capital Aviation, donated hangar space and fuel.

Just before sunrise the next morning, I left for Littlefield, Texas, 35 miles northwest of Lubbock. That two-hour, 35-minute flight took me over barren, rocky terrain with no outstanding features to use as check-points. I paid really close attention to compass and clock. Refueled at Littlefield's little field, I headed for the day's final destination, Abilene.

At Abilene's Elmdale Airport I landed to a warm welcome by manager Bill Masters, and his wife, Nancy, had lunch at their home and returned to the airport for a productive session with a reporter and photographer. The Masters had invited me for the night, but I found myself too weary to be a respectable guest. I opted for a nearby Motel 6.

Pilot reliving Lindbergh's tour of U.S.
—Dallas Times Herald

Next morning, an undemanding hour-and-a-half flight took me to Fort Worth's Hicks Airfield, some 15 miles northwest of the city's center. I talked with a small but warm group there, and within the hour took-off for Addison Airport, Dallas, landing at noon to a grand reception. Chaparral Aviation donated fuel and hangar space. Holly herself was on hand with Ozzie Font handling video coverage for ORBIS. Media interest included a TV crew from Dallas Channel 4.

As I stepped down to the ramp, I was delighted to see Wilson Tayloe, the third of my three closest World War II pilot friends. Now a successful Dallas businessman, Wilson invited Holly, the van crew and me to dinner at his home where we met his British "war bride," Mary.

After a pleasant stand down day September 17, I shoved off for Oklahoma City, an easy two-hour flight to City Expressway Air Park a few miles north of the city. After several press interviews, I decided to forego the planned overnight there. The flying weather was too benign to pass up, so when the PR program wrapped up, I left for Tulsa. An Oklahoma City TV news helicopter briefly escorted me northward recording footage for that evening's newscast.

Veteran pilot channels efforts against blindness
—The Daily Oklahoman

At Tulsa's Jones Riverside Airport, home of the National Biplane Association, I was greeted by members of the association and given hangar space. Some limited newspaper coverage was drummed up, but my day-early, out-of-schedule arrival turned out to be a bad idea PR-wise. I stood down in Tulsa until my scheduled September 21 departure. I spent some pleasant hours with Charlie Harris, president of the Biplane Association, and several of his enthusiastic members.

Tulsa was the home base of Oral Roberts, the TV evangelist particularly noted some years ago for locking himself in his prayer tower until several millions of dollars were donated to his cause. It had appeared he was doomed to stay up there until the remaining seven-figure sum needed was pledged by a single donor. The van had arrived, and Katherine and I visited Roberts's expansive grounds and talked with many pleasant people.

Thursday, the 21st, I flew the short 30-mile hop southeast to modest Hatbox Field, Muskogee, Oklahoma. A twin Comanchee landed just after I had, and who was flying it? None other than John Shue with his son, Scott, on their way home from the Reno Air Races. John had a copy of my itinerary, but his appearance at Muskogee the same time I arrived was a fortunate coincidence.

As our planes were refueled, we chatted about my troubles with the turn-and-bank indicator and the second-hand replacement I had bought in El Paso.

"I'm sure I'll be hitting bad weather somewhere along the way," I told John, "so I'm going to install the replacement here."

"I'll put it in for you right now," he offered. And so he did, coincidentally fulfilling his promise to come wherever and whenever the Waco had mechanical problems. In short order I was back in the air.

Another day, another state
—Arkansas Gazette

The weather forecast for my next destination, Little Rock, Arkansas, was not invigorating. For two hours I flew through areas of low cloud and reduced visibility to North Little Rock Airport. There Russ Rivenburg and his wife Sylvia, friends from Clifford Baptist, greeted me. Sylvia was a native of Little Rock, and they visited the city each year. After media including TV interviewed me at the airport and dinner with Sylvia's family, I overnighted at yet another Days Inn.

Next morning: off for Memphis, an hour-and-a-half leg in cloudy skies with five-mile visibility. Steve Charles, an ORBIS ophthalmologist at Memphis was to have arranged hangar space, but when I arrived he was out of town. I taxied to the terminal as planned, dismounted and was met by a crotchety lineman.

"You can't park here."

"Where do you think I might park?"

"Dunno." Then he pointed. "Maybe at yonder hangar."

I climbed back aboard and taxied to yonder hangar.

Another discomfited lineman approached. "Can't park here."

Not exactly a hero's welcome in Tennessee's largest city. Then I remembered Steve was to have talked with Memphis Aero about fuel and hangar space. The lineman sent me in that direction. Haven at last. I talked with the manager and was given hangar space, fuel and a lift to a hotel. Though no PR had been planned for Memphis, the director of ORBIS's community health programs, Mrs. Eun-Joo Chang-Prewitt met me at the airport with moral support and encouragement.

A strong east wind cut next day's ground speed to 60 mph for most of my 200-mile flight to Nashville. What should have been a two-hour flight took almost three. When I landed at Cornelia-Fort Airpark northeast of the city, the van was already on-site. In a welcome change from my Memphis experience, airport manager Ernest Colbert was the soul of hospitality. Holly arrived in the afternoon and put together a fine PR effort. With the next day scheduled for stand down, we visited the Grand Old Opry House and other landmarks of musical note. I was given a proclamation- and a Gold Record, highly unusual for a sometime saxaphonist of no repute whatever.

Retracing Lindbergh's visionary flight saves sight in 1989

—Birmingham Post Herald

On the 25th, low clouds and rain showers enlivened my one-hour, 10-minute flight to Chattanooga. After a moderate PR effort there, I was off again, this time for Birmingham, Alabama, landing in mid-afternoon. Red Barron Aviation offered a pleasant welcome, a reporter showed up for the customary interview, then Connie Barron loaned me a car for the trip to a motel.

Though some distance from Lindbergh's Jackson, Mississippi stop, my arrival at Yazoo City northeast of Jackson would have to suffice. A prominent Yazoo citizen and ORBIS supporter had prevailed upon us to make the September 26 stop there. Though rain showers and stretches of poor visibility made the two-hour flight from Birmingham a touch challenging, I landed at the planned time. Bob Bailey, his son, and a group from the local Lions club hosted my appearance there.

Shortly I bid the good people at Yazoo City farewell and shoved off for New Orleans, a two-hour flight above a solid cloud layer. As I passed over Jackson, I was startled to see the top of a radio tower go by. Poking up through the overcast, its tip was even with me 2,000 feet above the ground.

Katherine, Betty and Rip awaited me at Lakefront Airport, an airfield jutting into Lake Pontchartrain and surrounded on three sides by water.

Early ORBIS pilot Leonard Sandridge and a press rep joined us at Aero Services International. During our three days in The Big Easy, Aero Services helped change the Waco's oil, clean the spark plugs and adjust the brakes.

The spirit of Lindbergh lives
—The Times-Picayune, New Orleans

Next, a long pull to Jacksonville, Florida with a refueling stop at Crestview, 40 miles east of Pensacola. Weather: marginal VFR with clouds at 1,000 feet and, stretching it a bit, three-mile visibility. The countryside was fairly flat, but restricted military areas along the gulf coast called for precise navigation.

Past Crestview the cloud base began to drop—down, down . . . and I flew into steady hard rain. In just moments I had been pressed down to treetop level. Time to make the sensible 180 and retreat.

Then in the green wilderness some 20 miles north of Tallahassee, I caught a glimpse of a tiny grass airport. I made a quick turn, lined up on the north-south strip—the only strip—and squished *Spirit* down with a major sigh of gratitude.

I taxied to a stop near a solitary small airplane tied down by an empty, open-sided hangar. So far, I hadn't seen another human being. As the rain let up, I climbed down to walk through the soaked grass to a small shack with a sign: OFFICE. I stepped in to find an elderly couple eyeing me. In retrospect, I realize they weren't much older than I, but I was surprised to find they were the owners. I had happened upon a mom-and-pop aerial enterprise that looked like a set for a 1930s aviation movie.

Pleasantly accomodating, they told me to push the Waco into the hangar for the night. It didn't really need gas, but I topped off the tanks anyway.

"There's a motel a few miles up the road," pop told me. "Give 'em a call."

I phoned the place. "Can you pick me up here at the airport?"

"Sure thing."

Driven back to the aiport in the morning, I paid for the gas. "How much for the use of the hangar?"

"Well," the grizzled owner said, "I'll only charge you fifteen bucks for that."

Not a bad fee for a timely port in a storm—a storm with a name. I had been forced down by the fringe of Hurricane Hugo.

The weather had cleared for my one-hour, 40-minute flight to Jacksonville's Herlong Airport just southwest of the city. After a spot of

PR work there, I refueled and headed north for Atlanta Falcon Airport.

As I flew over the incredible expanse of Okefenokee Swamp, I found myself praying the old engine wouldn't "pack it up" and splash me down among the alligators. It purred on and the three-hour flight was problemless. At Falcon, the van crew and Len and Mimi Goodman, friends from Pan Am days, were on hand as I arrived. Katherine and I were soon joined by our son John, who was attending an Atlanta meeting of the Manufacturers of Business Aircraft.

October 3 I lifted off for Spartanburg, South Carolina, a two-hour trip in generally good weather—except for big stretch of ground fog enroute, carefully avoided. With excellent press at Spartanburg, the occasion was highlighted by the appearance of 25 students from the school for the blind. Everyone of them itched to "see" the Waco. I was glad to guide them around the plane, then with the help of their teachers, seated them in the cockpit, one by one.

Pilot travels Lindbergh's route to promote eye hospital
—Winston-Salem Journal

Next stop this same day: Winston-Salem, North Carolina. As Carol Torkington, a frequent Crystal Lake visitor, showed me around town, the aroma of tobacco seemed to lurk everywhere. After overnighting there, I left for Richmond, Virginia. Two hours later, I swung into Richmond International Airport's traffic pattern, an airspace so congested I felt barely tolerated by the tower operator. Taxiing to the airport's Virginia Eagles Air Museum, I was regaled by an almost overwhelming reception—Eagles officials, press, TV, radio, a lifetime membership in the museum, lodging at Embassy Suites and a dinner the next evening at the Jefferson Hotel, including the just-arrived van crew. All beautifully arranged by Marty Torkington, Carol's mother.

October 6, I left Richmond for Maryland's College Park Airport northeast of Washington. I had been pounding along on this self-imposed, demanding, sometimes exhausting aerial trek since July 22. Given my age and the limitations of my old airplane, some pessimists were still convinced I would never make it. Now, with the next stop only a few hundred miles from home, I was sure I would cross the finish line, and on schedule. Only seven days to go.

Halfway to College Park, the white silk scarf I had worn since the tour's beginning on Long Island whisked away in the slipstream. An omen? I called Approach Control, identified myself and my destination and waited for instructions on skirting the District of Columbia.

To my surprise, the pleasantly accommodating controller responded, "Maintain 3,000 feet, and you may take a direct route to College Park."

In excellent visibility, I headed directly across Washington, DC. Today, after the inhumanity of the Trade Center and Pentagon attacks, flying over Washington invites the appearance of armed F-15s. A few minutes after crossing the impressive panorama of the nation's capital, I descended into the historic airport where the Wright Brothers had conducted many of their demonstration flights for government and military observers. Already on site, the van crew and Holly Peppe watched me touch down.

In the cold, windy morning—and with Holly in the front cockpit—we flew the short hop to Baltimore Air Park. A goodly crowd had gathered to watch us land amid wind gusts on the uphill runway. I worked hard at setting *Spirit* down smoothly, a three-point landing videotaped for that evening's TV newscasts. And Ozzie Font had reappeared to record the tour's final legs.

Airport manager Alice Grow donated hangar space until the 9th when I left for Atlantic City with Ozzie as passenger. After a chilly hour aloft, we glided in low over the Trump Casino to touch down at Bader Field.

Aviator fights to save sight through flight
—The News Journal, Wilmington

After a press interview, we were off again, now bound for Wilmington, Delaware. There we were hosted by a Dupont family member and generated publicity aplenty. Ozzie left for New York. After a night in a Wilmington motel, I took off for Philadelphia's Northeast Airport. Holly, the van crew, and Rev. Dr. Claude Pullis and his wife Esther, ministry friends, helped generate a bunch of good publicity.

October 14 dawned bright and clear for the final leg of this grand adventure. One small glitch had arisen: I could not land back at Bayport Aerodrome where all this had begun. Major reconstruction had closed the field. I chose Brookhaven as a close alternate. I lifted out of Philadelphia at 10:40 a.m., flew at 1,400 feet until I reached Red Hook, New Jersey, then let down to 1,000, the required altitude for passing south of Kennedy International. I made landfall at South Beach, throttled back and landed at Brookhaven 15 minutes past noon.

Katherine, our son John, grandson Josh, a bunch of ORBIS people with Oliver Foot and media folks—a crowd of more than 100—surrounded *Spirit* near a huge welcoming banner. I found all of this an overwhelming and truly touching celebration.

The Lindbergh tour had been accomplished. ORBIS had been widely promoted coast-to-coast. But for me, the flight would not be truly over until I landed back at Clifford with Katherine aboard.

After a night on Long Island, we returned to Brookhaven to find the cloud base at a mere 300 feet, a dismally low ceiling. Wilkes-Barre/Scranton Control reported five miles visibility in haze and improving. We waited. And waited.

At noon, the cloud base at Brookhaven lifted to 500 feet. I decided to take off. With Katherine up front, we headed north—and low—across Long Island. We didn't make it to the north shore. Ceiling and visibility worsened to the point where the possibility of slamming into one of the island's many radio towers became a life-threatening risk. I swung back over Brookhaven and decided to fly south then climb through the overcast into clear air above. Worth a try—and this time I had a turn-and-bank indicator that actually worked.

Over the water we headed up into the overhanging fleece. At 4,000, we broke out above the cloud layer. I set course for Clifford.

A chilly hour later, the undercast began to break up. Directly below lay the Bear Mountain Bridge. On course. I lofted a thank-you to the Lord. Katherine confessed later, "I had been praying since take-off."

Just after 2:00 p.m., the Waco's wheels kissed the sod of home base. Dozens of people—many of them from the churches I had pastored—several men of the cloth and area press and TV reporters roared a welcome. I cut the switch. Katherine and I stepped down. Then all of us formed a great circle of prayer around faithful old *Spirit of ORBIS*.

Veteran pilot fulfills his lifelong dream
—The Scrantonian

In 88 days I had flown 18,900 miles in 180 flying hours, made 96 take-offs and landings and burned 2,166 gallons of fuel.

The van crew had driven 13,718 miles with no mechanical problems whatever and had rendezvoused with me 25 times. Without that unflagging support of Katherine, Betty and Rip, the tour would not have been nearly so successful.

In behalf of ORBIS, the Lindbergh tour reprise had generated interviews or news coverage in 86 newspapers, on 18 radio stations and 114 TV channels. Articles had appeared in *National Geographic, Flying, Airways, Discovery* and possibly other magazines.

In some areas during the tour, I had been depressed by smoke-belching stacks, clear-cut forest areas and some polluted rivers. Yet from my slow-moving aircraft at low altitudes, I could fully appreciate what a beautiful country this is, with kind and generous people everywhere I had touched down.

CHAPTER 34

A RISKY CASE OF "GET HOMEITIS"

After renewing my FAA currency requirement in Denver, I traveled via Pan Am to Vanna, Bulgaria to fly the ORBIS DC-8 to Frankfurt. The next day, I returned to the U.S. on Pan Am and rounded out 1989 with a few Clifford area flights in the faithful old Waco.

My weekly trips to ORBIS's New York office continued into 1990. Ray Brooks, a United pilot, had volunteered to fly with us, and I decided he might do well as a fill-in pilot. With a mission nearing completion in Douala, Cameroon, Ray and I met there to fly the DC-8 to its next mission at Ibadan in neighboring Nigeria. Required to land first at Lagos to clear Nigerian customs, we found the experience totally exasperating. Only Flight Engineer Pat Healy and I were permitted to leave the plane. To expedite the purposely dragged out clearance procedure, we eventually complied with the standard requirement to speed things up: baksheesh. Waiting palms were crossed with silver, and we were suddenly cleared for our 30-minute flight to Ibadan. The next day a hired car and driver drove Pat and me back to Lagos for our Pan Am flight home. Swarms of haphazard traffic domineered the road, but we made the 100-mile trip suffering only a flat tire.

In May, Katherine accompanied me to San Diego for an ORBIS flight from California to Honduras on the 13th. Oliver came along for the four-hour trip and sat in the cabin with Katherine.

"I much enjoy flying with Jack," he told her, "and he always makes smooth landings."

My approach to the airport at San Pedro Sula was on the money. Airspeed and sink rate right on. I flared out expecting to feel the wheels' gentle roll. But it was rock and roll. I discovered later the approach end of the runway was deteriorating. Pilots in the know were landing long to avoid the rumpled patch. I've always felt it poor form to make excuses for a shabby touchdown, but in this case . . . .

Katherine and I spent the day in San Pedro Sula. Warned to avoid certain areas, we were careful and watchful. Or so we thought. Despite our alertness, some nimble-fingered scoundrel managed to make off unnoticed with Katherine's camera.

Early in the year, I purchased a four-place, single-engined Cessna 172. Though it was 18 years old, the plane was in fine shape with not much time logged. At the end of May, Katherine and I flew it to Georgetown, South Carolina, for a two-day visit with my brother Don, long retired from the dairy industry. He and his wife Jean now lived on nearby Pawleys Island.

The weather forecast for our flight home was marginal with VFR conditions deteriorating to IFR in the middle of the route, then improving to marginal again. Two hours after leaving Georgetown on the return trip, we landed for fuel at Chase City, North Carolina. Nobody in sight, except one sad-eyed dog. We walked to the office. The door was locked. Another ghost airport.

"We're getting sympathy from the dog," I told Katherine, "but that's all we're going to get here." I checked our sectional chart. Sixty miles later, the airport at Farmville proved to be open for business. We refueled and pressed on—now in decidedly murky weather. Not an hour out of Farmville, I set us down at Orange County Airport near Orange, Virginia for an updated weather forecast. Solid IFR well past Harrisburg, Pennsylvania. I filed an IFR flight plan to Wilkes-Barre/Scranton at 7,000 feet.

When we climbed to that altitude, we were still in solid cloud—and now in heavy rain. As we passed over Harrisburg, visibility at the airport there was reported as one mile beneath a 200-foot ceiling. A few minutes later, we broke out above the solid cloud layer. To get us down through that undercast, I requested clearance for an IFR approach to Wilkes-Barre/Scranton Airport.

"Denied," came the response. "We have an airshow in progress." An airshow? "But you are cleared for a non-precision IFR descent to Seamans Airport." Which lay fairly close to Clifford. Then I spotted a good-sized break in the cloud layer, cancelled the IFR clearance, spiralled down over Harveys Lake a few miles northwest of Wilkes-Barre and flew VFR on to Clifford. A happy ending.

I continued my mid-week Bible study group at Clifford Baptist and made an occasional pulpit appearance. In June, I flew the Cessna to Shippensburg, Pennsylvania for a three-day American Baptist Retreat. The Shippensburg Airport was deserted—my third landing at a totally unoccupied field. I flew on to Chambersburg Airport, 10 miles away, where the manager kindly loaned me a car for the drive back to the retreat at Shippensburg.

Katherine and I made several more flights that year, one of them to Bridgeport, Connecticut in the Cessna. There we boarded a ferry boat to Port Jefferson on Long Island for a gathering of former Pan Am pilots. After lunch and a session of tall tales, we caught the 4:00 p.m. ferry back to Bridgeport, took off and flew westward in mid-June rain beneath low cloud. I zig-zagged along, looking for a break, found one and climbed through the cloud layer, only to find we were sandwiched between it and a higher layer. About 50 miles from Clifford, the bottom layer began to break into low scattered clouds, very low. In sight of Carbondale, we descended to pick our way around the cloud clumps—and so to Clifford.

That evening, I had a call from friend John Harris, who had driven us from the ferry slip to the airport.

"Ah . . . really good to hear your voice, Jack. How did the flight home go?"

"Well enough, John, but it wasn't a pleasant one."

"You had me worried. While I was driving home from the airport in the rain, I heard on the car radio that a plane had crashed right after take-off from Bridgeport—just about the time you would have taken off. Gave me a heck of a scare until I found out it wasn't you."

That same month, Katherine and I flew my old biplane to the Waco Historical Society Fly-in at Lavelle Farm, a private strip near Troy, Ohio. I circled the Troy area looking for the strip indicated on my chart, thought I spotted it and we glided down to land on the rough sod. No one around. Then a car drove in. Out hopped Jack Wilhelm, my contact with the Waco group.

"Saw you circling, Jack. This isn't Lavelle." He pointed. "Lavelle is three miles that way."

We were the first to land at Lavelle's corn-edged strip—this one not appearing on the map. At the exhilarating two-day get-together I was asked to speak on the 48-state tour at a dinner and the next day treated Troy's Mayor Campbell to a flight in the Waco. Then Katherine and I flew on to Mt. Vernon, Ohio, for the annual National Waco Fly-In. At least 40 of the venerable aircraft appeared, and again I found the 48-state tour to be of lasting interest.

On November 1, I invited Katherine along to San Salvador, El Salvador where I would fly the ORBIS jet to Jamaica on the 3rd. The city was in a state of unrest. Groups of young people roamed downtown, shouting and fighting. At dinner one evening, we were told someone had been killed in a recent skirmish right in front of the restaurant. But despite the widespread political unrest between the poor and the prosperous, there was outspoken appreciation in San Salvador for ORBIS's humanitarian work there.

In early March, 1991, Clifford Baptist asked me to serve as interim pastor until a permanent replacement could be found for their departing pastor. "I'll be glad to accept the offer," I said, " but for no longer than 15 months." That same month, Oliver asked me to journey to Ecuador, this time as advance man for a coming ORBIS mission there. The permitting process, aircraft parking clearance and access arrangements took about a week on-site. I returned to Clifford just before Easter to begin my pastoral duties.

Notable flights that year included the Waco's appearance in an airshow at Wilkes-Barre/Scranton Airport. My old biplane made a stunning contrast to the Navy's Blue Angels fighter jet team howling overhead.

The venerable Waco's most notable hop that year carried aloft Bishop Timlin of the Catholic Diocese of Scranton. By pre-arrangement, I welcomed him aboard at Wilkes-Barre/Scranton Airport. We had a good conversation then a fine flight over the Lackawanna/Luzerne Valley area. The bishop, himself an alumnus of Scranton Municipal Airport and an accomplished airman, did most of the flying.

With its aging DC-8 growing seriously tired, ORBIS began efforts to replace it with a much larger Douglas DC-10. I had never flown a DC-10, and having reached 70 in May, I was not eager to go through the rigorous training to qualify. Though Oliver urged me to stay on in a non-flying capacity, I felt the time had arrived to say farewell to ORBIS. I decided to bow out gracefully at year's end.

But first came a November reception at the United Nations Building in New York to formally recognize ORBIS's worldwide humanitarian work. Oliver, Holly, one of the ophthalmologists and I spoke in behalf of ORBIS, followed by several foreign diplomats who praised the organization.

On December 31, I resigned as chief pilot from Project ORBIS. At age 70+, I had joined a small group of septuagenerian pilots still flying airline four-engine jet aircraft. One of my friends claimed I was the oldest, but I can't verify that. I was gratified to have been a part of ORBIS's humanitarian mission. I had become convinced that helping and serving others was far more important than war in healing our unsettled world. And I had learned people everywhere have the same hopes and dreams.

Now my work centered around the church—Sunday services, weddings, visiting the ill and incapacitated, Meals on Wheels. But I flew the Waco and Cessna whenever possible.

In June, 1992, Clifford Baptist's search committee succeeded in calling a full-time pastor. My commitment as interim pastor ended and within days, Milt Massey and I flew the Waco to the annual and now overwhelmingly huge Oshkosh event. Ever-hospitable Bill Rose was our host overnight at Barrington. The next day we winged on to Oshkosh as a guest member of his squadron of classic planes. The big event was impressive, as always. At one point, Bill invited Milt and me to fly with him in his Grumman Goose to an island he owned in a Wisconsin lake. He generously asked me to fly the Goose and land on the lake. What memories that evoked. Conditions were just right for our glass-smooth landing. Not bad, if I can be just a bit immodest; I hadn't flown a Goose in 40 years.

On a side trip across Lake Winnebago for breakfast at New Holstein's big grass field, I was struck by a remarkable sight. On a portion of the field a dozen or so lawn mowers ceaselessly whirred back and forth. The hilarious result of a runaway computerized purchase order? No. "What you're looking at," I was told, "is a lawn mower test site.

Heading home, Milt and I had no problem at our first refueling stop, Plymouth, Indiana. But as we approached the next one at Wayne County Airport, Ohio, I noticed a big X on the single runway. The airport was shut down. We flew on to Akron/Canton, 20 minutes east, overnighted there, then took-off for Clifford in the morning.

Kind of thought-provoking when you're about to land and find your destination out of business with no prior notice anywhere. Without the major support of G.I. Bill students or any comparable program, many small airports were having a tough time.

In April, 1993 Katherine and I flew the Cessna to Florida to attend Sun-N-Fun near Orlando, something of a minor Oshkosh. We stayed at Mike Lyon's place at Eagles Nest, an aviation community, shuttling back and forth to the Orlando event. Our exciting time there was capped by our flight home. The dramatics began after we spent the night in Salisbury, Maryland. In a strong northwest wind with gusts well past 30 mph, our ground speed seemed like a fast walk. I realized we would have to make an unplanned fueling stop at Allentown, Pennsylvania. In a heaving sea of air, we rocked and rolled in there, refueled, and bounced back into what felt like heavy surf over the Pocono Mountains. Ground speed sank to about 50 mph.

Our approach to Clifford took us into some of the roughest air I had ever experienced in a lightplane—and into a stiff quartering wind. We did manage to land fairly neatly. When we taxied to my hangar, a pilot who had watched us claw our way in shook his head.

"I can't believe you would even *attempt* to land in that wind!"

Katherine, as on every one of our excursions together, proved the perfect passenger. No "back seat" driving, always comfortable aloft— and very good at looking out for other air traffic. After our arrival at Clifford that blustery day, she just smiled. "Nice landing, honey." Sounded as if she meant it. But I realized she was inclined to say "Nice landing, honey," for landings good, bad and indifferent. Who could ask for a more understanding passenger?

During a run-up before take-off at Knox County Airport near Mt. Vernon, Ohio, the old Waco suffered a significant drop on one of the dual magnetos. With Milt Massey as passenger, we were on a mid-1993 flight to the Bartlesville, Oklahoma, National Biplane Meet. I leaned the fuel/air mixture and the mag returned to normal. We took off, but the next morning at Richmond, Indiana, it faltered again. And again, a bit of fiddling cleared it. Refueling at Mt. Vernon, Illinois, I met a "round engine" mechanic. Together we found the problem to be a bad spark plug, promptly replaced.

As we landed at Springfield, Missouri, thunderstorms threatened. With no hangar space available, Milt and I lashed on the cockpit cover. The concrete apron lacked embedded tie-down anchors. We had to settle for decidedly unreassuring chocks. As we sat down to dinner at a nearby motel restaurant, lightning flashed, thunder crashed and sheets of rain pelted down.

But the old bird managed to ride out the storm. In clearing morning skies, we took off for the Oklahoma event. Just after we landed at Bartlesville, we watched another biplane land, pivot around in a tight ground-loop that wiped out a wingtip and damaged the landing gear. After three days of seminars, speakers—including yours truly—and a banquet, we enjoyed a placid flight home without mag drops or monsoons.

A flight later that year ended in a way it shouldn't have. I had flown the Waco to York for its annual inspection. Some days later, Milt drove me back there to pick it up. On that dull gray day, the visibility was barely . . . okay. As I followed the Susquehanna River north, the weather began to thicken. Clouds rested on the crests of the surrounding mountains. I circled Berwick—which no longer had an airport—deliberating whether I should make a 180 and retreat to Bloomsburg Airport 12 miles behind me, or press on. I knew the terrain flattened a bit up ahead, and . . . .

Rain began to hammer the Waco. Turning around in truly bad visibility was no longer a prudent option. Weaving among low scud clouds, I forged on upriver. I forged on upriver, pressing the envelope just a tad.

My only advantage: I knew the terrain. Through the gray muck cliff-hanging moments later, I made out Wilkes-Barre's river-edged Wyoming Valley Airport. I circled at no more than 300 feet, plunked in and taxied to the FBO ramp. A young fellow in charge on this dark and dismal day appeared amazed I had emerged from the murk to actually land there. We pushed the Waco into the hangar, and I called Katherine to come fetch her humbled husband.

A September flight that year was memorable for a more benign reason. In the Cessna, Katherine and I flew to where powered flight had all begun 90 years ago: Kitty Hawk, North Carolina. We stood on the site where the Wright Brothers had made some 2,000 glider flights then on December 17, 1903, the world's first three flights under power. As I reflected that Lindbergh had always been my aviation hero, I realized I should make space for Orville and Wilbur.

Later that day, we flew on to Norfolk, Virginia to visit Wali and Martha Azimi, close friends from our days in Afghanistan. Wali now flew for Continental Airlines. In 2001, he would captain his retirement flight with Katherine and me joining his family aboard, first class from Newark to Los Angeles.

Nineteen ninety-four began on a distressing note. With heavy weather cancelling any idea of flying to Hanover, New Hampshire, Katherine and I had driven there, then on to Boston with Woodie. His wife and our dear friend, Barbro, was hospitalized in Boston. Still seriously ill, she was released and we drove her home to Hanover. Sadly, about a month later she died in a nursing facility there, a heartfelt loss for all of us. Katherine and I promised to return in May when I would conduct a special service in Barbro's memory.

Clifford's version of a spring thaw held off until April when the heavy snow cover finally melted into mud. Only half the runway was usable. For a flight to Florida in the Cessna with Milt, I had to lighten ship for a short-field take-off by asking him to drive to Seamans Airport. I picked him up there, and together we launched southward from Seamans's fully-in-use runway.

Next came a curious link with Lindbergh—in Canaan, Maine. Larry Ross of that tiny town had acquired the crate in which Lindbergh had shipped the *Spirit of St. Louis* from Europe back to the U.S. Larry had read about my 1927 tour recreation. He invited me, along with several people who had witnessed Lindbergh's historic take-off, to attend "Crate Day" on his Easy Street property. The event was scheduled for May 21, the 67th anniversary of Lindbergh's departure for Paris.

Katherine and I flew in the Waco to Concord, New Hampshire, refueled, flew on to Pittsfield, Maine, the nearest airport to Canaan. Larry met us there and drove Katherine and me to a motel in Caanan. Next morning we were driven to his house on Easy Street to take a look at his historic artifact.

The 28-foot-long, 9-foot-wide and 8-foot-high crate had passed through several owners but had never been put to any significant use. Larry had done a fine job converting the big box into quite an attractive Lindbergh mini-museum. He asked me if I might oblige with a fly-over during his scheduled festivities. Glad to. I made a slow, low circle around Easy Street, adding—I hoped—a touch of aerial focus to Larry's unique exhibit.

From Concord we flew to Bradley Field, Massachusetts, visited our son, John, and his family, then on the 23rd, rented a car to drive to New Hampshire. At Woodie's home, wearing my black ecclesiastical robe at his request, I conducted Barbro's memorial service for a small gathering of their close friends. The next day, Woodie, Katherine and I, and two of his closest friends, carried her ashes to "Barbro's Hill." There she and Woodie had often shared a picnic lunch and read poetry. Every year since, Woodie, Katherine and I have revisited that secluded hilltop. A yellow rose bush planted there in Barbro's memory still blooms.

The next month, an aborted mission. Katherine and I flew to East Stroudsburg Airport, Pennsylvania, to attend a Pan Am fly-in. To our puzzlement, we found only one other Pan Amer there. "Where is everybody?" I wondered.

"Didn't you hear?" some bystander said. "The fly-in has been rescheduled for some later date."

So we climbed back in the Waco and flew home.

My next non-local flight took me to New Hampshire in the Cessna to pick up Woodie. From Lebanon Airport, he and I flew to Sugar Loaf, Michigan to visit our old friend and Pan Am colleague, Al Heligmann. A good trip in good weather—except for dicey landing conditions on our return to Lebanon Airport in a near 30-mph crosswind. Happily, nothing was bent.

I then treated area Sunday school children—who had memorized Bible verses—to local scenic flights. In late June, Milt Massey and I forged westward through a fairly sticky weather front. Destination, the annual Waco meet at Mt. Vernon, Ohio. Made it there safely but on the return trip several days later, the same weather front was now a solid cloud barrier shrouding the Allegheny Mountains between Western Pennsylvania's Du Bois and Clifford. We and Fred Schmukler, piloting another Waco stymied at Du Bois, stayed the night. Though next morning didn't look any better, we both took off hoping for the best but promptly running into the worst. Rain hammered down and the clouds ahead were low enough to have rocks in them.

We retreated back to Du Bois, hangared the two Wacos and rented a car. Milt and I dropped Fred at Wilkes-Barre/Scranton Airport and pushed on to Clifford. In much improved weather two days later, we drove back to Du Bois to fly the Waco home.

The last week in July, the Clifford Fire Company held its annual picnic, a hugely popular event attended by thousands of good folk from miles around. In this year of 1995, I was asked to salute the kick-off parade aboard the Waco. I flew low, slow and noisily down Main Street, fun for me but a mere blip among the myriad festivities.

My next command performance took place the following month at the big Wilkes-Barre/Scranton Airport 1995 airshow. Mine was one of seven Wacos on static display representing "Aviation of the Past."

A September flight in the Cessna took Katherine and me to New Hampshire where we picked up Woodie and flew on to Bar Harbor, Maine. There we were met by Dr. Dave Bradley, a friend and Dartmouth classmate of Woodie's and the author of several erudite books including *No Place to Hide,* detailing the nuclear threat to humanity, and *Robert Frost, A Tribute to the Source.* We spent several glorious days sailing with Dave and I snapped plentiful photos. Without having to worry about a Honduran camera thief this time, I somehow managed on my own to lose the camera and all my exposed film.

In April, 1996 I made the decision to discontinue all treatment for my prostate cancer. Not because further treatment was hopeless, but because after nearly eight years of medication, all tests were negative. In fact, such tests had been negative through the past four years, but my oncologist had believed if I stopped the regimen, cancer would return. He still thought my ceasing the treatment even at this late date would prompt a recurrence within three to four months.

I respected his opinion but stuck to my decision. In the decade since, there has been no recurrence. Was my recovery the result of the medications? The microbiotic diet? Prayers of family and friends? A positive, optimistic outlook? All of that combined? I will never know, but the ultimate effect is a happy one.

In May, 1996 I agreed to serve for one year as interim pastor for Trinity Baptist in Scranton. I was truly blessed by that year of wonderful people, a marvelous choir and choir director, Patricia Koch, fine Sunday School teachers—and a competent, committed church secretary, Pat Marlow. I continued flying locally when practicable. By arrangement with the church, Katherine and I flew to the annual mid-year Waco meet in Ohio.

Then at 3:00 a.m. the last Friday of August, I was struck with an agonizing chest pain. Heart attack! Through the pre-dawn darkness, Katherine rushed me to the Marian Community Hospital Emergency Room in Carbondale where the ER doctor diagnosed not a heart problem but a severe gall bladder attack. I was promptly prepped for surgery.

By late afternoon, I was in recovery. The next day, Saturday, I was released. On Sunday, I was holding forth The Word at Trinity.

And I was back in the air. This time with an exceptional young man named Brian Ewasko who lived with the Richard Collins family in Clarks Summit. Brian had an interest in flying and hoped to enlist in ROTC in college. I took him on several instructional flights in the Cessna. The encouragement I gave him noticeably increased his confidence in himself, and he went forward with his idea of a military career. He is now a 2nd lieutenant in the U.S. Air Force.

In June, 1997, the Waco, Katherine and I retraced the annual pilgrimage to the Waco Fly-In at Mount Vernon, Ohio. The next month, we flew Allegheny to Chicago, motored to Barrington to join Bill Rose for the annual Oshkosh extravaganza. We flew from his Barrington airstrip to Oshkosh in one of his Stearmans as part of "Rose's Raiders." As Katherine and I droned past the crowd in the "Parade of Flight," I was told the announcer noted, "The pilot of the Stearman is the pilot who flew General Jodl to Rheims, France to surrender the German forces in May, 1945." A brief moment of fame.

. . . Followed in mid-August by a long moment of humbling. Katherine and I flew the Waco to a Pan Am fly-in at Stroudsburg, Pennsylvania. One afternoon's events included a spot landing contest, touching down as close as possible to a mark on the runway. I wasn't all that eager to compete, but several people urged me into it. I taxied out and took off without any enthusiasm wondering—"Why am I doing this?" I flew the pattern, glided in—and masterfully managed to touch the Waco down so far from the mark I was awarded last place.

In June, another aborted flight; this one intended for the 1998 Waco get-together at Mt. Vernon, Illinois by way of Altoona, Pennsylvania. This time with son John sharing the flying, we faced grim weather from Altoona onward. We stayed the night there, woke to even worsening conditions, so we flew back home in sensible defeat.

Later that year Katherine and I did make it to the "Gathering of Eagles" at Kirkwood Airport, Kirkwood, New York, only 30 minutes north of Clifford. The landing strip was a bit too narrow for a couple of other incoming pilots who neatly took out the orange plastic runway marker cones with their landing gears.

In 1999, with Katherine feeling I might enjoy some flying time by myself, I flew solo to Ohio for the annual Waco fly-in, a smooth trip in excellent weather throughout. I also continued my many scenic, non-solo flights for friends, parishioners and other interested folks.

That summer I received an invitation from the Indianapolis Aero Club to serve as guest speaker in January, all expenses paid. The previous speaker had been famed World War II ace Francis Gabreski. In fact all previous speakers had been well-known pilots and aviation leaders. I felt everyone of them must have been more compelling than I would be. I accepted anyway, honored to be considered at all.

I was sent a round-trip ticket to Indianapolis, was met by representatives of the Aero Club who took me on a tour of the famous Motor Speedway—with a snappy ride around the 2 1/2-mile track. At that evening's banquet, I spoke for about 45 minutes and answered a bunch of questions. I left elated—and faced the new century with an appreciation for the truth in the adage that "an old man often feels like a young man with a mere temporary condition."

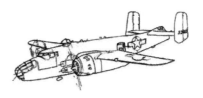

CLOSING THE CIRCLE

The year 2000 marked my 60th year as an active pilot. Now seemed the time to "close the circle," the time to hang up my goggles.

I have always considered Scranton Municipal Airport my aerial alma mater. In July, 1940 I first soloed there. At Scranton Airport, I received my commercial license and flight instructor rating—the beginning of a career that had taken me all over the world.

Started as a partnership venture on rural pastureland in the late 1920s, Scranton Airport grew into a gem of Pennsylvania aviation. Hundreds of pilots had trained at Scranton Airport, many of them moving into distinguished careers in military and civil aviation.

The airport boomed through the federal government's Civil Pilot Training Program. After World War II, thanks to G.I. Bill flight students, it boomed again. As that program tapered off, business flying became the airport's mainstay—but with a catch. The relatively short runways limited the size of corporate aircraft and were inadequate for corporate jets. The larger business aircraft began to relocate to more adequate airports in the area.

By 1970, the airport had seriously deteriorated. In 1973, Harold Swank, who had founded the airport 44 years before, retired. The city, the airport's owner since 1936, put the management contract up for bid.

Gene Scappatura, then manager of a small airport in nearby Fleetville, and the only bidder, was awarded the contract.

Scappatura did his best, but by the end of 1977, the Mayor of Scranton came to the unhappy conclusion the struggling airport was no longer of use to the city. Four days into the new year, crews from Scranton's Department of Public Works winterized the water lines and painted the fatal big X at the intersection of the runways. Scranton Airport was closed.

In the echoing hangar one plane remained; a Piper Tri-Pacer dismantled for replacement of its fabric covering but now caught in the abrupt closing of the airport. Thus the last plane out of Scranton Airport departed in pieces by truck.

Within a year, vandals trashed the neglected old hangar/office building into an eyesore.

Various uses for the airport site were suggested and abandoned until Glenburn resident Frank Colombo proposed converting the hangar into a factory for traffic signs and "Jersey barriers," those portable solid concrete fence sections used during highway repair and reconstruction work. Thus in 1981, Scranton Airport's hangar became a concrete fabrication plant. Operations soon crowded the old parking apron and much of the runway pavement with factory output and storage.

An annual get-together of Scranton Airport alumni and alumnae was all that remained of the airport's 50 years of operation. Near the end of the century, Bill Hallstead, my co-writer on this book, contacted the group, volunteering to write a history of the airport. Since he was now a resident of Florida, he would need a Scranton area partner in the project to handle most of the research. The ideal person for that task turned out to be Russell Hazelton, a resident of nearby Lake Winola.

Russ had begun his aviation career in 1954 as a 65¢-an-hour mechanic's helper at Scranton, paying his own way through commercial, flight instructor and instrument ratings there. He was accepted in the Air Force aviation cadet program, graduated to fly B-25s, then while a USAF Reserve 2nd lieutenant, was hired by TWA. After his mandatory retirement at age 60 as a TWA 747 captain, Russ had flown as a TWA flight engineer for three more years.

Immersed in the Scranton Airport history venture, he pored through the archives of the Lackwanna Historical Society, the Scranton Chamber of Commerce and newspaper libraries and compiled I-was-there material from dozens of former Scranton airport pilots. And through Russ's efforts, the University of Scranton Press agreed to publish the book.

As work on the book progressed, several of us airport alumni and alumnae—Bill Seamans, Matt Mackie, Nancy Bushko, I and several others, former Scranton pilots all—met periodically at Russ's home to discuss additional input for the history. All of us were dismayed at the inglorious manner in which the airport had met its end. A lockdown by work crews and the last plane hauled out dismantled on a truck.

Such a demeaning sequence, Russ and Bill agreed, had been a far from fitting way to salute a half century of flying at an airport that had hosted such luminaries as Wiley Post, Frank Hawks, Roscoe Turner and Jimmie Mattern—the airport that had, in fact, brought Scranton and its environs into the Air Age.

During one of these get-togethers Russ, a man with an inspiration, turned to me.

"Jack, how much room would you need to land and take off in your Waco?"

The "last landing and take-off" project was underway.

Russ and I met at the old airport site several times and found the current owner, "Butch" Columbo, most cooperative. For the day of the event, he agreed to evict the cows that frequently grazed on the only practical area for our event—a 1,500-foot north-south strip along the east fence. The surface was rough. Russ spent a lot of hours driving a big borrowed roller to smooth it down, and more hours publicizing the event.

On September 15, 2000, a clear 65-degree day with a gentle northerly breeze, I arrived overhead at 5 p.m. In the cleared eastern portion of the field, I spotted quite a large crowd. I throttled back and made two low passes, one of them beautifully caught on film for the cover of the forthcoming book, *The Rise and Fall of Scranton Municipal Airport,* Scranton University Press, 2001.

I landed south to north, taxied to a point near the crowd, cut the switch. WNEP-TV's helicopter then flew a photo circuit. I was interviewed by the press, questions and comments abounded—especially from those who had known Scranton Airport in its glory days. Faces from the past emerged—Bill Hutchins, Bill Seamans, Andy White, Roy Craig, Bishop Timlin, Harold Swank's son Hank . . . .

I realized I had taken my private pilot flight test here exactly 60 years and one week ago, coincidentally making the landings south to north. I was struck with vivid memories of Harold, Hymie Wintersteen, Mark Richards and so many others, a sentimental and quite emotional experience that many in the crowd visibly shared.

"For one glorious hour," reported the Scranton Tribune, "the Scranton Municipal Airport was back in business."

At 5:45, I climbed back in the old Waco, fired up the engine again, taxied into position and roared away in a properly respectful "last plane out" departure. I circled around for one more low pass then rocked the wings in a final salute. Fifteen minutes later, I landed at Clifford.

In 60 years of active flying, I have been most fortunate in pursuing a vocation that was my avocation as well. Its demands, though, necessarily forced me to miss quite a bit of an important part of my life by being away from my family much of the time. Yet Katherine has always been remarkably supportive—and often an eager participant.

Flying has been a spiritual experience for me, with God becoming very real. The heavens and earth indeed proclaim His glory. Especially through my work with ORBIS and pastoral ministry I have learned that love and service are the center of Christianity. Love your neighbor as yourself—and who is your neighbor? Anyone in need.

As I move toward the final transition to eternal life, my time as a pilot is expressed in the inspired last three lines of John Gillespie Magee's poem, *High Flight:*

And, while with silent, lifting mind I've trod
The high untrespassed sanctity of space,
Put out my hand, and touched the face of God.

FLIGHT CREDENTIALS

Licenses and Ratings
FAA Airline Transport Pilot with Ratings on Douglas DC-4, DC-6, DC-7 and DC-8; Convair 240, 340 and 440; Boeing 707, 720 and 747.
Airplane, single engine, land and sea; multi-engine, land and sea.
Flight Instructor, airplane, single engine, land and sea; and instrument flying.
Flight Navigation
Ground Instructor, navigation, aircraft engines, meteorology.
British Airline Transport with Rating on Boeing 707
Afghan Airline Transport Pilot with Ratings on Douglas DC-3, DC-4 and DC-6; Convair 440
Afghan Flight Examiner with Rating on DC-6.

Aircraft flown
Aeronca Chief, Champ and "T"
Piper J-3, J-4, J-5, PA-11, PA-14, PA-18, PA-22, Arrow, Vagabond, Cherokee 180 and Cherokee 300
Cessna 150, 172, 180, C-78, T-50 and AT-17
Luscombe 8A
Culver Cadet
Globe Swift
Ryan Navion
Bellanca Cruisemaster
Fairchild 22, 24, M-62, PT-19 and PT-26
Champion Citabria
Helio Courier
DeHavilland Tiger Moth and Beaver
Stinson L-5, 10A and SR-9
Noorduyn Norseman
Ryan ST
Airspeed Oxford
Fleet, Kinner 125 model

Waco UPF-7
Stearman PT-17
Travelaire 4000
Kinner Bird
Curtiss AT-9
North American AT-6 and P-51
Percival Proctor
Grumman Goose
Consolidated BT-13 and BT-15
Tupolev TU 104
Douglas DC-3, DC-4, DC-6, DC-8, C-47, C-53, C-54 and A-20
Convair 240, 340 and 440
Lockheed Constellation and P-38
Boeing 377, 707, 720 and 747
North American B-25, P-51
Republic P-47
Beech C-45
Avro Anson
Schweizer 2-22
Total flying hours: 28,306 logged; about 1,200 unlogged.

CO-AUTHOR

William Hallstead is the author of 21 books—including 6 suspense novels under the pen name "William Beechcroft"—and more than 400 articles and short stories, many of them aviation-oriented. He is a member of the Authors Guild and Mystery Writers of America. For several years he was a flight instructor, single engine land and sea, and a glider pilot, logging 1,100 flying hours.